MW00635222

CATHOLIC ACTIVISM TODAY

Catholic Activism Today

Individual Transformation and the Struggle
for Social Justice

Maureen K. Day

NEW YORK UNIVERSITY PRESS

New York

NEW YORK UNIVERSITY PRESS
New York
www.nyupress.org

References to Internet websites (URLs) were accurate at the time of writing. Neither the author nor New York University Press is responsible for URLs that may have expired or changed since the manuscript was prepared.

Library of Congress Cataloging-in-Publication Data
Names: Day, Maureen K., author.
Title: Catholic activism today : individual transformation and the struggle for social justice / Maureen K. Day.
Description: New York : New York University Press, 2020. | Includes bibliographical references and index. | Summary: "Maureen Day's "Catholic Activism Today" explores the role religion plays in individual transformation and struggle for social justice, paying specific attention to the phenomena of JustFaith Ministries (JFM) and its contributions to civic engagement"—Provided by publisher.
Identifiers: LCCN 2019029131 | ISBN 9781479851331 (cloth) | ISBN 9781479821419 (ebook) | ISBN 9781479886265 (ebook)
Subjects: LCSH: JustFaith Ministries. | Church and social problems—United States. | Church and social problems—Catholic Church. | Catholic Church—United States—History. | Social justice—Religious aspects—Catholic Church. | Christian sociology—United States. | Christian sociology—Catholic Church.
Classification: LCC HN39.U6 D39 2020 | DDC 303.3/72—dc23
LC record available at https://lccn.loc.gov/2019029131

New York University Press books are printed on acid-free paper, and their binding materials are chosen for strength and durability. We strive to use environmentally responsible suppliers and materials to the greatest extent possible in publishing our books.

Manufactured in the United States of America

10 9 8 7 6 5 4 3 2 1

Also available as an ebook

In memory of my father

David Riley O'Day

Let perpetual light shine upon him

CONTENTS

Introduction

We begin in an affluent California town known for its excellent schools, expensive homes, and beautiful parks. The small city has only a handful of churches and tonight Holy Trinity[1] is hosting an event. It is a typical Monday evening in the Bay Area. The weather is mild, it is overcast, and the traffic is terrible. The speaker is tall, lean, and in his mid-fifties, and wears khakis and a button-down shirt, the expected garb for a church function such as this. The thirty or so Catholics gathered to hear the presentation look like the usual suspects at a religiously sponsored suburban event: white, older, and middle-class. Some of those gathered are interested in the topic, and others are "grads"—as JustFaith Ministries (JFM) staff members refer to those who have completed JustFaith— excited to meet the man who created their beloved program. The room is typical for a church meeting, with whiteboards, ample folding chairs, and an assortment of snacks, ranging from brie to brownies. At first glance, the town, the church, the speaker, and listeners seem altogether ordinary. However, the speaker, Jack Jezreel, founder of JFM, wants the evening to be anything but.

With practiced oratory skills that combine enthusiasm with challenge and invitation, he begins. Speaking loudly and rapidly with wild gestures, Jezreel suddenly subdues himself, lowering his voice to emphasize a point, affording himself a long pause. He makes careful eye contact with those present, never glaring but giving the impression that the listener is part of a smaller, more intimate conversation. Those in the audience are riveted by his words: they sorrowfully shake their heads as he describes the plight of the poor, nod enthusiastically when he claims that God wants more for the world, and lean back with a reflective countenance as they consider their own role in the world's problems and graces.

Jezreel's talk focuses on transforming people who will go on to transform the world into the Kingdom of God. He tells the story of John Newton: a slave trader who underwent a dramatic conversion leading to his work as an abolitionist and the composition of "Amazing Grace." He defines *agape* as a "love without exception" that can and must animate the life of the Christian. He speaks of the necessity of Catholics to be involved in their social and political world specifically *as Catholics*. And he wonders aloud, rhetorically, "What *did* happen to John Newton?" How did he move from a person who profited from evil to one who worked so fervently against it? Broadening this question, he asks his listeners, "When twenty-one thousand people die each day because of hunger or hunger-related illnesses—three-quarters of them children—why do some get upset about this while others simply go about their day?" Why do some care while others do not? Jezreel encourages the listeners to bring JustFaith, the original JFM program, to their parish so that more people will come to care about and make a difference in the lives of the poor and vulnerable. Some here will indeed bring this program to their parish, organizing a small group of eight to twelve parishioners who will—for twenty-four weeks—directly witness and learn about poverty through a lens of faith.

JFM: A Window into Catholic Civic Engagement

Based in Louisville, Kentucky, JFM designs curricula that encourage Christians across the United States to become more involved in poverty and related problems. Churches use JFM curricula to facilitate small groups that gather for prayer, ritual, retreats, immersion experiences, and discussion of assigned readings. JFM hopes its programs will help participants to connect their faith to their social worlds, compelling them to improve society in significant ways. Its mission statement indicates a focus on both social justice and personal transformation, reading, "JustFaith Ministries forms, informs and transforms people of faith by offering programs and resources that sustain them in their compassionate commitment to build a more just and peaceful world." JFM has expanded from its Catholic origins to become ecumenical, although it enjoys far more success in the Catholic world; fewer than 1 percent of the program graduates are non-Catholic. As of this writing, JFM programs have enrolled more than fifty thousand program participants in more than fifteen hundred churches in the United States.

JFM is a recent chapter in a long history of Catholic civic and political engagement in the United States and illuminates much when placed in this larger context. Historian David O'Brien noted that we can observe three "styles" of Catholic public involvement when examining America's past: republican, immigrant, and evangelical.[2] The animating theologies, mission, strategies, and so forth of these styles have varied due to the different sociohistorical circumstances from which each emerged. This sociohistorical variance within the American Catholic experience creates differences *across* time among Catholic organizations but yields similar organizations *within* any given period. I argue that the contemporary American context has now given rise to a fourth style of Catholic public engagement; I call this style the "discipleship style."

This book examines JFM in the context of the discipleship style, shedding light on the organization as well as uncovering important trends about the role of contemporary American Catholics in the public sphere more broadly. To briefly outline the most fundamental characteristics of the discipleship style here, first, it has a personalist character, which tends to appeal to contemporary Catholics who, like other Americans, are less inclined to join civic organizations and more apt to be involved as single volunteers.[3] Furthermore, with increased professionalization among Catholics, they become involved in the causes that make the most of their own unique talents, helping them find personal and even deeper vocational meaning in their service work.

The individual-level engagement of volunteering tends to point participants to individual-level solutions, such as lifestyle changes, rather than to ways of becoming involved in macro-level change. This means that, second, discipleship organizations that emphasize justice, like JFM, are finding it difficult to translate their participants' enthusiasm for the personal into more structural contexts. Although JFM may be successful by many measures, such as getting programs into parishes and creating a sense of community among participants, the personalist emphasis distracts from and even undermines the organizational goal of attaining structural change.

Third, and importantly, the personalist qualities of the discipleship style assume a locus of moral authority rooted in the individual. American Catholics have increasingly come to understand themselves as sources of moral authority while decreasingly relying on the Catholic hierarchy for moral guidance.[4] However, this does not mean that the institutional church no longer has influence over Catholics. What it means is that the magisterium has become *a* source of moral wisdom among many; it is no longer *the* source. The church will continue to influence the faithful insofar as it offers cogent and compelling arguments for its positions.[5] This new moral posturing not only means that the church needs to earn allegiance from the faithful, but it also affords the magisterium an opportunity to dialogue with and influence individuals and institutions beyond Catholicism.

Finally, the republican, immigrant, and evangelical styles of the past each prevented a fully Catholic public engagement; in their own ways, they each segregated Catholic life from American life more broadly. The personalism of the recently emerged discipleship style instead encourages a more integrated approach, helping participants make their faith the foundation of their lives and, building from there, putting that faith into the world both personally and socially. What people do for a living, where they vacation, how they vote, their financial priorities, and who they spend their time with are no longer mere preferences. The discipleship style reframes these as ways of practicing faith. Organizations of the discipleship style, such as JFM, plant the believer firmly in the world, expecting faith to determine people's relationships to individuals and institutions. In sum, the personalism of the discipleship style integrates the different aspects of a person's life—work, family, politics, and so forth—while it imparts religious significance to them. These characteristics and their implications for understanding American Catholic civic engagement are central to this book.

This volume argues that while JFM and other discipleship-style organizations are largely successful in attracting Catholics (and others) to their programs and effecting change in participants' lives so that their faith and lives in the world are integrated, discipleship organizations are significantly less successful in fostering the ultimate aim of attaining social justice activism. Although JFM and others continue to valorize the kind of social engagement that has been encouraged throughout the long history of Catholic social thought, a personalist approach shifts participants' energies away from social mobilization. Moreover, the focus on the individual also challenges the institutional authority of the Catholic Church in the lives of contemporary American Catholics, shifting their perception of the church from a hierarchy that *controls* the laity to one that simply *influences* them as they live their individual lives. This trend has significant ramifications for the shape of the American Catholic Church even as it offers opportunities.

Methods and Demographics

This study is based on interview, survey, and participant-observation data gathered over roughly three years, from September 2011 to October 2014. I conducted sixty-one semistructured, in-depth interviews with program graduates and JFM staff, twenty-seven of whom were living in Louisville, Kentucky; twenty-five in the San Francisco Bay Area (one of these visiting from Colorado); and nine from the Los Angeles Area. They were not a random sample of graduates but a purposive sample. Most of the interviewees were selected because they actively support JFM through serving on the board, facilitating groups, or coordinating program graduates in their geographical region. I sought interviewees who were committed to JFM in some way so that they could speak more deliberately about the organization. However, I also interviewed what one might think of as more "typical" graduates, that is, those who completed the program but are not involved with JFM. These nine typical graduates show no significant difference in beliefs and practices compared to those more invested in JFM as an organization, indicating that these findings are generalizable to program graduates more broadly. Fifty-three of the sixty[6] interviewees returned their surveys (via post), yielding a robust response rate of 88 percent. In addition to surveys and interviews, I also conducted participant observation in four JFM programs. These courses account for the bulk of the field time and with various JFM events—such as speaking engagements, retreats, and service projects—yield more than 270 hours of participant observation. More details on the methods are available in appendix A.

For the most part, the interviewees were older, middle- to upper-class, and well-educated and of similar demographics compared to current participants.[7] Specifically, about three-quarters were fifty-five or older and half were sixty-five or older. Half made $90,000 per year or more, and only 13 percent made under $50,000. Ninety-two percent had a four-year degree, and 58 percent had a graduate or professional degree. Forty-one percent were male, and 59 percent were female. Forty-six percent were retired, 32 percent were employed full-time, 17 percent were employed part-time, and 5 percent were unemployed. Religious schooling was not as common among Protestants, but the Catholic participants were much more likely to have attended Catholic school—for example, nearly half attended Catholic universities compared to just 8 percent of Catholics nationally.[8] Fifty-one interviewees were Catholic (84 percent), and ten were Protestant (16 percent). Seven of the Protestants came from the United Methodist Church, two were Episcopalian, and one was Presbyterian.

Order of the Book

What follows is the story of JFM and what it reveals about American Catholics in the public sphere today. Chapter 1 describes the birth and development of JFM, showing the ways a small parish program expanded across the nation. It also provides a sociohistorical overview of American Catholic civic engagement. The Roman Catholic Church in the United States has seen a variety of social changes. Catholics and the church have responded to these changes through various styles of public engagement; these manifest both continuities and changes when compared to Catholics of today. This discussion situates JFM and the discipleship style within a historical context of Catholic civic engagement.

The second chapter discusses the culture of JFM. It outlines the Catholicity of JFM and the five core values of the organization. Although JFM has become ecumenical and a fair number of Protestant participants were interviewed for this book, the roots and the animating spirit of the organization are distinctly Catholic. In introducing the five core values of JFM—transformation, Christ-centeredness, community, justice, and compassion—chapter 2 explores their meaning for the organization and demonstrates the importance of these values in contemporary Catholic outreach more broadly.

Each of these core values serves as a lens for the remaining chapters. Chapter 3 focuses on transformation. JFM seeks to transform participants, encouraging them to care for the poor and vulnerable. The organization anticipates that these new ways of caring will, in turn, ripple outward as participants become more active in the world around them.

I call this strategy, which pours organizational energy into transforming individuals in the hopes of fomenting broader social change, a "ripple group" strategy.

Chapter 4 investigates the core value of Christ-centeredness and the ways that religious beliefs shape the outlook of the participants, creating a "theology of pragmatic reverence" that helps them to bring their religion to everyday life. A theology of pragmatic reverence provides a framework that helps them to see religious meaning in the ordinary, offering participants a lens that makes life more spiritually significant and morally compelling.

Community is the core value discussed in the fifth chapter. Many organizations that help Catholics bring their faith into the world form and encourage them through a community of similarly minded others. This chapter determines which communities act on the grads and which they act on. This navigation and negotiation of communities create a "dilemma of resistance" as participants attempt to bring their faith to civil society, discovering how to be—as the saying goes—in the world but not of it.

The sixth chapter explores the value of justice and the participants' understandings of the state and market. Although justice demands a structural approach to a social problem, many aspects of JFM programs focus on the individual, thus inadvertently undermining a more macro-level strategy. This charity-or-justice conundrum is the "dilemma of volunteerism." Additionally, participants are often unsure if social problems are best solved by abandoning the avarice of the market and the power of their social positions or if they should remain where they are, using their material and social resources for the common good. This difficult question is the "dilemma of efficacy."

Chapter 7 examines the ways in which JFM treats compassion as an affective response to suffering as well as a form of knowledge and experience. This chapter also discusses the role of stories and dialogue in the participants' formation—that is, the ways stories and dialogue shift participants' perceptions and evaluations of reality and their moral agency within it. In shaping the ways in which the grads understand and act in their world, stories and dialogue also lend insight into a Catholic understanding of moral authority in today's landscape.

Finally, the conclusion revisits the volume's core argument and its major themes as they have been introduced and realized throughout this text. It proposes questions for further research, identifies "loose ends," and suggests other arenas beyond Catholic activism in which this analysis would be useful.

This book tells the story of an organization that brings Catholics to the public sphere *as* Catholics. Although the reach of JFM is relatively small—fifty-thousand graduates are few compared to the seventy-five million Catholics in the United States—this volume also sheds light on greater themes occurring within contemporary Catholic public life. In the pages that follow, the participants reveal the ways Catholics and Protestants alike attempt to bring religious and moral meaning to their everyday lives despite the social constraints they face in this endeavor. Both their successes and the areas that warrant growth provide insight for understanding contemporary Catholic engagement in the public sphere.

1

JustFaith Ministries and the Discipleship Style

A Sociohistorical Context

The political events of the 1980s facilitated the eventual creation of Just-Faith Ministries (JFM) in 1989. President Ronald Reagan had just taken office and some of his policies—especially those on taxes, nuclear weapons, and the wars in Central America—upset small, but well-networked, groups of both Catholics and Protestants. American Catholics had been involved in peace efforts since Dorothy Day and the Catholic Worker Movement in the 1930s, but those voices tended to come from the margins.[1] Organizations such as Witness for Peace, Sanctuary, and the Pledge of Resistance brought public attention to these issues and mobilized Catholics and Protestants to confront their country's policies from religious bases.[2] In 1983, the American bishops published *The Challenge of Peace*.[3] This document condemned much of modern warfare, especially the use of nuclear weapons. Shortly thereafter, they released a second pastoral letter, *Economic Justice for All*, wherein they insisted that all have a right to a minimum standard of living, that people have an obligation to the poor and vulnerable, and that private associations, as well as the government, hold this responsibility.[4] The wars in Central America, nuclear deterrence, growing economic disparity, and the bishops' pastorals all lent Catholics a political opportunity to act *as* Catholics concerning issues of peace and justice.[5] JustFaith[6] emerged out of this period of heightened activism and awareness, when ideas like peace and the common good were at the forefront of the Catholic mind.

The parish is the most logical venue for organizations of the discipleship style as it is the sole institution that is both distinctly Catholic and regularly frequented by many Catholics; 46 percent of Catholics claim that they attend Mass at least two or three times per month.[7] However, for the vast majority of American Catholics, faith formation at the parish level is grossly inadequate. Rare exceptions aside, parishes' lack of adequate faith formation is a cultural problem that affects Catholics in terms of both their religious identity and their ability to connect their religion to their public lives.[8] How can parishes help Catholics make those connections between faith and social issues, seeing their religion as relevant to everyday life? How can parishes help contemporary American Catholics, who are products of a more individualist, middle-class socialization, make these connections? A parish in Louisville, Kentucky, offered an answer.

Epiphany in Louisville: The Emergence of JFM

Among Catholic mystics and contemplatives, Louisville is famous for an epiphany. In 1958, Thomas Merton—Trappist priest, engaged intellectual, and pacifist—was running errands in the downtown shopping district. On the corner of Fourth and Walnut Streets, Merton had an epiphany that he deeply loved all the world, understood his connectedness to God and all humanity, and saw, as the oblivious shoppers strolled by, their faces "shining like the sun."[9] Between a lamppost and a bicycle rack at that same corner, with Walnut Street renamed to Muhammad Ali Boulevard, stands an inconspicuous plaque marking the spot of Merton's epiphany. There is another epiphany in Louisville, one with less acclaim yet one that is more significant for these purposes: the Church of the Epiphany. Here Jack Jezreel began JustFaith in 1989.

Jezreel was born in the mid-1950s into a middle-class family in a suburb on the west coast of Florida. He won the religion award in first grade, and it seemed only natural to him and others, with his precocious devotion, that he should become a priest. In high school, Jezreel was advised to get his undergraduate degree in philosophy before going on to seminary. After taking the year off after high school to participate in tennis tournaments, he went to Furman University, then affiliated with the Southern Baptist Convention, on a tennis scholarship. While there, he realized that he wanted to enjoy married life and yet he was no less interested in serving God and the church. He became intrigued by what was then a new phrase: lay ministry.

He went to Notre Dame to pursue a Master of Divinity, and his education exposed him to many new and exciting ideas. He was especially impressed with renowned ethicist Stanley Hauerwas's class, which he took his third year. He had not even heard of Catholic social teaching, but Hauerwas's style brought it to life. Another extremely formative experience for him was an urban immersion experience his school offered. Although intended for undergrads, Jezreel thought it sounded interesting. It was taking place in Florida and coincided with his return home for the Christmas break, so he signed up. The experience transformed him:

> I ended up spending a couple days with some sisters who worked with migrant workers. And it was *really* eye-opening. I lived in Florida all my life. I'd never *seen* a migrant worker. And now I'm in a camp where people have taken a couple of pieces of corrugated tin, leaned them up against each other and there's ten people living in it. And it literally was within view of Cinderella's castle at Disney World, which was built while I was in high school. So, that experience made a big impact.[10]

Although impressed with the school and thankful for his education, he was—and still is—troubled that he could have completed his theological training without ever taking a course in social justice and thus would have been "completely oblivious to the fact that the Gospel had anything to do with poor people." Another formative experience he had at Notre Dame was his two-year involvement in the Rite of Christian Initiation of Adults (RCIA). He was very inspired by the fire and conviction of the women and men seeking full Catholic initiation and wished more Catholics shared their fervor.

The significance of the RCIA to Jezreel should not be understated. The Second Vatican Council (1962–1965) called for the restoration of this ancient rite of bringing adults into the faith.[11] In 1972, the Latin *Ordo Initiationis Christianae Adultorum* was published, and an English translation followed two years later.[12] Sometime later, in 1988, the National Conference of Catholic Bishops made a more aggressive push for the RCIA, publishing an official American English translation of the *Rite of Christian Initiation of Adults* as well as "National Statutes for the Catechumenate." This latter document established norms for the rite and mandated that parishes use this new rite for bringing adults into full church membership. As Jezreel understood the rite, it was a paradigm shift in what it meant to "be a Catholic." Rather than simply memorizing doctrines, program facilitators encouraged their candidates and catechumens to grow in faith, illustrating the processual nature of conversion. Various stages are built into the RCIA process that bring the non-Catholic—or the Catholic not fully initiated—more deeply into Catholic living. Most pointedly, the RCIA must ensure that participants receive "suitable pastoral formation and guidance aimed at training them in the Christian life," and this should come through the traditional emphasis on catechesis as well as community, liturgy, and evangelization through Word and service.[13] This cultural shift in understanding what it meant to fully enter the Catholic faith would inspire Jezreel in the years that followed.

Upon earning his MDiv, Jezreel, then twenty-five years old, began a job in adult faith formation at a parish in Colorado Springs. There he drew on his experience at Notre Dame to lead the RCIA program and continued to be marveled by the results. He happened upon an intentional community of Catholics and Mennonites living very humble and other-regarding lives. In his address at the 2012 Social Action Summer Institute in Louisville, Jezreel described his first dinner at the "hospitality house" in revelatory terms. "I sat down with ten formerly homeless men and women and we were all served by our host, Steve, who sat down last after everyone had been served. For this rather naïve, protected, insulated young man, it was blowing all my theological circuits. And I thought to myself, 'This just looks too much like the Gospel.'" He joined them and continued his job at the parish for another year, but eventually left the parish position and worked other jobs to support his new community. There Jezreel met Maggie, proposing to her, he jokes, on the romantic occasion of a jail visit. They had the first of their three daughters while living in community and left after his nearly six years in the spring of 1988 when they were expecting their second child.

Jezreel's next job was at Church of the Epiphany in Louisville, where he was hired as the minister of social responsibility. The parish was financially well-off, and Jezreel was unsuccessfully trying to reinvigorate a once-active social justice committee. Despite the support of the American bishops for peace and justice, his first year with the social justice group was a failure. He remembered with a laugh, "Nothing I did worked!" He could not get more than four people on the steering committee, and his programs attracted only a handful of people out of a parish of one thousand families. And too often he felt the few people attracted to social justice were angry and grouchy rather than animated by Christian love and joy. Still, he had hope when he remembered the strong, enthusiastic Catholics coming out of the RCIA programs of his past. They were, in a word, transformed. He wondered how to bring that excitement and conversion to social justice.

In his second year, beginning in fall of 1989, Jezreel had the idea to combine the transformative aspects of the RCIA with Catholic social teaching. He would use the pedagogy of the RCIA: the engaging speakers, personal transformation, relevant readings, Catholic prayer and ritual, discussion, community building, and retreats. Yet, instead of teaching the fundamentals of Catholicism, Jezreel would expose them to Catholic social teaching. He made a rough outline of what he planned to cover over the course of the thirty-five weeks and called it JustFaith. Perhaps, he thought, these dozen or so people who do not yet see how their faith relates to the poor will be transformed with this new approach.

Jezreel was intentional in crafting the materials that would draw the participants into new beliefs about poverty, peace, and justice. While his notes were vague, he led the groups himself—with an occasional co-facilitator—and ensured that things went according to plan. The dozen or so parishioners read a variety of books that pushed them to see the relevance of faith to everyday life, the merits of and differences between charity and justice, and the dire situation of the poor. They struggled with the new insights that these books brought to them and they reexamined their priorities. They prayed together around candles and offered one another affection and blessings. They met people who recounted firsthand the very hardships they were reading about. They went on immersion trips so they could witness the tragedies and hope within their local communities.

Jezreel also used the small-group framework when designing Just-Faith. Small groups permit a greater depth to conversations, allowing for more intense community building. Jezreel wanted the participants to increase their knowledge of a topic and care more deeply about certain issues as well as develop strong affective ties to one another. Having a smaller group facilitates this intimacy.

Besides Jezreel's well-designed program, an important political event occurred this first year that made JustFaith more salient for the participants. Only a few weeks into the first session, six Jesuit scholars, their housekeeper, and the housekeeper's daughter were murdered in El Salvador for the Jesuits' work in aiding the poor of their region. Jezreel recalls that this event was very emotional for the group: "When it happened it, I remember it was just *tremendous*, tremendous sadness." Jezreel recalls that his participants did not know if Nicaragua was in Africa or Latin America. JustFaith gave them a place to learn more as well as a moral frame for understanding these events. Their sadness was transformed into conviction, and once their thirty-five weeks had passed, they were determined to do something to change the world around them.

These participants' dramatic transformations to care more deeply for the poor and vulnerable did not happen just for the first JustFaith group at Epiphany. Year after year, each set of graduates took on new projects for the parish and this made social justice and charity front-and-center issues. The grads made significant lifestyle changes, such as job switching or buying more modest homes. They donated more to their church, giving the parish an even larger budget. For five or six years, the parish council president was a JustFaith grad, which brought poverty and outreach needs to many discussions and not just charity budgets. The Church of the Epiphany's social mission attracted others to the parish, causing it to grow even larger, with members who wanted a faith that would invite them to be active in the world.

In 1995, after being in Louisville for seven years, the Jezreels moved an hour's drive away to bring up their children in a more rural environment. Jezreel continued commuting to work for another year, but when they bought a new piece of property, even farther away and without electricity or running water, working at Epiphany became impossible, and he devoted his time to farming their land. Although JustFaith stopped running temporarily at Epiphany, it continued in a handful of other parishes, some outside of Kentucky. These early JustFaith parishes ran the program with very little support; Jezreel simply gave his facilitating notes—three pages for the whole thirty-five weeks—to all who asked for them. These early groups began through the impetus of grads who relocated and offered JustFaith at their new parish or through neighboring parishes that had heard about the program through word of mouth.

While Jezreel was cultivating the earth, he was also planting the seeds for a larger, more organized JustFaith. In the early to mid-1990s, the Catholic Charities USA office had noticed that many of the services they offered communities were being coordinated and fulfilled by social workers rather than parishes. The staff there wondered how they could bring parishes to work alongside those social workers in a more intentional way. One staff member in particular, Megan Kennedy, led an effort to discover the ways in which some parishes had bolstered their social outreach. She traveled to different parishes in the United States to catalog a collection of "best practices" that would suggest ways to bring charity back into the parishes. She caught wind of Church of the Epiphany's JustFaith and was amazed by what Jezreel told her: the parish had many hands on deck, the budget had grown immensely, and the parishioners were engaging their local community in a variety of ways. After Jezreel left Epiphany, Kennedy invited him to several regional meetings each year to discuss the ways parishes could bring more of their members to social justice, peace activism, and general outreach. Kennedy's successor, Pamela Evans, continued promoting Jezreel as an excellent and dynamic speaker for Catholic social outreach, and by 2000, he was speaking at as many as ten major venues annually, which meant that larger and more numerous organizations learned about Jezreel and his work.

The needs of the Jezreel family seemed to coincide with that of Catholic Charities. Although Jack thoroughly enjoyed farming, Maggie was ready to return to work, requiring that they move to a more populated area. Evans and others at Catholic Charities USA believed JustFaith was a great way for Catholics to learn about the church's teachings on peace and justice. Catholic Charities also noticed that they had more volunteers than before and that many of them had graduated from JustFaith. Realizing that they could directly benefit from promoting the program, they explored the possibility of some sort of sponsorship. Initially, Catholic Charities was hesitant, unsure about how to fund the project. Fortunately, a graduate from the first year it ran at Epiphany donated "*major* seed money" to Catholic Charities, and that, in addition to smaller donations from other grads and program registration fees, supported the project, with Jezreel working from his new Louisville home as the lone staff person. Jezreel's job was to promote and create a JustFaith program that parishes across the country could run themselves. Catholic Charities helped JustFaith gain national attention by promoting it in the local Catholic Charities offices as well.

Pat Dillon, a parishioner at Epiphany who had become an active Just-Faith facilitator, called Jezreel soon after to ask if there was anything she could do to help him get "JustFaith National" off the ground. He explained graciously that the project consisted of writing manuals, giving workshops—things he could only do himself. Over the course of the day, he realized all the organizational help he could use and the next day called her back, offering her a very busy and very unpaid position. Luckily for Jezreel, Dillon brought valuable skills from her previous employment. She had published a book on medical care, lending an editor's eye to the materials. She had worked in a significant leadership position with the Hospice of Louisville, overseeing 150 employees and a budget of several million dollars, a testimony to her organizational skills. Dillon had also taught at a major California university for twelve years and knew how to create a curriculum, eschewing Jezreel's casual style in favor of a more professional and thorough document, growing the three-page syllabus into complete plans for each meeting.

They divided the labor according to their skills, with Jezreel's charisma and vision placing him in charge of promoting JustFaith and Dillon's organizational and management skills helping the co-facilitators. They trained the co-facilitators at diocesan workshops and offered phone support to any facilitator who was having trouble. Jezreel and Dillon spent most of their time developing the curriculum, writing it as the program ran, sending out a six-week segment, and then prayerfully, yet frantically, working on the next installment, staying just ahead of the JustFaith groups. This early curriculum was not as detailed as the 350-page JustFaith program that JFM offers today, but the early program is quite similar to it in substance. Jezreel and Dillon did not have permissions for prayers from copyrighted works, for instance, but they suggested particular prayer books for purchase and recommended specific prayers from them. There were several faith-based social justice videos covering a variety of topics, from world hunger to Catholic social teaching. They worked with the Catholic Campaign for Human Development (CCHD)—the social justice arm of the United States Conference of Catholic Bishops (USCCB)—to develop a "Journey to Justice Day," a day to meet people from CCHD-funded projects and learn more about local efforts to promote justice. Recognizing that this program would be run by volunteers, they shortened it from thirty-five weeks to an even thirty and reduced the number of retreats from three to two. The main concern Jezreel and Dillon had was that many parishes did not (and do not) have a full-time social justice minister who would have the theological background to explain Catholic social teaching. They hoped that the detailed curriculum and the thorough facilitator training would create uniformity in the groups' experience, which would yield the same level of transformation and social engagement that Epiphany experienced.

The program was a huge success. In the first year, Jezreel expected a dozen groups and was elated when sixty-eight signed up. The following year, there were 156 groups. In the third year, enrollment had grown to 230 groups, and the organization was finally in a position to offer Dillon a paycheck. Dillon reflects: "It is a remarkable story. I don't know if as you're writing it you find it as remarkable as it was living it, but it was and continues to be just an amazing story about a small, little organization that has had a big impact and how it started was just amazing." Those involved in the early days of JustFaith still cannot believe that what began in 1989 as a small faith-formation program at Epiphany has become a national phenomenon.

Some of this early and rapid spread of JustFaith was due to the highly organized nature of the Catholic Church. Parishes are grouped into dioceses that have central offices, some of which have a director of peace and justice or a director of parish social ministry. JustFaith, when it really began to take off, often spread through the diocesan offices of social justice. These gatekeepers would recognize the name Catholic Charities, be very receptive to the format (study and prayer) and content (orthodox Catholic social teaching), and would quickly disseminate it to either all parishes or at least the ones they knew would be most interested, saving JustFaith the resources that promotion requires. Besides creating a more detailed curriculum, Jezreel and Dillon put a lot of energy into communicating with diocesan leaders. The two main venues to which they initially gained entry were the Catholic Social Ministry Gathering, under the USCCB, and the Social Action Summer Institute, sponsored by numerous Catholic agencies. These are both major Catholic conferences that gather parish leaders—mostly laypeople—to learn more about ministry tools and opportunities related to social outreach. Additionally, in 2002 Jezreel established a national advisory board, the members of which also helped to promote the program in their areas.

In early 2004, Jezreel thought they could take on the project for which so many grads had asked: a faith-and-justice-based high school program. Jezreel had become good friends with Mike Campbell while working at Epiphany. Campbell was in charge of the youth ministry at Epiphany at the same time that Jezreel handled the adult and justice programming. He was currently working for the diocese as the director of youth formation and had just received a peace and justice award from the National Federation for Catholic Youth Ministry, giving him some clout in the Catholic youth ministry world. Jezreel approached him to see if he would contract out to develop a program that could offer high school students a similar transformative process. At this same time, Jezreel and Dillon realized that they had outgrown the resources Catholic Charities could offer. Catholic Charities was going through a hiring freeze while more than 275 JustFaith groups were meeting. Catholic Charities was finding it difficult to spare the administrative time that JustFaith National's communications and bookkeeping required. Jezreel saw this as an opportunity to become their own 501(c)3, JFM. This also gave them a chance to change their relationship with other organizations. Rather than being *sponsored* by Catholic Charities and being *funded* by CCHD and having an *informal* relationship with Catholic Relief Services, JFM could become *partners* with them. These organizations would give JFM a certain amount of money and would promote it as they were able. In return, these partner organizations were integrated into the curriculum, such as providing guest speakers or having organizational publications as assigned reading. Also, these partner organizations gained access to graduate addresses for donation solicitations and to notify the grads about local opportunities for engagement.

Once they realized that they were going to be an independent organization, they approached Campbell with, instead of a contract job, an invitation to join their staff to create JusticeWalking, more commonly called JWalking. They also hired a JustFaith grad, one who underwent a drastic lifestyle change because of the program, to be the business manager. A former member of Campbell's youth group came on as an administrative assistant, putting their staff at five members in 2005. At this point, JustFaith was truly a national phenomenon, having run in 108 dioceses and with more than seventy-five hundred graduates. Despite the breadth of the organization, it was still run as though it were a small project, with everyone working from home and getting together for meetings in Jezreel's living room. With two new hires in 2006, they decided to move into a small office in northeast Louisville. They gradually knocked down walls, expanding their space as more staff members came on board.

Some Protestant congregations had heard of JustFaith and, from 2001, were running the program, designed for Catholics, with their own denominationally specific modifications. Some Protestants took JustFaith at their Catholic spouse's parish and were excited to later bring it to their own congregation. However, often a pastor resisted the program because it contained too much Catholic theology. JFM wanted to create a curriculum that approached faith-based justice work from a Protestant perspective, allowing the program to reach more people.

Jezreel drew on his experience at his Baptist undergrad and the Catholic/Mennonite community, as well as the insights from an advisory committee of about a dozen Protestants from multiple traditions who had been through the Catholic program. As part of this endeavor, they partnered with Bread for the World, a multidenominational hunger lobby that asks congregations to write letters to politicians in the hope of affecting international policies on poverty and hunger. Jezreel, the consummate optimist, believed that Bread for the World's extant relationships with Protestant churches would cause the ecumenical version of JustFaith to take off: "I had anticipated that the Bread for the World sponsorship [would make a difference], and the fact that JustFaith Catholic was getting into so many Protestant churches with no promotion for us. And I thought, 'Well, if we promote it, if we create a resource exactly *for* the Protestant network, if we had Bread for the World's name on it! Like, oh . . . we'll be overwhelmed!'" Bread for the World was also an excited partner because volunteers or guests at events would often say that they learned of Bread for the World through JustFaith.

Instead, Bread for the World's relationships with its congregations proved to be weaker than the raw numbers indicated. For example, a congregation might have only one or two people actively involved in the hunger issue while the remainder of the congregation is less interested in poverty and, therefore, not interested in a program like JustFaith, ecumenical or otherwise. Actual registrations proved to be a tenth of what Jezreel anticipated, with twenty groups when they launched the ecumenical version in 2007 and never more than thirty-nine in a year. Despite a variety of efforts, including bringing more Protestants to their board and staff, registration for the Protestant program was fairly flat and then decreased even further. More recently, however, the enrollment for the ecumenical program has been increasing with twenty-five groups in 2017 and twenty-nine groups by August 2018.

Contributing to JFM's lack of success in the Protestant world are two other factors that one would not run into among Catholics. The first is that many of the mainline denominations, which tend to have theologies friendly to peace and justice, are rapidly losing members. Pastors concerned with simply keeping people coming to church are unlikely to offer them a difficult, long, intense program that invites members to shake up their understanding of the world. The data support this theory. The Protestant congregants in this study enjoy vibrant communities with extensive ministry offerings—one of them with a staff of over thirty—and are clear exceptions to their denomination's rule of membership loss. Second, many Protestant denominations have a more congregational polity, without the regional gatekeepers and centralization that helped JustFaith spread in the Catholic world.[14]

The same year JFM offered an ecumenical version of JustFaith, it also began a new program called JustMatters. These "modules" are much shorter and focus on a particular issue, like prison reform or climate change. The following year, in 2008, it launched Engaging Spirituality, a program that incorporates centering prayer with Catholic social teaching.

Donors have been very generous to JFM, but their financial support appears to be waning. JFM has enjoyed ample monetary support over the years, with over half of its revenue coming from program graduates. The 2012 fiscal report shows that the total operating expenses were $1,282,723, and the organization enjoyed a roughly $61,000 surplus. More recently, it has not enjoyed seven-figure budgets. Organizational budgets continued to be impressive, and the staff size peaked in 2014 with twenty-three employees. The 2015 revenue dropped to $960,087 and then fell precipitously to $468,269 in 2016. The 2017 revenue was likewise low, but there were also fewer staff, making the 2017 budget deficit much lower than that of 2016.

Registrations began to drop around 2010 and remained fairly steady, with 4,300 to 5,100 participants each year from 2014 to 2016. The 2017 IRS Tax Form 990, however, only reports three thousand participants. One Louisville grad who took JustFaith in 2006 spoke six years later, unaware that the program's enrollment had dropped even then: "They live by attraction versus promotion, and I think when people see [inspirational] people, one of two things happens, they think, 'Why, I don't want to attempt to do that,' or they think, 'I want what that person's got, the peace they've got, the understanding they've got.'" This attraction-over-promotion strategy aptly describes JFM in the beginning, with parishes banging down the door and the tiny organization scrambling to keep up. But later on, JFM would need to promote its programs in order to reach out to Catholics less aware of the social teachings of the church. One of the JFM staff describes the easy success of JustFaith in the beginning as that of low-hanging fruit:

> So you have a parish where maybe there's some tradition of social justice or progressive theology or whatever, and you have some people who say "We've been waiting for something like this for a long time. Where do we sign up?" . . . then all of a sudden, that ten percent of those folks, the liberals or the people who are inclined to doing this kind of work, they're done. And the rest just say "*Thirty weeks?* Are you kidding me? Why would we want to do that?" . . . That's why we're kind of right now going through a bit of an ebb in terms of the numbers for registrations.

The idea of saturating the most available segment of the market has a good deal of merit. Without active recruitment on the part of the grads, especially if they are lacking the support of the pastor, JustFaith's parish presence eventually diminishes.

Structural factors also played into the decline. The recession of 2008 hit corporate America, as well as the churches and nonprofits. This forced dioceses to prioritize their mission and consider what the most critical positions were when making staffing cuts. Many elected either to close their offices for peace and justice or to combine them with other outreach programs, eliminating or diluting the attention given to justice issues. Because of these organizational changes, JFM lost much of its institutional support. The future of the organization depended on a very deliberate self-promotion at the same time that it recognized that many of the most culturally available Catholics, that is, those with an interest in the church's social teachings, had already taken JustFaith. Even while the organization is clearly showing signs of difficulty, that program participants—more removed from the organization—remain grateful and enthusiastic is important to note.

Low enrollment explains the latest addition to JFM's offerings: Good-NewsPeople. The staff designed this program with the intention of reaching large numbers of "middle-pew" parishioners—so called because their parish involvement lies between the most and least active in the parish—by asking a parish to commit to ten groups with ten participants each. This larger net, with content designed for moderately active Catholics, helps JFM reach a new and larger audience that it was not privy to before, offering a chance to awaken in thousands of participants a concern for the poor. A second strategy was to look for new gatekeepers. With the elimination of many diocesan social justice offices, JFM turned its attention to the parish level and its directors of religious education (DREs). Pope Benedict XVI proclaimed 2013 the Year of Faith, and the staff of JFM created a resource for DREs that would help them celebrate and enact this theme through prayers, opportunities for action, quotes from popes, scriptural reflections, and the like. GoodNewsPeople caused a significant increase in the number of participants the year of its launch—roughly nine thousand—but JFM was not able to sustain this enrollment in the years that followed.

JFM has created a variety of programs for those interested in understanding Christianity's, especially Catholicism's, notion of the role of the church and the Christian in the world. JFM gives participants in all programs group guidelines, asking them to "honor differences ... listen intently ... practice sacred listening ... respectfully seek clarification ... [assure that] everyone has an opportunity to speak ... [and] participate fully."[15] This emphasis on listening, interpersonal respect, and so forth are common to all programs. A fair number of the interviewees mentioned that these guidelines allowed for motley assortments of individuals—with a variety of ages, experiences, political leanings, and theological beliefs and practices—to come together for the JustFaith process. Although there is much learning, with the readings drawing on social science, theology, ethics, and other fields, understanding JFM programs as a "class" akin to a university course, where the main objective is to acquire knowledge, would be a mistake. The small size of each group facilitates dialogue and reflection, helping people incorporate their experiences and those of others into the process. It is as affective as it is intellectual, with the primary purpose being the transformation of the whole self. There are also important differences in the programs, such as duration and topics covered. Appendix B covers the programs in greater depth.

Styles of Public Catholicism

JFM and the significance of the discipleship style in the American social landscape are best understood as a small chapter in the voluminous history of Roman Catholics in the American public sphere. It is part of the long tradition that includes hospitals, schools, civic associations, and nonprofits that brought Catholicism outside the walls of the parish building and into the parish territory. The needs and mission of the church and its members have changed throughout its five-hundred-year history in the United States, giving rise to different kinds of institutions and varying missions. Because the discipleship style emerges from this tradition, understanding the ways in which it builds on and departs from the organizations that precede it is helpful. This sociohistorical overview shows the ways that both Catholicism and American culture have shaped one another, contextualizing contemporary American Catholic civic engagement.

Like the discipleship style, earlier styles of public Catholicism— republican, immigrant, and evangelical—emerged from specific sociohistorical circumstances, and each style has adapted and persisted to this day. These styles have unique theological emphases, approaches to the wider society, and understandings of the mission of the church. Each style thus brings different assets and liabilities for understanding the role of the church in the public square. Although the three earlier styles differ in obvious ways, they share something in common: each has created a dualism in the lives of the faithful, separating what it defined as the "holy" from the "world" in different ways. This causes Catholics to confine the expression of "holiness in everyday life" to priests, lay ministers, Catholic schoolteachers, employees of a Catholic charity, Catholic Workers, and so forth, thus weakening what could be the full thrust of Catholic engagement with the world. JFM, however, as an organization of the discipleship style, provides Catholics with new religious tools so that they may bring their faith to public life in a consciously Catholic way.

Although a distinctive style characterizes particular eras, that each of the three earlier styles was the prevailing style of its time, not the exclusive style, is important to note. There were certainly other styles operating less obviously in Catholic thought, as well. Exploring these three historical styles illustrates the consistencies and departures in the discipleship style, providing the historical backdrop and social context to understand the more recent emergence of what I identify as now a fourth style: the discipleship style. (Summaries of each of these styles are at the close of this chapter in table 1.1)

The Republican Style (1750–1820)

The republican style has its roots in the strong democratic impulses that characterized early European immigrants on the Atlantic coast. Because of the suspicions Protestants harbored toward Catholics, Catholics divided their lives into private and public realms, isolating their religion from their civic lives. This strategy prevented Catholicism from influencing public life, yet it nevertheless allowed individual Catholics to hold both a strong Catholic and American identity, albeit not simultaneously. The ideas of participatory government, individual liberty, religious tolerance, egalitarianism, and an optimistic view of the reasonableness of others shaped the law and customs of the country, including the beliefs and practices of the Christian faithful. Although this litany of republican virtues seemed inimical to much in official Catholic teaching at the time, American Catholicism would be deeply influenced by these values and perhaps no institution reflects the American Catholic identity of the laity of this time better than lay trustees, that is, boards of the lay faithful who participated in parish governance with the pastor.

Lay Trustees

The democratic impulse was strong among American Catholics, and it was something they desired in their civic life as well as in their parishes. However, it caused a bitter conflict between the laity and much of the hierarchy. At times, the lay trustee issue was a thorn in Jesuit bishop John Carroll's side, saying he "would sooner see a whole Congregation leave the communion of the Church than yield" to their choice for pastor.[16] At other times, he saw its merits and initially supported the lay trustee system because it promoted a republican form of Catholicism. The conflicts surrounding the trustee issue were unique to Catholics. Protestants tended to argue over doctrinal matters, whereas for Catholics, the primary struggle was over power.[17] The laity wanted to fund their church as well as participate and share in the decision-making.

The movement for lay participation needed institutional support, and it found that in John England. Three months after being consecrated bishop in his native Ireland in 1820, he arrived at his post in the Diocese of Charleston. England was a strong supporter of the lay trustee movement and finessed the democratic leanings of his people to be more compatible with Rome's hierarchical model, saying he wanted the laity to be "empowered to cooperate but not to dominate."[18] He drew up a constitution for his diocese spelling out the requirements of being on the board of trustees, of which the pastor was president. Some issues the pastor could not veto, and in severe cases, the board could petition the bishop for removal of the pastor. England worked hard to establish trustees in each parish and held regular meetings with the clergy and laity, who would discuss issues of the diocese, with all matters subject to the final authority of the bishop. In this way, both the autonomy of the laity and the episcopal authority could coexist. Many clergy were against the idea of trustees, saying it was a Protestant custom. Parishioners pointed out that the idea had precedent in feudal Europe, where kings and landlords who endowed churches reserved the right to appoint or dismiss clergy.[19] Why, they argued, could not the people who collectively financed a church enjoy the same privileges?

With church authority that was somewhat shared, there were often major clashes. Sometimes the bishop simply moved a disliked pastor to another parish. In other cases, the laity did not get their wishes, and when they were especially defiant, the bishop would place the parish under interdict and excommunicate the parishioners.[20] Conflicts could last as long as twenty years and sometimes even turned violent, with one exceptionally heated conflict ending in a riot, leaving roughly two hundred parishioners injured. These exceptional incidents aside, historians have uncovered a rich tradition of successful lay involvement in both the organizational and the decision-making life of the parish. Without a doubt, lay trustees led to conflict in some cases, but more often, they were competent, accomplished, and a great asset to the early American Church.

The energies that gave rise to lay trustees met strong opposition and eventually dissipated. Once America won independence, the country's vigorous promotion of democracy began to wane.[21] Furthermore, the new wave of immigrants brought a more monarchical view of the church, adding momentum to the movement away from lay trustees and other forms of democratization.[22] In addition, in 1829, at their first meeting as a national body, the American bishops voted to eliminate lay trustees and move all church property into the hands of the diocese, a first step in the process of centralization.[23] The combined influence of the increasing federalism, the monarchical mores of the immigrants and the clear objection of the clergy marked the end of any notable lay involvement until the founding of the St. Vincent de Paul society in 1845. The trustee question set a precedent for how the church would later understand its public mission, underscoring the role of the laity in engaging society on behalf of the whole church.

Modern Expressions and Evaluation of the Republican Style

The bifurcation of private life from public life, Catholicism from civil society and politics, is one of the defining qualities of the republican style. In their attempt to resolve the American Catholic tension, they separated the two, showing themselves that they could assimilate and still be good Catholics and signaling to others that Catholicism was not a threat to American life. Shaped by Anglo-American Catholics, the Enlightenment, and anti-Catholic prejudice, the republican style had a very strong, yet very private, piety, consisting mainly of devotions, study, and personal works of mercy. Compared to the church in Europe, Catholics had a great deal of opportunities for lay involvement within the actual running of parish life.

This style manifests in contemporary public Catholicism. The bishops use the republican style—with its nontheistic use of reason and natural law—when addressing a wider audience, such as to "people of good will." For example, in the 1983 American bishops' pastoral letter *The Challenge of Peace*, they discuss their arguments and conclusions differently depending on whether they are writing within a republican or evangelical framework. When engaged in a republican style, the bishops offer a nuanced portrait of world affairs with the secularism of natural law. When drawing on the evangelical style, they tend to use more prophetic and biblical language, giving clearer directives to modern Christians.

The strength of the republican style is obvious: it draws on language, norms, and values that are generally accepted by and that appeal to the whole American people rather than to just Catholics. It fits well with many American civic values. It is pluralistic through the removal of any sectarian language, preferring instead the rhetoric of natural law and a theologically vague notion of God. It dovetails with a very American notion of liberty, as freedom *from*; by defining faith as a private affair, the republican style limits religious influence so that it does not infringe on the beliefs of others. This style encourages rational civic participation through nonconfrontational political involvement (e.g., congressional letter writing), helping Catholics understand themselves as citizens. The republican approach is rooted in both the Enlightenment's optimism that people are at root reasonable and the importance of political participation. In these ways, the republican style attends to the diversity of the American people and carves out a political space for Catholics to solve problems in a secular context.

The weakness is that it might not be compelling or distinctly Catholic. In *The Challenge of Peace*, the bishops were strong and clear when they used the evangelical style, unequivocally condemning nuclear war. Later in this same letter, they drew on the republican style, acknowledging the complexity of the issue and offering little sense of how rank-and-file

Catholics or the church as a whole might bring faith to bear on work or politics. This style brackets faith, relegating it to the realm of private devotions with little significance on a person's life in the world. The republican voice, in its effort to appeal to all people, can appear assimilationist as it lends humanist ethics and provides Catholics little direction as to how they might bring religious beliefs into the public sphere. Additionally, pushing religion into the private sphere is problematic for the mission of the church. The organizations of the republican style put Catholics into public life as *Americans*, not as *Catholics*. There is, hence, no way for the church to evangelize the wider society in the republican style. In sum, although the republican style helps American Catholics enter public life in some ways, in other ways, it risks losing elements that are central to the faith.

◆

The Immigrant Style (1820–1920)

The story of the immigrant church is a story of embattlement. There was a great deal of prejudice in the Catholic world, with Protestants against Catholics, Catholics against Protestants, and Catholic ethnic groups against one another. This prejudice, this "prickly apartness" as historian Charles R. Morris calls it, drew sharp in-group boundaries that animated Catholics and the church for roughly a century.[24] At this time, the issue of lay trustees withered. The church was no longer concerned about authority, turning its attention instead to the great masses of Catholics emigrating from Europe. As Catholics grew from a small fraction of Americans into the largest denomination by 1850, Protestant churches responded to this wave of poverty by offering services with "bread in one hand, and the Gospel in the other."[25] Catholic leaders feared this would draw members away, so they created many organizations to care for the arriving poor.[26] There was a great deal of institutional support for these organizations, with cooperation among bishops, sisters, and laity. It was not long before the situation of the poor overwhelmed the wealthy and middle class. The long-term solution to alleviating poverty was education, but the public school system, as a *de facto* Protestant institution, would undermine their children's faith. The majority of Catholics believed that the only choice was to build their own schools, yielding the most robust institution of the immigrant style.

Protecting the Faith: The Catholic School

After the American Revolution, public schools began to open more steadily, especially in the northern states. The United States had one of the highest literacy rates in the Western world, reaching 90 percent in some regions, and by 1870 every state had public elementary schools.[27] Public schools were also undergoing a cultural shift, with Americans understanding them as educative institutions as well as a primary locus of socialization for American values.[28] Recognizing the impact schools had on youth, Bishop John Hughes of New York made the creation of schools the church's principal task.[29] Undaunted by the denial of public funds and aware of the Protestant tenor of the public schools, he believed the only choice was to call upon Catholics to sacrifice in order to fund the schools. By 1840, Hughes had five thousand children enrolled in eight Catholic schools, but roughly twelve thousand remained without Catholic education.[30] Nodding to the anti-Catholic sentiments in the public schools, he wrote, "I think the time is almost come when it will be necessary to build the school-house first, and the church afterwards."[31] By 1865, 75 percent of the city's parishes had schools.[32]

Most school boards and local government bodies were transitioning from a general Protestantism to the secularism of the Blaine Amendment.[33] Once public schools became more areligious, Catholic schools would become a refuge from another kind of Catholic fear: the perceived secularism of the age. Bernard McQuaid, bishop of Rochester, called it a "mongrel morality, this code of compromises and concessions, a bit from Tom Paine, another from Jesus of Nazareth, some sentences from Benjamin Franklin, then Saul of Tarsus, something too from atheist Frenchmen, all sifted and sorted by a school board nominated at a ward caucus and elected amid the turbulence of party strife."[34] Thus, the push for Catholic schools had different motives depending on the historical context, with secularism perceived as a greater social threat during this period relative to the past. In the Plenary Council of 1884, the bishops wrote that teaching religion in school was of central importance for moral living:

> To shut religion out of the school, and keep it for home and the Church, is, logically, to train up a generation that will consider religion good for

home and Church, but not for the practical business of real life. But a more false and pernicious notion could not be imagined. Religion, in order to elevate a people, should inspire their whole life and rule their relations with one another . . . From the shelter of home and school, the youth must go out into the busy ways of trade or traffic or professional practice. In all these, the principles of religion should animate and direct them.[35]

The bishops were arguing that religion should be the *basis* of one's life, informing all other aspects, and not merely a private issue, relegated to home and church and isolated from public life. Catholics, however, did not have the cultural tools to put this ideology into practice. The republican style put religion into public life only as a general public morality with nothing particularly Catholic; elements specific to Catholicism were to remain private or among Catholics. The immigrant style was defensive against the wider culture, resulting in a parallel Catholic universe that reacted to the wider culture to secure specific rights and protections for the practice of their Catholic faith. These republican and immigrant discourses shaped the ways the bishops approached the school debate. Republican-style Catholics, like Archbishop John Ireland, wanted to have all schools funded by public money, teaching academics during normal school hours with optional religious—and church-funded—courses after school. Other bishops of the immigrant style, who became the dominant voice in the school issue, feared that the secularization of the regular school day would lead to improperly instructed Catholics and too much Catholic assimilation. On close inspection, neither camp listened to the pastoral letter published by the bishops in 1884. Neither strict separatism nor the bracketing of religious instruction would create a mind-set in which Catholics would make their faith the basis of both their public and private lives. From the immigrant perspective, the Catholic and American identities were mutually exclusive. The parish school, Catholic to the core, epitomized the immigrant style of Catholic engagement in this period.

Modern Expressions and Evaluation of the Immigrant Style

Protestant hegemony, a secular school system, and the resurgence in nativist activities shaped immigrant-era Catholics' engagement with the wider American society. The immigrant style required Catholics to set themselves against non-Catholics, justifying the social isolation and sacrifice Catholic schools and similar parallel institutions brought with them. Even among today's American-born Catholics, remnants of the immigrant style persist in contemporary Catholic political activity. Like earlier days, the single-issue advocacy of the Catholic school system was a rally for the church and gave the immigrants a strong sense of being together with their church in an embattled conflict. Similarly, as O'Brien notes, certain issues—abortion, same-sex marriage, contraception, and others—and community organizing have mobilized some Catholics with a similar single-mindedness. Rather than being the embattled Irish facing the Know-Nothings or the embattled Catholics facing Protestant-dominated schools, there are the embattled Catholics protecting the unborn from a culture of death and the embattled poor confronting oppressive laws and the interests of the powerful. Just like their predecessors, they construct a Catholic worldview that contrasts with an outgroup, make great sacrifices to further their cause, and are uncompromising in their struggle.

A strength of this style is that it does not need consensus; the immigrant style does not seek a middle ground. It reacts when its interests are threatened and it mobilizes its resources with great enthusiasm. It always involves the laity, partly to demonstrate the Catholicity of their position and partly because there is strength in numbers. This sectarian subculture lent Catholics many advantages, such as a separate space to practice the traditions and customs of their homelands and helping the church to foster in-group identity. This also preserved the church's unity despite the diversity of cultures and interests that would have manifested more strongly otherwise.[36] These strengths are visible in the modern church as well. Catholicism has moral, cultural, and organizational resources that groups can draw on, allowing them to be more effective and understand their political actions in religious terms rather than simply secular. Those against abortion or same-sex marriage on the right and the community organizers of the left are also successful in minimizing the significance of Catholic political diversity or dissent by defining *church* through a position on a particular issue.

The weaknesses are that this style is focused on ends, is fueled by embattlement, and does not consider the message of transformation and love in the Gospels. Those of both the immigrant and evangelical style identify enemies, but evangelicals will try to love their enemy whereas those of the immigrant style will manipulate the power dynamic to further their end. Another weakness is the way these Catholics focus on particular causes instead of the common good (although they may couch their arguments in the language of the common good). Unlike their republican counterparts, immigrant-style Catholics are ideologically driven to the point of losing sight of potential compromises. Because of the reactionary, special-interest approach, immigrant organizations hamper their ability to affect the wider culture, which is a major setback from an institutional perspective. As far as opening a way for Catholics to enter public life as Catholics, the immigrant style fails because, although Catholic organizations mirror those in the wider society, they are hostile to that which is non-Catholic, limiting the scope of the church's relevance.

Evangelical Catholicism (1920–1960)

In the early 1900s, the church's desire to understand "evangelization" helped birth this evangelical style of engagement. Catholics of the immigrant style understood evangelization as bringing more Americans into the church. More and more Catholics, however, began to think of evangelization as bringing their Catholicism to bear on pressing social issues.[37] This style also emerged from Catholics' gradual movement into the middle class.[38] With greater resources and questions of war and economy looming large during World War I and the Great Depression, they began to look outside themselves and bring a critical eye to the problems in their communities, nation, and world.

In 1931, Pope Pius XI released *Quadragesimo Anno*, subtitled *On the Reconstruction of the Social Order*, in which he proposed a new economic system. Rather than capitalism or socialism, Pius XI advocated for a guild-based system, which would involve both owners and workers in decision making and would make the common good, rather than individual gain, the primary focus. This papal encyclical was the first to use the phrase "social justice," meaning a justice that applies to the common good, intended to be a moral guide for both personal and collective decisions. Unlike the 1891 reception of *Rerum Novarum*, the first social encyclical, *Quadragesimo Anno*, was warmly received. Lay Catholics were in different circumstances and now had strong bishops who had become more progressive and were intent on bringing justice to the pulpits. The laity helped develop this emerging evangelical style, which is perhaps most clearly articulated in the Catholic Worker movement.

Creating Christian Alternatives: The Catholic Worker

Just as lay trustees are representative of the republican style and the sectarianism of the ethnic parish and its adjacent school epitomizes the immigrant style, the Catholic Worker offers the clearest organizational articulation of the evangelical style. On May 1, 1933—the feast of St. Joseph the Worker—Dorothy Day, Peter Maurin, and a few others peddled the first twenty-five hundred issues of the *Catholic Worker* for a penny a copy. Soon the periodical was reaching readers across the nation, with 190,000 readers in five years, and (mostly younger) followers were establishing small houses of hospitality for living among the poor they served.[39] Poverty was, as Maurin and Day saw it, Jesus's central concern and so they made it theirs. They were angry at the exploitation of the poor and lived in voluntary poverty, which joyfully freed them from material constraints. The perfectionism of the Gospels motivated them, not the minimalism of the republican style's natural law tradition. They believed in material relief but thought it was more important to create relationships with those they served. In the end, they did not look to results other than the transformation of self and love of God and one another, and they believed this love would radically transform the world. Another essential ingredient for the evangelical pilgrim is community. Community insulates Catholics from the wider world and its evils; it is how they celebrate the sacraments, and it is where they dispense and receive love and mercy.

The Catholic Worker movement brought Americans a new way of being Catholic. After World War II, American Catholics would have to confront pluralism and freedom in ways they had not in the past.[40] Due to cultural shifts that underscored the importance of the individual, both in American society and in the documents of the Second Vatican Council, Catholics would find themselves drawing not only upon doctrines but also personal experience. They would be just as Catholic but understand their religion within the broad Christian tradition. With an emphasis on Christ as revealed in the poor and an approach that was personal and pragmatic, the Catholic Worker Movement would help the American Church more deliberately embody these new values and vision.

Modern Expressions and Evaluation of the Evangelical Style

The clearest contemporary expression of the evangelical style is the Catholic Worker Movement and similar live-in communities, such as Jonah House. Whether the issues are personal morality or ones of justice, the evangelical solution is to withdraw from the evils of society and turn toward the ways of the Gospel. Having a personal transformation, reinforced in a community of like-minded believers, grants a small Eden, generating light to dispel the darkness outside. The evangelical style also manifests culturally in official church documents. *The Challenge of Peace* illustrates this prophetic language in the portions condemning war unequivocally.

The greatest strength of the evangelical style is the primacy it places on scripture. It looks to the Gospel and the challenges it poses and sees an invitation for daily living. It makes religion the foundation of life, allowing faith to determine the relationships to other aspects of life. By doing this, it brings the wisdom of scripture and tradition to society, critical and comfortable with being unpopular. Another obvious strength is the raw, intense conviction Catholics of this style demonstrate to others. They show an unfailing dedication to the Gospel and a level of hope that compels them to action despite the slim odds of success. Catholics are often impressed by the dedication and alternative lifestyles of those who live in intentional community.

In the end, the weakness of the evangelical worldview is that, although many admire the holy laborers, outsiders often deem their outlook idealistic and impractical. They may inspire individuals, but they cannot persuade the public as a whole through their radical language and deeds. Furthermore, the style has little room for compromise; they cannot table their faith for the sake of common ground or public good, for it is the very foundation of who they are. Because their faith is the basis of their convictions, they are captive to their Christian audience and are limited as to what they can effectively do for the wider public, which is problematic for a religiously plural society. Exacerbating this, their perfectionism often pulls them out of mainstream institutions, the very institutions they argue are in such need of change. Although the church has more influence on public institutions in this style compared to the immigrant style, they still have little to no influence over the most powerful structures in American life.

The Discipleship Style . . . and JFM

Each style discussed earlier arose from social circumstances that caused Catholics to remove their religion from the wider society. The republican style dealt with anti-Catholic sentiments by privatizing religion. The immigrant style rejected non-Catholic America and embraced the Catholic poor by creating a subculture with parallel institutions. The evangelical style saw the problem in secular structures and—finding them incompatible with their faith—rejected many institutions and attempted to supplant them with faith-based models. However, these other styles provided Catholics religious meaning through the ubiquitous institutions that made them cognizant of their faith as they came home from work at the Catholic hospital, dropped off outgrown clothes at a St. Vincent de Paul, and helped a child rehearse the corporal works of mercy for tomorrow's test. Now Catholics do not enjoy the same institutional vitality, with many Catholic organizations run by paid professionals instead of parishioners' labor. Given the dearth of distinctively Catholic institutions and their presence off parish grounds, if today's organizations use the styles of the past, American Catholics will not easily bring their faith to their daily lives. Contemporary Catholics navigate different circumstances that have given rise to a new style of engagement that "works" given these social realities: the discipleship style. JFM employs this style, which allows Catholics' faith to influence their lives rather than bracketing it from other spheres.

In the latter part of the twentieth century, American Catholics experienced three major shifts that undermined the efficacy of the three historical styles and became the roots for this fourth style: increased geographic mobility, greater individual moral authority, and rising socioeconomic status. These changes diminished the bloc approach of the historical styles, offering a new style of Catholic organization that approached public life in a more personalist way. The first of these roots, an increase in geographic mobility among Americans generally, dispersed Catholics, weakening the ability of parishes to form the stable relief societies they relied on. Important trends in past American culture, such as anti-Catholicism, had the effect of cementing in-group bonds among Catholics, which fostered the social capital that facilitates community and institution building. With greater geographic mobility, however, Catholics have found long-term community and institution building more difficult. As people relocate more frequently, they forgo civic associations and more long-term projects, preferring instead the role of the volunteer, with its low commitment and easy exit.[41] Similarly, this increase in volunteering comes with a corresponding decrease in those "working on a community project," the latter of which describes the sort of shared endeavors typically undertaken by organizations of the earlier historical styles.[42] This increase in geographic mobility required that Catholic organizations create an alternative to the tightly knit aid societies of the past, a more informal way for individuals, rather than groups, to get involved in one's community.

The second social root of the discipleship style is Catholics' greater emphasis on individual moral authority. This has changed the way Catholics understand and use power, both individually and institutionally. Because of the dearth of clergy, republican laity held a good deal of power through the lay trustee system. With the immigrants, power was centralized in the hands of the bishops. In the era of the evangelical style, parishes and small communities were important places of Catholic power. In each period, although the locus of power changed, Catholics themselves were relatively cohesive and followed the designated leaders more or less willingly. Catholics now are increasingly likely to say that moral authority resides in individuals.[43] Admittedly, Catholics were never as united as most Americans assumed they were. However, by the 1970s, their dissent and division became public. Because they increasingly attribute moral authority to individual selves, they have come to exercise greater agency and choice in engaging the public sphere. They have consequently gravitated to more personalized service commitments, which has two important repercussions. First, it scatters Catholics, diffusing collective Catholic power. Second, this vocational approach to service commitments diminishes direct magisterial power as Catholics focus their energies on issues that they personally feel are important rather than taking cues from their priest or bishop.

The final root of the discipleship style is Catholics' increasing socio-economic status. Catholics' place on the American social ladder has fluctuated considerably. The Catholics of the republican style were relatively wealthy. Catholics of the immigrant era were much poorer. They saw a modest rise in education and income during the time of the evangelical style. Catholics have continued to improve their socioeconomic status and now approximate the national averages in education and income.[44] These increasingly professionalized Catholics are looking to channel their efforts into something that is personally meaningful and makes the most of their talents.[45] Organizations of the discipleship style mobilize individual Catholics to pursue volunteer commitments according to their specific skills and desires.

In sum, these three social shifts—geographic mobility, individual moral authority, and increased socioeconomic status—were roots for discipleship-style organizations, encouraging Catholics to engage society as individual actors rather than through the historical styles' associations. Some discipleship organizations were born out of this time, like JFM or an American Sant'Egidio movement. Others were virtually unknown and then increased in popularity, such as Opus Dei, which grew from having centers in eight US cities in 1975 to seventeen in 1995.[46]

Discipleship-style organizations seek social change through the transformation of individuals. Responding to the more personalist trends among American Catholics, discipleship organizations provide new outlooks and values for their members. These organizations reason that perceiving religious meaning in the world will change the way individuals act in society. Discipleship organizations, like JFM, hope that these new patterns of behavior will ripple out and transform society as well. Like the other styles, the discipleship style has a drawback for the institutional church. As noted earlier, this personalist emphasis allows Catholics to enter public life in a meaningful way, but they do so as individuals. The institutional church does not have the same control over the laity as it did in the past as the laity are free to pursue the causes they as individuals—rather than the church corporate—deem important.

Losing magisterial *control* is not the same as losing magisterial *influence*, a subtle but important distinction explored later.

Also, three dilemmas are inherent to this new style. The first is the dilemma of resistance. This is the tension of being in the world but not of it. It is navigating being both fully in the world, as the republicans were, while still living in strict accordance to higher principles that might cause one to turn away from the world, as the immigrants and evangelicals did. The discipleship style calls Catholics equally to both. The second dilemma is the dilemma of volunteerism. The discipleship style's emphasis on a transformation of the individual, one-on-one relationships, intimacy of the discipleship community, and so forth creates a culture that privileges individual acts of care rather than the corporate acts of justice that social movements work toward. The dilemma of volunteerism asks whether *individuals* can be effective agents of significant *social* change. The final dilemma is the dilemma of efficacy. Catholics now match, if not exceed, fellow Americans in education and income. As they engage society, they do not know whether they can most effectively alleviate poverty through a more direct approach, like social work, or indirectly by remaining in their position of greater wealth and power and using their influence and generosity for the benefit of the poor.

In sum, personalism matters. Personalism gave rise to the discipleship style, and it provides the basis for the four major characteristics of American Catholic life today: (1) individual rather than bloc engagement, (2) executing individual-level rather than structural solutions, (3) a growing sense of an internal locus of moral authority, and (4) seeking personal and religious meaning in volunteer commitments (and beyond). These characteristics have consequences.

Conclusion

Discipleship style organizations, like JFM, offer participants a chance to engage society in a deliberate and meaningful way. Although discipleship organizations—which include Opus Dei, Ignatian Volunteers, Sant'Egidio, and others—differ from one another in the specific issues and ideas that they bring to their participants, they share a desire to bring Catholicism to public life in an authentic and meaningful way for those involved. For example, JFM focuses on poverty, peace, and justice and encourages participants to engage in direct service as well as structural reform. Members of Sant'Egidio, another relatively new Catholic organization, are also concerned for the poor, but they devote much of their energy to the elderly, those with AIDS, and the homeless in a context of mercy. Discipleship organizations differ in their details but are similar in that they are animated by a religiously grounded vision of the world.

Both the similarities and differences among organizations of the discipleship style come into relief when examining their respective organizational cultures. A common thread to these organizational cultures is that they work with, rather than against, the social context of contemporary American Catholics by exposing participants to religious tenets on social ministry. Moreover, discipleship organizations, although often not a part of the institutional church, are still deeply rooted in their Catholicism. This is especially important as these Catholics are navigating a world that is not as connected to Catholic institutions as it was in generations past. The next chapter explores this culture, which accounts for much of the success of discipleship-style organizations, in greater depth.

TABLE 1.1. Features of Styles of Public Catholicism

	Republican	Immigrant	Evangelical	Discipleship
Sociohistorical roots (wider society, power, and class, respectively)	• Anti-Catholicism • Lack of clergy/ strong lay leadership • High socioeconomic status	• Anti-Catholicism • Strong episcopal leadership • High poverty rates	• Attention shifts to wider American culture • Strong parishes • Increasing socioeconomic status	• Geographic mobility • Moral authority in individuals • Solidly middle class and professional
Examples of Organizations	• Lay trustees • Devotional societies • USCCB	• Hospitals and schools (historically) • Anti-abortion groups • Community organizing groups	• Catholic Worker • Jonah House • Plowshares	• JFM • Opus Dei[1] • Sant'Egidio

(continued)

TABLE 1.1. (*continued*)

	Republican	Immigrant	Evangelical	Discipleship
Character-istics (Ch. 3 & 4, organi-zational model and relationship of Church and society)	• Nontheistic engagement with the world • Private Catholic, public citizen	• Parish societies and Catholic institutions serv-ing Catholics • Embrace Church, reject America	• Parish soci-eties serving all in need • Rejection of dominant structures	• Discipleship communities • Religious worldview
Strengths (Ch. 5 & 6)	• Fits well with American values • Encourages civic activism	• Emphasizes unity and mini-mizes diversity • Articulates clear moral imperative	• Focused on Scripture • Strong convictions can inspire others	• Brings religious meaning to world • Engages society in per-sonalist way
Weaknesses or Challenges (Ch. 5 & 6)	• Little distinctly Catholic • Minimal-ist ethics of natural law	• Reactionary rather than leading • Focus on issue rather than common good	• Little room for compromise • Christian mores pre-vent reach-ing wider audience	• Dilemma of resistance • Dilemma of volunteerism • Dilemma of efficacy
Challenge of Church in the World (Ch. 7)	• Unable to evangelize society	• Unable to influ-ence society	• Unable to in-fluence most powerful institutions of society	• Unable to control where laity expends efforts

[1] These organizations and others are discussed briefly in Chapter 2.

2

The Culture of Catholic Civic Engagement

Catholicity and Core Values

The room is cheery: children's art plasters the walls for the parish's "Little Church," the primary use of this room. In stark contrast to the cotton-ball sheep and block letters in primary colors, the JustFaith Ministries (JFM) Prison Reform group sits, quiet and solemn, around a table. There are seven people—five are women—and aside from me, all are in their fifties or older. The facilitator lights a white pillar candle, gathering the focus of the group. Beside the candle sits a basket of apples, and as it is mid-October, they are ripe and inviting.

After a brief welcome and invocation, a co-facilitator reads a portion of Genesis: God commands Adam not to eat of the tree of knowledge of good and evil. The other co-facilitator takes an apple from the basket and connects those present to the sin of Adam, citing Paul's letter to the Romans: "Through the disobedience of one, the many were made sinners." She reminds participants that they are spiritual descendants of a long line of sinners and criminals. Those present take a strip of paper, offering an addendum to introducing themselves, with a woman beginning, "I am Veronica," and adding, "Spiritual descendant of Eve, and I stole fruit I was forbidden to take from the tree of the knowledge of good and evil, a thief." This continues around the table until roughly one dozen criminals are brought into spiritual company.

There is a thoughtful pause, and a co-facilitator reads new words from Paul, again from Romans. However, this time, instead of culpability, they are words of redemption: "Just as through one transgression condemnation came upon all, so through one righteous act acquittal and life come to all." To acknowledge their sinfulness in a more concrete way, they pass the basket around, and each takes an apple and reads in unison with the others that they are complicit in "the Sin of the world . . . [God,] Look not on our sin, but on the faith of the people gathered here before you." After more prayer and readings from scripture, they finish this opening prayer by drawing a cross on their forehead and praying, "Open our minds"; then crossing their lips, saying, "Speak to our lives"; and crossing their chest, asking God to "soften our hearts."

As this is the first meeting of the series, they discuss group guidelines for respectful dialogue, such as honoring differences and a commitment to participate fully. A participant offers an additional guideline to not overspeak, allowing time for all to talk. The group quickly confers and agrees to adopt it. There is an obvious shift in mood from the seriousness of the earlier ritual to the current discussion, with faces becoming more animated and characterized by an obvious curiosity of one another. The two co-facilitators introduce themselves and their interest in a faith-based approach to contemporary incarceration. Others do the same, some explaining that they have friends in prison or prison-related work. The co-facilitators have completed the thirty-week Just-Faith course, and everyone else is new to JFM programs. They talk about the possibility of a project at the end of the six-meeting session. The idea garnering the most support is an educational event for the parish and wider community, bringing in speakers with experience in restorative justice. At break, the facilitators bring out store-bought cookies, juice, and sparkling water to share, and each person signs up to bring snacks for a future meeting.

The group reconvenes to discuss the introduction to the assigned book, focusing on the questions supplied by JFM in the materials. Some questions have to do with scriptural perspective: "Why do you think so few have noted this scriptural theme [of criminals and prisoners throughout the Bible]?" One participant elicits nods when she says that people simply do not recognize biblical figures as prisoners because in emphasizing their holiness, they overlook their sins. Other questions were more introspective: "Is it really necessary to undergo some sort of personal tragedy or trial in order to be as strongly motivated as [killers like David, Moses, and Paul] were?" The group does not believe that everyone needs some sort of great tragedy to befall them to serve God in a more significant way but that some obviously do have a conversion experience after "hitting bottom." The participants' answers are unsurprising given that many have had experiences with what they perceive to be a broken prison system and they believe that society harbors a strong bias against the formerly incarcerated. Their education, a concern for the marginalized, and a desire to leave space for a variety of spiritual needs and experiences shape their responses.

The group becomes more formal again as they prepare for the closing prayer. After a moment of silence, the participants echo, line by line, the co-facilitator's words as she reads them from her paper. She finishes by inviting the group to recall this prayer throughout the week as they "walk, work and wonder." Everyone takes an apple from the basket and holds it up as the other co-facilitator reads, "All crimes have consequences . . . Jesus has shown the way back to God, around the table of the Eucharist, where we find the fruit that restores, forgives, brings us back together." The other facilitator reminds the group that the Sign of Peace offers a second chance at life and that it is to be extended to all. The group members exchange smiles, hugs, and handshakes and head home following a few minutes of chatting and an invitation to take an apple. After an evening of meaningful conversation and good feeling, the bright décor of the room seems to match the mood of the group after all.

As this vignette from the JustMatters module *Prison Reform: The Church of the Second Chance* illustrates, the institutional form JFM programs take is the small group. Many Americans are familiar with small groups, recognizing them as an institutional form that promotes a culture of intimacy and personal growth. This culture comes with certain expectations that facilitate group interaction and build a sense of cohesion among the members. The contribution of small-group culture to discipleship organizations cannot be understated as this community becomes the vehicle for personal and social transformation. Because of the expectations of intimacy within small-group culture, what begins in the vignette as a tentative gathering of strangers quickly becomes a primary site of spiritual formation. This community also builds affective bonds, especially when group members share personal stories and laughter over homemade snacks in later sessions.

Besides the small-group structure, other aspects to JFM's culture are appealing given its US context. The faith-based peace-and-justice content of JFM's programs obviously attracts progressive Christians. JFM also attracts those with weaker political convictions owing to two aspects of its organizational culture, which is the focus of this chapter. First, having a Catholic identity is essential to any discipleship organization.

Although JFM is officially an ecumenical organization, it has Catholic roots that shape its organizational choices. Second, JFM names five core values that guide the organization; these also illuminate the values of other discipleship organizations.

The Catholic Identity of JFM

A distinctly Catholic spiritual identity animates all discipleship organizations. Although JFM is officially ecumenical and has never operated under the control of a diocese, its Catholic identity is unmistakable. A Methodist grad of the ecumenical program made this humorously apparent when she asked if JFM was ever going to have a Protestant version. When I told her that her church had only run the ecumenical version—the one she participated in—she had a moment of confusion and replied, unconvinced, that it seemed Catholic. Her perception of a Catholicity to the program may have been because, as a full-time lay minister at her church and the wife of an ordained minister, she was more sensitive to a Catholic undertone or some theological minutiae that another Protestant might have missed. Despite the ecumenical efforts of JFM, given the Catholic roots of the program, the dominance of Catholics on its board and staff, and the fact that more than 99 percent of the grads are Catholic, JFM's Catholicity is quite palpable in the organizational identity. JFM and the grads place the organization within the context of the institutional church. Whereas other studies have shown that groups that dissent from church teaching—either to the right or to the left—are deliberate in cultivating a Catholic identity, that orthodox organizations also have to carefully construct their Catholicity in light of criticism from their co-religionists is striking.[1] JFM demonstrates its Catholic identity through the ways it handled past situations that threatened to place it outside conventional definitions of Catholicism and in its response to conservative Catholics who claim that JFM is unorthodox.

Claiming a Conventional Catholic Identity: Navigating Institutional Events

JFM reveals its Catholic identity through the way it responds to events in Jezreel's biography and in JFM's history. Before JFM existed, even before there was a JustFaith National under Catholic Charities, Jez-reel had many speaking opportunities to spread the church's message of social justice. He likened himself to an itinerant preacher, speaking to anyone who invited him to share the church's teachings. In addition to the many talks at organizations that are closely or directly affiliated with the Roman Catholic Church, Jezreel also spoke at the controver-sial Call to Action (CTA), an organization of Catholics that advocates for major reform of the church and society. CTA began as a lay-bishop initiative, and very quickly, its proposition to reform church doctrine and ecclesiology led many Catholics to distance themselves from the movement. Because of its founding roots, however, some dioceses have been more supportive of CTA than others. In 1996, for example, when Jezreel first spoke at CTA, he did so at the invitation of a staff member of the Archdiocese of Chicago. He spoke at CTA two other times, once for a national conference in 1997 and another for the West Coast CTA Conference in 2000. Jezreel claims that he spoke at these venues, first, because he was unaware of the politics that were happening at the time and, second, and more important to Jezreel, because he would have gone anywhere to share the church's teaching:

> I say this with a smile on my face, if the Ku Klux Klan called our of-fice and said, "Is this where that Jack Jezreel guy is? Well, we want him to come talk about Catholic social teaching." Would I go? Yes, I would go. And then would somebody say, "Jack spoke to the Ku Klux Klans-men. That means *he's* a Ku Klux Klansman!" . . . We shouldn't presume that because someone is speaking with, or connecting with somebody of an organization, or a tradition that is different than ours that that is an unhealthy thing. I would argue that whenever I have the opportunity to talk about Catholic social teaching, or even to talk about JustFaith, with anybody, I ought to take the opportunity.

Jezreel later qualifies that he is not implying that CTA and the Ku Klux Klan are in the same moral category, but his point is that he believed he should preach the good news of the church wherever he was able.

As appealing as this model of evangelization is for some, becoming JustFaith National in 2001 forced the organization to consider the im-pression a speak-wherever-invited policy could give to fellow Catholics.

Catholic social teaching is already suspect for some politically conservative Catholics and JFM did not want to appear dissident for speaking at an organization that some saw as outside the scope of Catholicism (the bishop of Lincoln excommunicated all members of CTA in his diocese in 1996[2]). Jezreel no longer speaks at CTA and is adamant about his own orthodoxy, then and now:

> The presentations I gave at Call to Action look a lot like the presentations I gave in front of a group of bishops. I mean I think they're nearly identical . . . I've often said this: I have given a thousand or more public presentations and *half* of them have been recorded: videotaped, recorded, publicly made available, some of them on YouTube. And I just ask people find *one* sentence of *one* talk where you can find something that wasn't faithful to the Catholic Church. Find *one* sentence of one talk. So far, not a one. I have published materials. I have articles. You can find them anywhere. Just find *one*, one line, one line! So far, nothing.

A second event happened in 2010 when it became public that one of their board members, a Catholic deacon deeply committed to social justice issues, had become involved in a womanpriest church. The situation was difficult for the organization, and the man stepped down from his position on the board. Jezreel remembered:

> [He] made a commitment as a deacon. And he made a choice that just wasn't consistent with that. On the one hand, I would say, [he] didn't steal money . . . he didn't even verbally assault anybody. His heart was telling him that this [womanpriest church] was a place where he should pray and that's where he prays . . . I don't feel like I'm in a place where I can condemn [him] for a decision on where he would pray, but on the other hand, it was inconsistent with the choice he made to become an ordained deacon of the Catholic Church. So, as an organization that has responsibilities to many other organizations, it wasn't a good fit for it, it wasn't. It was a really regretful situation.

Because this Catholic board member had placed himself outside of the official church, the organization had to grapple with its own sense of what it means to be a Catholic organization. The conventional Catholic identity of the organization prevailed over a more pluralist and interdenominational identity it could have sought to foster.

These institutional choices, to distance themselves from movements or situations that are problematic for some Catholics, both constrain and enable the organization.[3] The choices constrain JFM in that it cannot exist as a more radical reformer of the church, nor can the organization ally itself with Catholics of that ilk.[4] However, these choices enable JFM to plant itself more firmly within Catholicism, mainstream and promoting the church while reforming society. These choices prove to be far more effective in garnering support than those of organizations that attempt to change the church through the posture of an intrainstitutional movement.[5] According to their websites, intra-institutional movement organizations like Voice of the Faithful (VOTF)[6] and CTA[7] have memberships of about thirty thousand and twenty-five thousand, respectively, while JFM boasts more than fifty thousand graduates. Considering the time and discipline that any JFM course demands and the ambiguous definition of membership for VOTF or CTA (people could regularly volunteer or they could simply be on a mailing list), that is an impressive figure. From an organizational standpoint, remaining firmly within the church and seeking only external reform have both assets and liabilities, and in this situation, it serves JFM well. Social utility should not overshadow the religious dimension to JFM's choice: staying within the church allows the organization to remain true to its founding vision. This stance enables JFM to invite participants to become more profoundly Catholic through their church's social justice teachings, reforming society as conventional, yet strengthened, Catholics.

American Catholic Dissent from Social Teaching

The primary way the organization fosters a Catholic identity is to consistently draw on official elements of the Catholic faith, such as Catholic social teaching, the theology of the Eucharist, and prayers. A brief look at the reception of social teaching among Catholics nationally helps to fully understand the criticism of JFM. Long before organizations like Catholics for Choice, Dignity, and the Women's Ordination Conference began pushing for changes within the church on abortion, homosexuality, and women's ordination, respectively, Catholic social teaching invited public dissent from the fiscally conservative. *Catholic Mind*, a popular Catholic periodical, ran an article in 1956 that discussed the problems clergy were having with fiscally conservative Catholics in their rejection of Catholic social teaching.[8] This took place during the Cold War so the juxtaposition of the church's progressive economic teachings with its anti-Communist teachings could have been confusing for some of the laity. Having both of these teachings to draw from concealed the political rift among Catholics, as dissenting conservatives voiced their opposition to social teaching in anticommunist terms. In another article, *Catholic Mind* wrote that Catholics can be liberals as long as they are not "radicals, leftists, pinkos, and even Communists."[9] The article went on to state that Catholics can also be conservatives so long as they are not "reactionaries, sometimes charter members of the lunatic fringe."

Catholic Digest, another popular Catholic magazine, promoted free-market capitalism when it published an article by Senator Barry Goldwater: "One of the foremost precepts of the natural law is man's right to the possession and the use of his property . . . This attack on property rights is really an attack on freedom."[10] The timing of this article is especially interesting, given that Goldwater was running for the Republican nomination in the 1960 presidential election. To run this article so close to an election might be a subtle endorsement for a fiscal conservative over John F. Kennedy, the Catholic nominee. *Catholic Digest* was not alone in their socially conservative leanings. The *Wanderer*, a mainstream Catholic publication that turned conservative at the onset of the Cold War, went so far as to explicitly endorse Goldwater.[11] Shortly after the publication of *Mater et Magistra* in 1961, American dissent moved from the rank and file to major leaders. William F. Buckley, editor of the *National Review*, argued that the encyclical proposed too large a role for the state.[12] He initiated a discussion on the role of legitimate dissent and claimed that fellow conservatives were joking to one another, "*Mater, si, magistra, no.*" In sum, conservative Catholics were the first in the American Church to assert a theory of dissent through their opposition to Catholic social teaching. This dissent illustrates the beginning of a more personalized sense of moral authority for American Catholics and coincides with the emergence of the discipleship style.

This historical dissent from social teaching is no less prominent today and has affected the reception of JFM. Catholicism has a vast array of teachings that have implications for politics and moral life. Some of these are quite friendly to Catholics who follow a Democratic way of thinking, such as articulating criteria by which people might justly immigrate, opposing the death penalty, being stewards of the environment, and a highly stringent set of criteria for declaring a war morally just. Other positions are more favorable to Republican Catholics, such as opposition to abortion, same-sex marriage, and euthanasia. Catholic teachings, in sum, do not neatly fit into either political camp. Sociologist Michael Cuneo found that Catholic conservatives are not monolithic, and he illustrates this by making a distinction between orthodox Catholics and what he calls "conservative Catholics."[13] These Catholics attend Mass in churches that are in communion with Rome, as opposed to schismatic groups that establish their own magisterial authority. Unlike orthodox Catholics, defined here as those in agreement with the whole of church teaching, conservative Catholics usually disagree with the church's position on several issues, most notably the economic teachings.[14]

Conservative Catholics' Arguments against JFM

Conservative Catholics who dissent from the church's social teaching would not like an organization such as JFM. JFM experiences some difficulty due to these conservative Catholics who call JustFaith an "infiltration of the Catholic Church by socialist-Marxists"[15] or claim that "Jezreel's program is nothing but a platform for an ultra left wing social, political, and economic agenda that is NOT consistent with traditional Catholic social teaching."[16] The framing of JFM as heterodox is important to conservative Catholics.[17] A "JFM-as-heterodox" frame positions their pro-war, fiscally conservative, charity-over-justice, or other stance as authentically Catholic. Also, it draws boundaries around themselves and their church in a way that excludes JFM and those who support its programs.

To be clear, there is very little official opposition to JFM. They have received mixed support from bishops, with one bishop strongly encouraging every parish in his diocese to run the GoodNewsPeople program and another bishop forbidding the programs within his diocese, but there is rarely a diocesan stance on JFM. The vast majority of the websites that oppose JFM are statements by lay Catholics, and these circulate the writing of a single journalist, Stephanie Block. She claims that her eighteen-part online series on the JustFaith program exposes an unorthodox portrayal of Catholic social teaching. Block's writings are an excellent representation of conservative opposition to JFM because of the volume of her writings and her concrete evaluations.

The vast majority of Block's complaints fall under the scope of two larger criticisms: that JFM misrepresents Catholic social teaching and theology and that JFM promotes organizations that engage in practices contrary to Catholic teaching. Both of these are serious criticisms for an organization that understands itself as orthodox and faithful to Catholic social teaching and Catholicism generally. Examining Block's understanding of Catholic social teaching before looking specifically at her criticisms of JFM, as this contextualizes her complaints, is helpful. The American bishops, for example, have developed "Seven Themes of Catholic Social Teaching" to be used as stepping-stones to learn the wider body of social thought, offering tools for the newly acquainted to probe and discuss contemporary issues.[18] Block argues that these are either wrong or deficient. For example, she claims the seventh theme, Care for God's Creation, "proposes a preposterous task. There's no such mandate in Catholic social teaching or in the Scriptures. Stewardship of the galaxies and management of angels, to name a few elements of creation, is an awfully grand enterprise that's completely out of our league."[19] When the themes are not impossible, they are "deficient" because they do not convey the whole scope of Catholic social teaching.

Block also takes issue with the very understanding of Catholic social teaching. *The Compendium of the Social Doctrine of the Church* states, "Evangelization would be incomplete if it did not take into account the mutual demands continually made by the Gospel and by the concrete, personal and social life of man. Profound links exist between evangelization and human promotion . . . This is not a marginal interest or activity, or one that is tacked on to the Church's mission, rather it is at the very heart of the Church's ministry of service."[20] Here the church teaches that evangelization itself is inadequate if it neglects justice, mercy, and love. Another paragraph more clearly states the purpose of Catholic social teaching: "The immediate purpose of the church's social doctrine is to propose the principles and values that can sustain a society worthy of the human person. "[21] This demonstrates the church's belief that material, social, and personal goods *are* religious in nature and an integral part of the church's mission. Social teaching is not a "tacked on" collection of writings without spiritual significance nor a means to conversion. Block has a different understanding of Catholic social teaching: "So we must observe what Catholic social teaching says about itself—that 'social action is an integral part of her evangelizing ministry' and is an 'instrument of evangelization.'"[22] Here she claims that the primary mission of the church is religious, which is correct according to the documents, but then incorrectly concludes that social teaching is a mere means to a greater end: conversion. This interpretation of Catholic social teaching affects her interpretation of JFM.

Block's first criticism, that JFM promotes a theology that is contrary to Catholicism, appears throughout her work. An example of this is JFM and Block's use of the "Reign of God."[23] Block takes issue with a talk Jezreel gave at Seattle University in 2007, which is one of the assigned readings for JustFaith participants. In it he said that "this reign of God is the reign of service, justice, generosity, compassion, peacemaking. Jesus calls disciples to THIS vision . . . he is pointing toward a new possibility, as described in this vision of the Reign of God." Block calls this a "liberationist perspective," and notes that "[t]he Catechism of the Catholic Church, on the other hand, describes the 'Reign of God' (the Kingdom of God) as fulfilled by 'God's triumph over the revolt of evil' which 'will take the form of the Last Judgment after the final cosmic upheaval of this passing world.' These are two, very different 'visions.'"[24] Jezreel presents a vision of the Reign of God as something that we should strive to attain in the present world, whereas Block contends that the Reign of God will only be achieved with the passing of the present world during the Last Judgment.

As far as orthodoxy goes, they are both drawing on accepted elements of Catholicism. Catholicism has developed an extensive theology over the centuries, with a wide collection of christologies (understandings of Christ), ecclesiologies (understandings of the church), eschatologies (understandings of the "end times"), and so forth. Some elements appear to contradict others, yet they remain part of the deposit of the faith. This results in Catholics who either hold these parts in tension or emphasize one part over another.[25] This is simply a case where Jezreel and Block are drawing on two distinct, yet both orthodox, understandings of the

Reign or Kingdom of God. Some Catholics, including many grads, dwell in the tension, referring to the Kingdom as "the already and the not yet." Block and Jezreel, instead, emphasize one over the other, with both articulations found within *The Catechism of the Catholic Church*: "The Kingdom of God lies ahead of us. It is brought near in the Word incarnate, it is proclaimed throughout the whole Gospel, and it has come in Christ's death and Resurrection. The Kingdom of God has been coming since the Last Supper and, in the Eucharist, it is in our midst. The kingdom will come in glory when Christ hands it over to his Father."[26] It continues, illustrating both Block's and Jezreel's emphases and tying Jezreel's understanding to the mission of the church: "In the Lord's Prayer, 'thy kingdom come' refers primarily to the final coming of the reign of God through Christ's return. But, far from distracting the Church from her mission in this present world, this desire commits her to it all the more strongly. Since Pentecost, the coming of that Reign is the work of the Spirit of the Lord who 'complete[s] his work on earth and brings us the fullness of grace.'"[27] As the official documents of the church illustrate, although Block and Jezreel hold different eschatologies, neither one is heterodox.

Block's second criticism is that JFM promotes organizations that engage in practices deemed immoral by the church. There is significant distance between the organizations and the immoral acts, which calls into question the degree to which JFM is culpable. For example, one of the books that participants read in JustFaith is *Credible Signs of Christ Alive*, which offers six case studies of Catholic Campaign for Human Development[28] (CCHD) grant recipients that are working for social justice in their communities.[29] The first case highlights an organization that is working for minimum wage increases and better working conditions for migrant workers in the poultry business, the Delmarva Poultry Justice Alliance (DPJA).[30] Block actually has nothing negative to say about the work of DPJA and directs her attention to other neighboring organizations and their founders. She writes that one of the founders of DPJA, an Episcopalian priest, is also active in anti–death penalty, gay rights, labor, and women's reproductive issues. Although the scope of DPJA is exclusively labor issues, this piece of personal information could cause the reader to be suspicious of DPJA's work. She continues by saying this Episcopalian priest also found La Red Health Center, which provides much-needed health care for the workers and other lower-income residents of the community. She adds that, despite the good works of the clinic, they are outside the scope of Catholic moral teaching as they refer some clients to other clinics for contraception and sterilization procedures. Block continues, writing about the founder of a second agency that originally founded DPJA (even though, at the time of writing, it is independently run). Block reports that this founder has spoken at CTA and contributed to a book on community organizing that focuses on defeating the "radical right" in one's community. Although Block says nothing negative about the particular organization that CCHD is highlighting, she concludes that "its mentors and founders procured these goods [economic betterment] with the blood of poor children." She previously states that La Red and DPJA are independent organizations but brings them together in concluding that "[t]he CCHD-funded Delmarva Poultry Justice Alliance runs La Red Health Center, providing (or referring) its low income clients with 'reproductive health services,' including abortion-producing contraceptives and sterilization."

The critiques are similar for the other five organizations in the book. The first organization fights for living wages alongside other local organizations. One of these other organizations also works for lesbian, gay, bisexual, transgender, and queer rights. Block claims that the first organization—the only focus of which is poverty-related issues—should no longer be funded because it cooperates with this other organization in poverty advocacy. A second organization lobbied for legislation that is proving far from effective—disappointing but not contrary to Catholic doctrine. Another organization violates middle-class manners in demonstrating outside a politician's or other opponent's home. A fourth organization advocates for the rights of undocumented workers. Although the church does not condemn liberation theology *tout court*[31] and Block does not cite any specific aspects of liberation theology this church employs that are rejected by the church, she argues that the final organization is non-Catholic because it "is a disseminator of liberation theology." Block reports no agency practices that are inconsistent with Catholic teaching; still, she argues against their orthodoxy.

Block is the most articulate and thorough of JFM's opponents, and the point of using her work is to show that much of the backlash comes from people who are most likely loyal and sincere Catholics who fall into one of three camps. There are those—of whom Block is most likely representative—who unwittingly reject major parts of their church's teachings on social justice as they interpret it through a conservative lens. Others are aware of their church's teaching and knowingly reject it. Finally, some are unaware of their church's teaching and have no idea that their political beliefs are in conflict with it.

Maintaining Orthodoxy: Response to Conservative Backlash

JFM responds to accusations of heterodoxy with some success. One strategy is used only by the staff: they underscore the close collaboration JFM has with official Catholic organizations. The other strategy, used by both staff and grads, is to avoid politically loaded words and to empha-size shared religion and concern for the poor. As for the first strategy, the staff are more aware of web pages that call into question the orthodoxy of the organization and are quick to point out JFM's formal and intimate ties with other organizations that are official bodies within the Catholic Church. They partner with CCHD, Catholic Relief Services (CRS), and Maryknoll[32] and are sponsored by Catholic Charities USA. Finally, they are listed on the USCCB's website as one of the sixteen organizations that compose the Catholic Social Ministries Gathering, which is "com-mitted to the Church's social mission to explore common issues and concerns of global and domestic policies on life, justice, and peace that challenge our nation and world."[33] The staff also note that cooperating with these organizations holds them accountable to orthodoxy, unlike Block or other critics who are not responsible to any official Catholic authority. In short, JFM argues that these important endorsements make them, first and foremost, a Catholic organization.

Both staff and grads respond to the political division among today's Catholics by minimizing language of "liberals and conservatives" or "Democrats and Republicans" and focusing on religious commonalities or shared concerns for poverty. Cathy Meyers illustrates this strategy:

> I have had lots and lots of work with small groups in doing presenta-tions with church groups and stuff like that, and whenever it would break down into like the Republican and Democrat I used to say, "That's not why we are here. That's not why we are here, I don't care if you are a

Republican or Democrat, conservative or liberal. On the basis of what we say we believe let's go to the Lord's Prayer." And I will pull back to the Lord's Prayer: Thy will be done on earth as it is in heaven. Now that's what we are trying to do.

If a group is politically diverse, party loyalties can render conversation unproductive. Meyers helps draw the group back to a common point, the Lord's Prayer, so that the small group can keep God's will in mind rather than the will of a political party.

She also uses religious belonging and the Eucharist to illustrate common bonds between Catholics:

> Our programs are not driving people to be Democrat or Republican, to be liberal or conservative. It is driving people to say, we all are of our own free will members of this Catholic Church and on the basis of walking into your parish every Sunday, you say you have something in common with everybody else walking in. It is that commonality that we are trying to get people to have conversation around. You go to the communion table and at that table you say, "All are welcome here, everybody is welcome." And your participation in that saying you have this in common, it is that commonality that we are trying to get people to be in conversation about as it focuses on the issue of poverty.

Although most Catholics follow party lines before heeding denominational teaching, JFM is trying to reverse that, saying that religious identity should trump any party loyalty and offering common ground for productively discussing poverty, war, immigration, and related issues. Grads and staff typically combine these, reducing the importance of political ideology while emphasizing faith to build common ground around concern for the poor. Underscoring their commitment to the Gospel rather than a party, JFM avoids naming a party or group as a threat to peace and justice, discussing problems of violence and greed rather than pointing fingers at the military or the "1 percent." In this way, JFM attempts to bring participants the Gospel without naming enemies.[34]

One of the problems with discussing civic and political issues is that many sincere Catholics are completely unaware of the church's body of social teaching. Describing the social teaching of the church as its "best-kept secret" has become cliché. Gina McCormick, a Southern California grad involved in her local Catholic Worker, recommends that churches use JFM programs to educate Catholics on the tradition while making social teaching more mainstream: "I think the Church really, really needs to let the faithful know how important social justice is. It's good as 'the best kept secret in the Catholic Church' and to make it more palatable, for people, because a lot of people look at it as a left-wing thing, 'Oh, you know, they are radical, they are not being good Catholics' or what have you . . . [The Church could] encourage JustFaith Ministries and maybe offer other ways to learn about doing the right thing, doing what Jesus did and serving." Much of the division among Catholics, she believes, results from so few being educated on the social teachings of the church. A priest corroborated this, saying that many of his colleagues are reticent to preach on social teachings as parishioners might become upset or even leave the parish. Grads accurately perceive that social justice is unfamiliar to most Catholics. In 1987, shortly after the release of the US bishops' pastorals, 29 percent and 25 percent of Catholics had heard about or read the peace or economic pastoral, respectively.[35] Although initial exposure was minimal—reaching fewer than one in three Catholics—six years later, those percentages dropped even further to 18 and 19 percent, indicating that priests and lay leaders did not reinforce these social justice documents and they subsequently faded from Catholic memory. JFM and the grads have a weighty task as they attempt to minimize political friction while emphasizing a shared faith and concern for the poor as a way to introduce Catholics to their church's social teaching.

JFM's "Core Values"

JFM articulates its organizational moorings through five core values: transformation, compassion, community, justice, and being Christ-centered. Although JFM chose these five values, they reflect important elements of discipleship organizations broadly.

Transformation

Mike Campbell has been working at JFM for a number of years. He has a gentle and quiet demeanor and, despite having left Scotland more than twenty years ago, speaks with a strong accent. He lives in a lower-income area of Louisville with his wife and children and has cultivated a small backyard into a grove of over forty trees. As he sits in a room in the JFM office building, he shares many formative experiences that have shaped his own personal faith journey, from his time in seminary to encountering the indigenous people of the Amazon to the theological insights that came from his then preschool-aged children. He is thoughtful and has a wealth of experiences to draw from as he reflects on each question. Transformation is a recurring theme for Campbell, whether for himself, his community, or his inner-city backyard-turned-woods. Paraphrasing a speaker from GoodNewsPeople, Campbell says, "Sometimes you got to wake people. And if you can't wake 'em you've got to shake 'em." He asks rhetorically, "How many people *want* to be asked to uproot themselves? But *that* is fundamental to our story. Abraham did it. Moses did it. Jesus did it, you know: Uproot yourself and go into the desert and find a new way of living."

Transformation is the *modus operandi* of the organization. Jezreel modeled JustFaith after the RCIA, the formal rite and conversion process for those wishing to become Catholic. The idea is to transform participants in a holistic sense, fundamentally altering their worldviews and lifestyles. Transformation begins with a new awareness that, through choices and structures, participants' own lives hinder or help the lives of others in ways visible and invisible. In bringing participants closer to the lives of the poor, JFM programs personalize previously abstract suffering. Transformation is most fully actualized when the grads become more active in their communities in ministries of mercy and justice, thereby transforming society. The idea is to transform both people and institutions.

Informed by personalism, discipleship organizations place a strong emphasis on individual transformation. As Catholics' education level rises, those who seek volunteer opportunities will do so in a way that uses their individual talents in a way that is personally meaningful. The challenge for discipleship organizations is to convince Catholics to *begin* to get involved. Catholic Christian Outreach provides resources to college students to deepen their own faith and go out and evangelize others. The Jesuit Volunteer Corps recruits recent college graduates for a one-year service program, with the young adults so transformed that they are "ruined for life."[36] Although not all discipleship organizations would use language as strong as conversion or transformation, ongoing spiritual and moral formation remains central. This transformation shifts the participants' values so that they invest more of their time and money into things that benefit others, making both people and society more compassionate.

Compassion

Chris Miller is no stranger to compassion. Having grown up on a small farm in a family that "didn't have a whole lot," he knows the importance of caring for others in need. His face warms over as he remembers the trust and reciprocity: "We never locked our doors at night. If we needed to borrow something from [a neighbor], we'd just go and help ourselves and put it back." Miller attends the Church of the Epiphany, and after going through JustFaith, his notion of compassion changed, expanding from simply being altruistic to also include political activity for marginalized groups. He is now active in Catholics in Alliance for the Common Good—an organization that tries to promote Catholic social principles in the public sphere. Inside the office of his brick home in Lyndon, Kentucky, Miller explains the centrality of compassion in his JustFaith journey: "Well, I think [compassion is] the very essence of those who accept JustFaith teachings, gospel teachings. We have to have empathy and, consequently, compassion for those on the margins of society."

JFM believes the programs must instill compassion in the grads for real transformation to occur. From the Latin "to suffer with," compassion is not pity, prophetic anger, or the amelioration of an unjust situation. Instead, compassion is entering a situation deeply enough so that one feels some modicum of the victim's suffering; another's pain becomes one's own. This pain foments a desire to care for others and challenge the structures that perpetuate injustice. As a result of JustFaith, grads care about different things, saying that they have become less desirous of material possessions and more concerned with loving their neighbors.

Compassion is an emotional response to a particular person or event. It is deeply personal and relational and affects the scope of what a person cares about. Other discipleship organizations might choose a different phrase to discuss a similar concept, such as Sant'Egidio's use of "friendship with the poor," to capture the selfless relationality that compassion inspires for JFM.[37] Compassion, however, is an emotionally draining enterprise. For grads volunteering at a homeless shelter, feeling the trials that their friends are enduring is heart-wrenching. JFM believes that individuals cannot bear this weight on their own, asserting that one must have a community of like-minded others to offer support, encouragement, prayers, and joy.

Community

Grad Tammy Czap lives with her husband in a one-bedroom apartment just blocks from the University of California. She is intelligent, gregarious, and quick to smile. Tammy earned her PhD in education and will occasionally teach as an adjunct professor but prefers to spend her time on the various projects and groups she is a part of, from mentoring a young girl living in poverty to monitoring the wildlife at a local sanctuary. Having completed JustFaith and co-facilitated a module, she is quite familiar with the programs and has recently become the JustFaith coordinator at her parish. She remembers the care and commitment she felt for her group even before she was halfway through: "I had an opportunity, and someone said that I should've quit that [JustFaith] group . . . I don't really know why, but I made a commitment to the group so I didn't feel good to leave people." Before one can attribute her decision to Catholic guilt or an overbearing superego, the otherwise articulate Tammy Czap struggles to find the right words to describe her strongest motivation for staying: "I also felt that there was something in the group that I was getting that was different from any other group that I had experienced. I can do sort of prayerful reading on my own, but there was something about that group. Why I would say to someone, 'It must be grace.' If you look at the factors you might think it was this or that thing, or something else. Grace!" After a quick laugh at herself, she adds, "It's a mystery!"

Community serves many purposes for the grads, and Jezreel emphasizes the affective role of community, as well as its utility: "This Gospel thing, it ain't for solo artists. The best way to *do* the work of compassion is in community. It can be that the best way to effect transformation is in community." Community is the pot that all the ingredients simmer in and so itself is morally neutral. Communities, as associations of individuals, can be a source of problems, finding—like a white supremacist group—unity and coherence through a common enemy. But instead of JFM pointing its groups inward and *against* something, as some communities might, it believes JustFaith communities orient members outward and *for* something: for compassion, for others, for justice, and, most fundamentally, for Christ. The evangelistic nature of the program encourages them to bring these values to their other communities, transforming the mundane into an opportunity for discipleship. Their JustFaith community also plays a key role in helping them sustain their personal transformations.

Discipleship organizations likewise find gathering in community a source of renewal and formation. Members of Sant'Egidio will gather in community for prayer, socializing, education, and discussion of outreach efforts. Opus Dei members gather weekly for formation, monthly for recollection, and annually for a retreat. Although they have the option of cooperating as communities in their ministries, most discipleship group members engage their service commitments individually. Remember that the historical styles of public Catholicism operated in a church that was relatively cohesive and had many organizational expressions. Today's weaker institutional ties and Catholics' desire to find individually meaningful service opportunities allow discipleship communities—that is, the small groups that cohere and form the local members of a discipleship organization—to play a critical role in the formation and maintenance of the group's values. These regular gatherings help reinforce the values and charisms of the group, helping them serve others as well as see the spiritual relevance of that service. Discipleship communities act as a nexus, ultimately embedding the individuals and their personal priorities into a larger Catholic social and moral universe.

Justice

Southern California grad Margaret Wagner is a retired high school counselor and occasionally leads retreats and spiritual direction at a bucolic location in Orange County. The cool of her living room this morning provides a vivid contrast with the heat the August day promises. Wagner sips a full-bodied rooibos tea as she considers the role of justice in society: "Well, I think starting with a viewpoint that we are responsible for each other, 'What happens to you happens to me' is the basic premise to start with and then I think that informs the kind of policies we set and so forth." Wagner believes that responsibility is both a personal and a social virtue that should affect the way individuals and society understand justice. Wagner's life demonstrates these dual concerns. A lot of her time right now goes to her daughter, who will be having breast cancer surgery within the week. She is also heavily involved, along with other JustFaith grads from her parish, in opening a fair-trade store. She continues: "We have limited resources obviously, we have to recognize that. How we spend those resources I think is very much informed by our basic view of the world and humanity. And I think that's very much informed by my faith."

Justice, in the sense that JFM uses it, is a measure for a community to examine its own righteousness. The biblical understanding of justice is not a concept that readily translates from its Hebrew origins into the English language. It is not retributive or distributive justice, concepts many Americans are familiar with. Biblical justice is closely related to the Hebrew notion of *shalom. Shalom*, meaning peace, indicates the absence of tension as well as the presence of this biblical notion of justice, which is better understood as "right relationship."[38] The extent to which individuals and social groups successfully live in right relationship with one another and God demonstrates their ability to live justly. This biblical notion of justice, rather than a secular conception of justice, grounds the grads in a faith-based understanding of their activism, helping ensure that they properly make the connections between religion and their daily lives.[39] JFM's notion of justice is also a particular type of civic engagement: charity satisfies the needs of immediate persons, and justice reforms the structures of society. By claiming this as a core value, JFM underscores the importance of systemic change.

Although discipleship groups would assent to the biblical notion of justice and right relationship, not all emphasize justice as a method of civic engagement. A more generic "outreach" or "service" would be the universal core value of discipleship groups. For Opus Dei members, their outreach happens wherever they find themselves, especially in their workplaces. Jesuit Volunteers work in full-time placements at schools, shelters, legal aid centers, and so forth that provide services for marginalized groups. Catholic Christian Outreach believes its university students will graduate to become future leaders who will influence society, "radically affect[ing] our world."[40] Sant'Egidio members hope to bring peace to their world and build relationships with those experiencing vulnerability, such as the aged. All discipleship groups value outreach and encourage their members to integrate their faith into their daily lives.

Christ-Centered

It is a sultry summer evening in Louisville, and the last of the season's fireflies are lighting the darkness in the quiet Louisville neighborhood where Episcopalian Adam Rousseve lives. In his youth, Rousseve made documentary films and lived in a collective in which they educated one another on political issues. He later had a "conventional" life when he worked for the state and raised his family. Rousseve now incorporates elements of each of these lives, living in a typical suburban home while protesting wars, sharing his possessions, and cultivating artistic expression. Deacon Diana Stewart drove over to join him. Stewart had recently been ordained a deacon and serves a community that began as nearly all Burmese refugees. Rousseve and Stewart are heavily involved in their diocese's peace and justice division and work with a host of local interfaith organizations. They co-facilitated the ecumenical version of JustFaith with an assortment of Episcopalians, Catholics, a Methodist, and a Presbyterian in 2009. When asked how they sustain their many commitments, Stewart answers, "The story that helps me stay focused is when Peter walked on the water. You remember and the storm came up. Jesus said, 'Come on over here,' and Peter gets up out of the boat and walks over to him. And he was walking on the water! But a storm came up and he got afraid and he took his eyes off of Jesus and he wasn't able to walk on the water. And I just keep saying to myself, 'Keep my focus on Jesus.'" A nodding Rousseve interjects contemplatively: "Wonderful." Stewart elaborates: "If my focus is on Jesus I can do anything. And so whenever I am troubled or afraid or whatever I am doing, I just remind myself to keep my focus on Jesus and I don't have to worry about it. And, to me, 'focus on Jesus' means caring for people. It's just real simple—it's just caring for people."

The final value of the organization is a commitment to being Christ-centered. This value hones all the others as the transformation, compassion, community, and justice the grads strive for demonstrate their commitment to Christ. The JFM curricula focus on Jesus, and the grads are eager to discuss their favorite Gospel stories. Central to JFM's notion of Jesus is Christian love, which is not a therapeutic sort of love. Instead, Christian love helps grads recall their baptismal promises to be priest, prophet, and king in the world. This more demanding Christ-centered love encourages grads to more closely study the Gospels to understand their own role as disciples of Christ, as Stewart illustrates in "caring for people" as her way of focusing on Jesus. Being Christ-centered also illustrates the patently Christian nature of JFM: their programs are for churches to use as a Christian tool and the curricula do not translate into interfaith or secular contexts. All these things reinforce that Christ is to be the centerpiece of the grads' lives.

Even discipleship groups that are more narrowly Catholic and do not include Protestants in their ministry maintain this primacy of Jesus—a broadly Christian, rather than a more exclusively Catholic, focus—in their spirituality. Catholic Christian Outreach teaches that "[t]his relationship [with Christ] is primary and central, influencing all decisions and every aspect of their life."[41] Opus Dei more often speaks of Christians and the teachings of Christ than Catholics and the teachings of the church in its literature[42] and counts non-Catholics among its membership.[43] Jesus Christ models Christian living for these Catholics, and these organizations encourage their members to follow Christ through a language of discipleship. Most important, Christ is the foundation of these organizations and their members' lives. These five values illuminate the moral foundations of JFM as well as the larger discipleship style of which JFM is a part.

It would be easy to think that a personalized following of Christ would cause fragmentation within discipleship organizations; if they are welcome to follow their own vision of Christ, what coheres them? However, this plurality of visions is accommodated on the level of the institutional church as well as that of individual discipleship organizations. First, Catholicism legitimates unity within diversity in a variety of ways, easily recognizable in its religious communities. Religious orders or congregations live according to particular charisms—that is, distinct spiritual gifts—that shape the character of the community. Distinct as these are, they all fall under the Catholic umbrella. The same can be said of saints; the saints include martyrs, children, bishops, hermits, religious sisters, priests, parents, virgins, slaves, and royalty. Each is held up by the church as an example of holy living and model of discipleship. The church recognizes that there are many ways to follow the one Christ, allowing for a variety of ways of being Catholic.

Second, discipleship communities are able to form their members in a way that allows for both unity and diversity. Although discipleship communities invite their members to contemplate their own gifts and roles in the world, some vocational responses are more culturally available than others. Because the spiritual writings, the religious practices, the encounters with those on the margins, and so forth are often managed by the discipleship community, members will gravitate to particular visions of discipleship over others. This formation, intentionally or not, constrains members' sense of what is morally and spiritually possible. In illuminating one aspect of Christ, discipleship communities obscure others, creating a bounded diversity within a discipleship community. Bounded diversity yields similarity even amid difference.

JustFaith: Who Is It For?

This culture indicates the target audience of their programs, as these elements will appeal to some populations more than others. The goal of JFM is transformation—of both the person and society—and the form the programs take is the small group, capitalizing on the community this offers. Transformation helps participants become aware of the injustice in society as well as convinces them that the injustice is something they can change; sociologist Doug McAdam calls this "cognitive liberation."[44] By cognitively liberating Catholics, JustFaith hopes to begin a more robust civic engagement. The programs also offer community to the participants, connecting them to one another and others in meaningful and supportive ways. This emphasis on community and transformation lend insight to JFM's target audience.

Not everyone needs transformation—as compassion for the poor—or community; some people are already sympathetic to poverty issues and enjoy lives rich in relationship with others. Those living closer to poverty

THE CULTURE OF CATHOLIC CIVIC ENGAGEMENT | 65

and systemic injustice are less likely to feel an affinity for a program like JustFaith. Poorer and working-class Americans would be aware of the injustice in their hardships. They may not know *how* to change it, but JFM programs do not offer resources on the nuts and bolts of actually producing change. The participants, therefore, will not benefit much from JustFaith without some extant political savvy. These skills, such as letter writing or organizing a meeting, are more developed and utilized among the middle class.[45] Additionally, JFM assumes that participants possess the time and education for lengthy and sometimes difficult reading assignments, further pegging their audience as middle class. Finally, not all Americans lack community. Lower-income Americans are usually closer to family, create support networks of kin and neighbors, and have less need for the support small groups offer.[46]

JustFaith is, in short, a program for middle- and upper-class Christians. This is no institutional secret as Jezreel spoke openly:

> We started this work very clear that we were coming from a middle-class, white perspective and that our constituency that we were trying to reach were white, middle-class people, to help to make bridges with people of color, to make bridges with people who were poor. In some ways, ours was a liberation theology for the middle class. One time I had a very, very candid conversation with the staff of Bread for the World National, went up there, gave a presentation. A woman of color said, "I don't think these materials are suitable for poor black communities." I said, "You're *exactly* right!" And she was taken aback by that. I said, "That's exactly right!" And, and there was a bit of a sort of politically-correct gasp, and I said "No, no. I'm just trying to be honest with you," and I explained to them [the transformative goals of the program]. And then five people came over and said, "You cannot believe how hopeful that was for you to say what you said." Because there's this presumption [that] whatever we do has to be geared toward everybody and everybody has to be included. And I was like, "No . . . this came out of a church where everybody's white and rich! I'm trying to figure out how to convert them! So that they become *allies* with [the poor]."

Further demonstrating this, a member from the Phoenix JustFaith coordinating group presented at the Social Action Summer Institute in 2012.

In response to a question similar to that at Bread for the World, she replied that there was one lower-income parish in the diocese that ran JustFaith and that it "didn't work out." Being a program of conversion, not an empowerment or training series, JustFaith seeks to bring its message to resourced Christians who, for various reasons, do not yet act to alleviate poverty. Glaring exceptions aside, such as the successful running of JustFaith in a Louisiana state prison,[47] JustFaith is geared for and attracts white, educated, middle-class, or wealthier Catholics.[48]

Conclusion

The culture of JFM demonstrates much about the organization. The Catholicity of JFM is important to its identity; it places itself firmly within Catholicism, despite the framing of some who would place it outside. The core values of JFM—transformation, community, compassion, justice, and Christ-centeredness—remind the staff and board of directors of their mission and identity as well as shape the programs.

This culture also illuminates much about discipleship organizations more broadly, as they share much in common. The Catholicity of discipleship organizations animates their institutional choices. JFM's core values are specific to its mission and discipleship organizations will have some variation of transformation, community, compassion, outreach, and Christ-centeredness as their own central values. This larger discipleship culture is especially attractive to professional, white, American Catholics.

Discipleship organizations reveal to participants the relevance of religion in their everyday lives, aiming to give their lives greater meaning and strengthen their religious identity. This shift in outlook requires nothing short of a transformation of the participant. The next chapter explores this notion of transformation that is fundamental to the entire enterprise of JFM.

3

From Private Belief to Public Call

Transforming American Catholics

The sun is still fairly high in the clear sky, a pleasant May afternoon. At the facilitators' spacious home in the Oakland hills, the participants gather into the living room for the final moments of their thirty-week journey. In the company of candles, soft music, and a spectacular view of the San Francisco skyline and the Golden Gate Bridge, a facilitator asks participants to reflect on the "desert times" in their lives. Participants ask themselves, "What are the things that prevented me from bearing fruits of justice in my ministries? What now holds me back from committing my life to justice?" They disperse to write in private what they must let go of so that they may move forward. The participants reconvene in the living room in contemplative silence.

A facilitator invites the members of the group to come forward, one at a time, to share with the group what they need to let go of before placing the paper into the fireplace, where the logs are now burning. One by one, the participants approach the fire and announce the obstacle that they will leave behind as they drop their strip of paper into the growing flames. One needs to let go of a sense of inadequacy, another finds herself impatient, and a third says he needs to stop judging others. As the participants each reveal their impediments, a common thread emerges in the sharing: each of them understands their biggest obstacle to living a life of justice as an internal trait, a character flaw that prevents them from being a holier self.

Committed to abandoning the proverbial beams in their eyes, the participants look to embrace a new way of hope through those who have led lives of justice. Two readers alternate in a litany of holy men and women from both contemporary and ancient times. This "cloud of witnesses" includes traditional saints: "Mary . . . mother of peacemakers" and "Francis of Assisi . . . a rich man who chose to have nothing." There are also figures from the Hebrew scriptures: "Amos and Micah and Hosea, voices for the oppressed" and "Esther, intercessor for the powerless." There are Protestants, "Martin Luther King, prophet and dreamer of the Beloved Community," and non-Christians, "Gandhi, the Mahatma, nonviolent warrior." There are magisterial leaders of the church: "Oscar Romero . . . martyr for justice" and "Pope Paul VI, apostle and teacher of peace." People bow their heads as they hear each of the thirty-nine names read slowly, prayerfully. Following each invocation, the group responds in unison, "Pray for us."

After letting go of their obstacles and stepping among the holy ones, they are sent. A reader beseeches, "The harvest is ready. Whom shall I send? . . . The world is waiting. Whom shall I send? . . . The world is hungry. Whom shall I send? . . . The vineyard is ready. Whom shall I send?" There is an emphatic pause. Breaking the silence, two facilitators remind those present that their tradition uses oil to mark new beginnings, such as at baptism or rites for the dying. Just as they turn away from old ways and come into new lives, this oil will seal the commitment the last thirty weeks has fomented. Participants come forward to be anointed with oil, an outward sign of this transformation. Smoke from the incense curls and moves slowly upward as the participants approach the facilitators. Dipping his thumb into a bowl of oil and marking the participants' forehead with a cross, a facilitator says, "David, blessings of peace, courage, and compassion as you continue your justice journey." After all are anointed, there is a period of graceful silence. The grads refer to their handouts to pray in unison, closing by acknowledging, "I am reborn."

This scene illustrates the culmination of the participants' transformation. JustFaith Ministries (JFM) looks to "form, inform, and transform" its participants.[1] The emphasis rests on the final word, *transform*, as Jezreel explains: "JustFaith was really born by trying to sort of adapt what at the time was *the* single most robust experience for a Catholic in a Catholic parish—which was the RCIA [Rite of Christian Initiation of Adults]—the *longest* thing, really the *best* thing, and adapt it and then enhance it. So that what you end up with is still that same paradigm of conversion. If you read the rite, you know that the paradigm is not education; the paradigm is conversion." While there is an educational component to JustFaith as there is in the RCIA, the primary focus of both programs is the transformational aspect. In fact, the entire enterprise of JustFaith rests upon the transformation of participants' beliefs and practices. For JFM, without this personal change, the hope of changing society falls completely flat.

After roughly 1970, American Catholicism began to lose its institutional strength, and now those who seek civic engagement generally do so as independent individuals. This situation poses two challenges for contemporary Catholic organizations. First, Catholics no longer engage their world in organized groups as they did in the past. Because today's Catholics are seeking personally meaningful engagement, if Catholic organizations want the laity to become more active in public life, they must offer venues that allow for individual engagement. The second challenge is getting participants to frame their engagement as more than just good citizenship. Discipleship organizations need to provide their participants with a worldview that illustrates the religious significance of these acts. These challenges warrant institutional adaptations, causing discipleship organizations to share two important characteristics. First, they mobilize individuals for civic engagement rather than instigating group efforts. Second, they offer Catholics a worldview that understands everyday life as religiously significant, rather than bifurcating life into the public and American realm, on one hand, and the private and Catholic, on the other. Bringing Catholic engagement to the public sphere requires more cultural work today than it did in the past. Catholics must experience a shift in outlook to see not only that their engagement is needed but also that their engagement has religious significance. Discipleship organizations must, in short, find a new strategy to achieve a distinctively Catholic social transformation.

Strategies for Transformation: The "Ripple Group"

Some organizations defy the conventional analytical categories used to understand them, requiring that academics create new categories or nuance the old ones.[2] Identifying where an organization focuses its efforts and its ultimate target of change provides a new way to understand social phenomena. An organization can expend its efforts either at the micro-level, such as individuals or families, or at the macro-level, as in laws or customs. Similarly, an organization seeks change at either the micro-level or the macro-level. Organizing these variables into a 2 × 2 typology

TABLE 3.1. Four Types of Pro-Change Organizations

		Focus of Organizational Efforts	
		Individual	Structures
Ultimate Target of Change	Individual	Support Group	Cultural Movement
	Structures	Ripple Group	Social Movement

yields four types of pro-change organizations: social movements, cultural movements, support groups, and ripple groups (see table 3.1).[3] Discipleship organizations are representative of what I call a ripple group. Ripple groups are groups that strive to effect social change through the concerted transformation of individual actors. To be clear, this typology yields ideal types as each, to varying degrees, devotes resources to, as well as seeks, change in both individuals and society. In reality, these groupings are not so neatly bound and will bleed into one another. This typology remains analytically useful, however, because as organizations privilege particular foci, these shape their strategies, goals, and so forth.

Support groups focus organizational energies on individuals as well as see them as the ultimate target of change. These groups meet in small, intimate settings and often discuss very personal matters as the members help one another to some improved psychic state. The hopes are as numerous as the problems are. Members of Alcoholics Anonymous help one another toward sobriety, Weight Watchers members encourage one another to shed pounds, and a bereavement group helps its members through the grieving process. Support groups usually have a very specific goal of change within the person.

Movements focus their organizational efforts on larger, structural phenomena. The most familiar type of movement is a social movement, which can be small or large depending on the scope of change, from local to international. Social movements focus their organizational resources on structures, such as laws or norms, and see these as the ultimate target of change. Examples of social movements include the civil rights movement, which advocated for nonracialized legislation and full-inclusion of black Americans, and various feminist movements, which looked to secure women's equality and make illegal practices that are antiwoman, such as spousal rape.

Cultural movements focus organizational energy on structures in order to target change in individuals. The environmental movement is an example of a cultural movement, which, for years, sponsored events and educated youth on the importance of conservation and now enjoys a generation that is more personally conscious of recycling and its role in climate change. The vegan movement counts a modest organizational membership in the tens of thousands, yet because of educational campaigns in the mass media and encouraging the food industry to increase the availability of vegan options, there are roughly 1.7 million vegans across the country.[4] These cultural movements seek structural changes, mostly educative or normative, in order to bring about changes in individuals' lifestyles.

Ripple groups, of which JFM is an example, focus their organizational energies on transforming individuals, with society as the ultimate target of change. Like support groups, ripple groups use the small group as their institutional vehicle for social change. By transforming and reinforcing people's values in a small group, participants in a ripple group come to share a plausibility structure that helps them make sense of the world.[5] This new plausibility structure changes the attitudes and behaviors of group members. The ripple group strategy further assumes that transformed individuals will, in turn, transform society. In *Habits of the Heart*, sociologist Robert Bellah and his colleagues discuss the importance of personal growth and concomitant social obligations in the formation of a morally healthy society: "Personal transformation among large numbers is essential, and it must not only be a transformation of consciousness but must also involve individual action."[6] As people truly transform, their new attitudes manifest in their social participation. The Bellah team continues, underscoring the importance of community in this process: "Individuals need the nurture of groups that carry a moral tradition reinforcing their own aspirations."[7] Genuine community, they contend, should transform the self as well as push individuals to go beyond themselves and the group to transform the wider world. As the effects of this transformation ripple outward, the impact will grow ever more substantial. A ripple group could be an isolated phenomenon whose probable impact would be very local, or it could be a series of cooperative groups spread across a geographic region, which would have more far-reaching effects.

The feminist consciousness-raising groups of the sixties and seventies are an example of a ripple group that sought to show women their value, challenging the male-centered norms of the wider culture. Another example is Opus Dei, which gathers its members regularly for spiritual strengthening and encourages them to take their faith into the world to serve God and all humanity. The thread that unites ripple groups is the channeling of organizational resources toward individual transformation with the expectation that this will ripple out to social change.

JFM's social form as a ripple group is apparent in its tagline, present in various promotional materials: "JustFaith changes people. Those people change the world." JFM does not engage in any efforts of social transformation itself, focusing instead on transforming individuals, as Jezreel says: "JustFaith Ministries does not feed the hungry. It does not clothe the naked. It does not visit those in jail or anything. We don't do that. The hope is that we can light a fire that inspires people to get involved in the Church's social mission." JFM's ultimate goal is not simply to transform individuals, as it is in a support group. The final hope is that these transformed individuals—grads with new outlooks, moral groundings, and faith commitments—will bring their new values to their everyday lives, causing the ripples to grow as positive social change occurs.

Why Discipleship Organizations Would Opt for the Ripple-Group Strategy

Underlying ripple groups is a notion of personhood that is a compromise position between classical liberals—held by most Americans—and communitarians: people are socially embedded individuals.[8] The hope and expectation that a single individual can have a significant impact on the world reflect the individualistic element. This individualism also privileges people's freedom to discern their own moral course. This is not to say, however, that people are without obligations to one another or develop without others. These notions of duty, sociality, and reciprocity are salient ideas among communitarians, which is a strong element within the Catholic tradition. The social and individualist aspects are apparent in the ways ripple groups identify and solve social problems: when a ripple group identifies a social failing, the group's plausibility structure compels each person to ameliorate the problem, albeit with ample freedom that respects each individual's personal discernment. For example, JustFaith groups identify poverty as a pressing social problem, and group members respond in their own ways, with one volunteering at a soup kitchen, another at an inner-city school, and so forth.

Also underscoring the sociality of the human person, ripple groups believe all individuals have some form of social influence and are a part of some social network. These relationships provide opportunities to transform other people and one's communities, illustrating the evangelistic aspect of ripple groups. In *Habits of the Heart*, Robert Bellah and his colleagues also discuss the self as both socially embedded and individualist when they acknowledge the trepidations of their American audience: "What [Americans] fear . . . is that if we give up our dream of private success for a more genuinely integrated societal community, we will be abandoning our separation and individuation, collapsing into dependence and tyranny. What we find hard to see is that it is the extreme fragmentation of the modern world that really threatens our individuation; that what is best in our separation and individuation, our sense of dignity and autonomy as persons, requires a new integration if it is to be sustained."[9] Individuality is nurtured—not threatened or stifled—through a sense of embeddedness in society. The self, these sociologists and ripple groups contend, is a socially embedded individual.

Ripple groups' notion of the socially embedded individual dovetails nicely with the discipleship style. The public styles of the past required a more communitarian approach, which does not mesh well with the more individualized sentiments of contemporary American Catholics. Organizations of each of O'Brien's historical styles, with their strong communitarian flavor, created collectivist models with little room for individual public action as Catholics. Organizations of the discipleship style, however, mobilize single persons, creating a conduit to bring the individual into public engagement as a Catholic. The ripple group, therefore, is a form that many find appealing because of its appreciation of the sociality of the individual. First, it focuses on the individual and takes seriously the social reality of a more mobile and less collectivist world. Second, despite its attention to the individual, ripple groups also revivify "communities of memory," embedding the individual in a language of commitment, tradition, and history.[10] Although not all ripple groups are discipleship organizations (e.g., feminist consciousness-raising groups), because of the affinities, discipleship organizations will most likely adopt the strategy of the ripple group.

Again, ripple groups seek social change by changing individuals, operating under the assumption that these transformed individuals can alter their social worlds. Because of this, understanding the way a ripple group changes society begins with understanding the transformations it evokes (or not) from the members.

Types of Transformation among JustFaith Graduates

Sociological studies of conversion are helpful for understanding the individual transformation that occurs in ripple groups. Adherents and demographers might privilege a definition of conversion that includes a change in religious affiliation. Sociological definitions, instead, emphasize a changed worldview. Jerald Brauer defined *conversion* as "a profound, self-conscious, existential change from one set of beliefs, habits, and orientation to a new structure of belief and action."[11] Richard Travisano wrote that it is "a radical reorganization of identity, meaning, life."[12] Max Heirich called it "the process of changing a sense of root reality."[13] Furthermore, a variety of experiences, not just those strictly "religious," can change a person's worldview, which can result in a new worldview while denominational affiliation remains unchanged.[14] Given the absence of denominational switching among the grads, the sociological interpretation—rather than demographers' religious identity definition—takes seriously their claims of transformation. JustFaith encourages participants to reorient their understandings of the world, allowing this new outlook to affect the way they engage society.

Conversion experiences are not uniform among the grads. The graduates discussed five motifs of personal transformation: religion-centering transformation, political transformation, religio-political transformation, intensification, and motivational transformation.[15] These are not rigid categories in which utilizing one motif precludes identification with another. Most grads draw on multiple motifs when discussing their personal transformation, and sometimes one type of transformation causes another. These motifs each emphasize particular aspects of the grads' worldview, aspects they believe are central to Christian living. Because the motifs refer to Christian values more broadly, these are personal accounts as well as normative statements about the Christian community, illustrating grads' understandings of evangelization and the social mission of the church today.

Religion-Centering Transformation

Religion-centering transformation means applying Gospel values to the whole of one's life. People experiencing this type of conversion move from a life that limits their faith to a Sunday activity toward one in which their faith influences all aspects of their lives.[16] Sociologists David Snow and Richard Machalek highlight that a convert's primary worldview need not be new; it could be that a previously peripheral worldview has become central.[17] This changed importance of religion gives rise to new relationships, practices, and understandings of the world. It is not the *newness* of the worldview that is important in assessing whether someone has undergone conversion but the new *position* of a worldview. Every grad experiences this motif,[18] demonstrating its centrality in the JustFaith moral universe, as Jezreel says of JFM: "We're trying to bridge the relationship between the Scriptures and response to the Scriptures. We're trying to bridge the relationships between Eucharist and what happens after Mass. We're trying to bridge the relationship between Catholic social teaching and Catholic social mission." JFM and other discipleship style organizations are ultimately trying to integrate the spheres of religion and public life that the historical styles segregated.[19]

Similarly, rather than understanding faith merely as praying or attending church, religion-centering transformation makes religion primary, framing the world with new religious and moral meaning. Under this logic, all life should reveal the good news of the scriptures, as Lucy Russell, a retired Louisville preschool teacher, shows: "[St. Francis of Assisi] preached the Gospel, but he always told his followers, 'Preach the Gospel at *all* times, and sometimes you will even have to use words.' And the conversion experience I had in JustFaith was showing, the way I live my life preaches a Gospel that is more real than anything I could ever say, or write, or profess. Because if I'm not living consciously, making choices based on my Gospel values then I'm just preaching with words, but not with my life . . . But I'm espousing to follow my brother

Jesus." Russell's transformation allows her, through living her faith, to proclaim God in a way that she believes is more authentic as it reaches all aspects of her life. For the cynic who argues that she mistakenly attributes a holiness to the profane or waters down her faith, recognizing that she does not simply assume that her life has religious meaning is important. Instead, Russell's transformation includes rigor and intentionality. She states that living the Gospel requires her to live more "consciously" and to make deliberate choices to follow God. In making faith central and grounding the rest of their lives in that faith, the grads work to make their lives witnesses of Christ's love, which also lends their lives meaning.[20]

Political Transformation

Political transformation is either the changing of political beliefs—for grads, making poverty a central, rather than peripheral, priority—or a substantial increase in political awareness. Many of these interviews take place in the San Francisco Bay Area, which is much more liberal than the nation as a whole. To hear people talk about becoming a Democrat after a long loyalty to the Republican party was unusual, simply because so few began as Republicans, but it did happen.[21] Matthew Collins, a Bay Area grad who retired from a long career in the oil business, was typical of this motif:

> I was more on the conservative side going into JustFaith, and I think it really opened my eyes personally, both to the needs and the depth of suffering that's within our country, in the world . . . It was much more personal for me and, you know, definitely opened up my heart more than before. And then also made me realize on a political level that I probably would have been more prone to vote Republican on a lot of different things because of some of the moral stands they took [rather] than the financial policies that they kind of endorsed. But from that time forward it became increasingly hard for me to kind of side with them on so many different things. And the latest budget negotiations [government shutdown of October 2013], just being a case of point, just drove me absolutely nuts. So I would say for myself personally it's pushed me much more from the conservative to liberal political standpoint.

This grad articulates a new political understanding, one that ties the suffering of many people intimately to economic policies, forcing him to abandon his Republican loyalties for something he now finds more compassionate.

A more common political transformation was becoming increasingly aware of the scope and severity of issues. Contemporary Americans have more years of education than previous generations, yet they know no more about politics than Americans in 1940.[22] Grads whose political acumen increases come to care about that newly acquired knowledge. Whereas some conversion stories are riddled with a painful and arduous "dying" leading up to the conversion, JustFaith grads do not share such stories nor was anything like this observed in the groups.[23] There is, instead, often a sense of disquiet or alarm as people become more aware of the suffering in the world and their role in it. Grads welcome this knowledge, and they focus on the new life this knowledge brings rather than the death to old ways they abandon. Some grads mention that they initially did not think the environment was an important issue or that they did not realize that human trafficking was something that happened in the United States. Others become more aware of numerous issues, as Maggie Patrickson, a college undergrad preparing to work with neurologically atypical children, has:

> There could be actual content living in Haiti if we address this situation of poverty across the world. Like people in Haiti could actually live real lives and not be so poor, so incredibly poor, that they just start starving and dying and everything. And then people who go on to Mali wouldn't live on top of dumps and people of Sudan wouldn't be worried about their kids getting put into those child soldier stuff and Somalia wouldn't have to worry about AIDS—that's one of the biggest places for AIDS. And Tanzania and Mauritania, the Muslims still are—I mean, no one talks about Mauritania. But the Muslims are still keeping the Africans as their slaves and no one goes in there.

"No one talks about Mauritania." Whether or not one agrees with Patrickson's list of social priorities, her knowledge of global issues is impressive. This twenty-year-old went through JWalking in high school and is better versed in global politics, as demonstrated by her litany of social ills, than the vast majority of Americans her age; a recent survey showed that half of Americans ages eighteen to twenty-four cannot identify New York and that nearly two-thirds cannot find Iraq.[24] No doubt that her participation in JWalking contributed to her knowledge and desire for further learning.

Religio-Political Transformation

Religio-political transformation is coming to perceive the theological relevance in political commitments. Some grads were active in justice or poverty issues prior to JustFaith but did not have a strong religious understanding of their convictions. This motif is far more common among San Francisco–area grads, many of whom already held concerns for poor and marginalized groups due to their political milieu. However, a considerable number of progressive grads did not previously connect their political convictions with their religious beliefs. Either they were not aware of the social implications of scripture and their denomination's tradition or they did not have the cultural facility to draw on religious ideas to understand and discuss peace and justice issues.[25] Liz Harris, a Methodist grad who works in faith formation, recalls conversations with her conservative in-laws:

> And so [my husband and I] became, in the [extended] family, the voice of social justice. Now that's not how they thought of it! [smiling] . . . and that became empowering for us. To have the experience of being willing to challenge something and take it back to the Bible, to the faith that Jesus calls us to have. And these are very conservative Christian people who are working from the same document we are, but who have understood that document in a different way. To be able to take it fundamentally back to the Bible and say "How does that fit with Jesus?" It was just really empowering for us. So I think for us it really became a confidence of being willing to speak out first in our family unit, but then more broadly and being willing to challenge people's views that seem inconsistent with our understanding of the people of faith God calls us to be.

Due to conservatives' more frequent use of religious rhetoric in public discourse, many religious liberals feel a cognitive dissonance as they seek to be true to both their religious and political beliefs.[26] Some progressive Christians leave their denomination because they cannot reconcile the two.[27] JustFaith is an invaluable resource for these people, helping them take parts of their lives that seemed unrelated or even contradictory and integrate them in an empowering way. This new religio-political relevance enables them to confront conservative co-religionists on religious terms.

Intensification

Some conversion theorists argue that scholars should study the intensity of adherent belief. Sociologist Arthur Greil claims that, occasionally, when researchers speak of conversion, they miss that the convert is actually embracing a worldview or ideology that is congruent with a previous value system.[28] Greil calls this "recruitment" rather than "conversion" because the person is simply becoming organizationally affiliated rather than embracing a new ideology. Anthropologist Henri Gooren also proposes that people have "conversion careers" in which, over a lifetime, their religious commitments vary in intensity.[29] These both illuminate the fourth motif of intensification, that is, a deepening of an already-held religious or ideological commitment. These intensified grads are similar to who they were previously, yet they grew in faith and increased their service commitments. Many grads say that JustFaith deepened their commitments without being able to pinpoint the precise changes. Margaret Wagner, a retired high school counselor and part-time spiritual director in the Los Angeles area, offers a clue when she says that JustFaith deepened her faith "by reinforcing a view, a worldview that I already had by providing avenues and resources and so forth to live out more fully this vision that I already had." She had a vision of what was just or caring, but prior to JustFaith, she did not know how to enact those ideas, nor did she have a milieu that strengthened her values. Wagner also highlights an Aristotelian truth: what we do shapes what we feel, think, and believe.[30] Sociologist Ziad Munson found the same ideological strengthening among pro-life activists.[31] Many people who were ambivalent or pro-choice with regard to abortion would find, after engaging in antiabortion activism through the invitation of a friend, that their beliefs became strongly pro-life. Munson's other interviewees, who were strongly pro-life but not active in the cause, had a much weaker grasp of their values and revealed considerable ambivalence about abortion when challenged. Similarly, JustFaith exposed Wagner to organizations that gave her ways to act on her convictions, ossifying her beliefs and making them a more important part of her life and sense of self.

Intensification also manifests as a widening of one's worldview. Many participants were already concerned with a particular issue, such as homelessness or climate change.[32] JustFaith exposed them to many more problems that contribute to suffering in their communities and world, expanding participants' notions of what was worth caring about. This suffering reinforces their commitment to their particular justice issue at the same time that it encourages grads to pursue new opportunities, as Pete London, a retired Bay Area grad who has taken a variety of JFM courses, illustrates: "At the beginning they tell you that, 'Oh, you're really going to change and you're going to make commitments to do extra stuff.' And I was thinking, 'Not for me, because I'm already doing enough. I'm not going for that, I'm going just to get the knowledge.' But I ended up signing up for [a juvenile detention center ministry]. And I guess I signed up for the [women's equality group] while I was going to JustFaith, too." Although London is incredibly active in his parish, holding major leadership positions, he added two more ministries to his schedule, even becoming the lone male member of a group that seeks women's equality. JustFaith exposes grads to issues and relationships that invite them to a deeper involvement.

Motivational Transformation

The fifth and final motif is motivational transformation, an increase in the desire to be publicly involved. Many said that before JustFaith they helped out as they were able. Following JustFaith, service to others became urgent and compelling. Motivational transformation explains more directly the increase in social action among the grads. Because few Americans are significantly involved in their communities, any ripple group that hopes to change society must instill both awareness and desire in its participants. JFM staff member Cathy Meyers remembers her work in a previous job: "When I was [working] at the [United

States Conference of Catholic Bishops; USCCB] and I had done a presentation for several other bishops and [one] said, 'Cathy, that was a very good presentation, but you are talking all about "how to."' And he said, 'My people are not at the "want to" stage.' I think that was such a good response and I think JustFaith offers both. We offer a way to get people to the 'want to.' . . . I think our programs address why should I want to do this and then all of our programs end with action steps." JFM believes JustFaith provides concrete ways to get involved as well as lends a desire to do more, even in the face of profound social apathy. JFM staff member Christine Philips tells a story of the organization's success in encouraging involvement: "I first heard about JFM when I was working here in town as a community organizer, which is hard work and it is hard to get people involved . . . And all of a sudden we have this influx of people who were volunteering to do stuff with our organization and we were all kind of confused . . . they were eager to even get involved in fund-raising, which even of the involved people in this organization it was hard to get people . . . People were so interested, and they kept talking about this JustFaith program that they went through." That an abundance of enthusiastic volunteers could leave a community organizer "confused" is not just amusing; it also demonstrates JustFaith's ability to instill a desire for civic engagement.

Marie Baker, a grad and former staff member, demonstrates the intensity of this heightened sense of motivation:

> It just made me feel more enriched and enlivened. And it also gave me, the courage and conviction and the *need* to feel like I needed to go and do something. I can't just sit here and live my little life in my little box. That's not what I'm supposed to do. That's not fair to me and that's not fair to the rest of the world. I still don't always know what that is or how to do that. But I know that I *have* to do that in some way. That I can't just be okay sitting back and watching the rest of the world do what it does without making some kind of contribution.

Grads offer a variety of reasons for why they become more involved in their communities, with Baker pointing to a sense of courage, duty, and fairness. Despite their diversity of backgrounds and understandings of the program, grads hold in common an increased awareness of their world, especially through becoming attuned to the suffering of others. This new scope of caring is ultimately what transforms the participants, their practices, and, it is hoped, the world.

Transformation as a Socially Embedded and Individualist Process

These transformations are both social and individualist. Looking first to the personal, each of these motifs illustrates a shift or intensification in care. Religion-centering transformation makes the message of the Gospels primary, approaching all other commitments through the lens of faith. Political transformation changes grads' political values, encouraging them to include the poor among their priorities or expand their knowledge, both increasing care. Religio-political transformation shifts into frames that highlight the religious meanings in political choices, prompting grads to a greater level of concern for political issues. Intensification draws grads more deeply into their previous beliefs and invites them into new issues as well. Motivational transformation changes the way grads see their place in the world in relation to others, understanding themselves as connected to others and sent to extend that care as service.

Experiences of transformation are also social and, viewed from this perspective, these transformations are normative and reveal grads' understanding of Christian mission. These motifs imply expectations of authentic gospel living for Christians and recommendations for the church. Religion-centering transformation says that there is no "religious realm." Instead, Christians must make their faith the foundation of their lives, and churches should remind the laity that God calls them, along with the ordained, to lives of holiness. As grads learn more about their world, political transformation illuminates the harsh realities of the poor, shifting their political priorities and understanding of the role of the church in the world. Religio-political transformation allows the grads to understand political problems and solutions in light of the Gospel, rather than segregating faith and politics, and recommends that churches do the same. Grads who have experienced intensification claim that holding Christians to minimal expectations does little for churches or society. Instead, intensification calls Christians to their moral maximum, to holiness. Motivational transformation mandates that churches bring their congregants out of the building to connect with Jesus through the poor.

These Catholics embrace a notion of personhood that acknowledges people as socially embedded individuals even while they engage a society that places more weight on individualist elements. Again, discipleship organizations are shaped by personalism. Using the word *personalism* over *individualism* highlights the unique-while-communal understanding of the human person, affirmed by sociology—as discussed earlier—as well as Catholicism.[33] Within the conversion motifs, we see grads negotiating some of the characteristics of the discipleship style. First, in their relationship with the institutional church, grads want their churches to be bolder in their stances, to demand more civically and morally from Catholics, and to be active formers of the faithful and reformers of society. Second, grads do not see this as political maneuvering. Rather, grads seek to integrate their sacred and secular lives and realize that their churches are spiritual resources for this endeavor. Their transformations have both personal and social repercussions as they discuss a shift in their personal values as well as their denominational expectations. If properly coordinated, transformations of socially embedded individuals have the potential for structural change. The new demands grads place upon themselves and their churches illustrate the ways a ripple group can affect the world at the macro-level.

Measuring the Ripples: Transformation in the Grads and Beyond

Ripple groups foment change in society by focusing organizational energy on individuals. The ripple group affects participants' beliefs, creating a *cognitive personal transformation*. Analogically, this is the pebble thrown into the pond. Participants in successful ripple groups will be significantly different people, with new attitudes, values, and worldviews. For JustFaith grads, this means caring differently about the world, especially the poor. Just as ripples grow larger as they leave their center, this analysis goes beyond the subjective self to changes in practices or the *practical personal transformation*. JFM expects this cognitive change to yield a transformation of the grads' behaviors. Although JFM staff claim that a cognitive personal transformation begets this practical personal transformation, a close look at the survey data that follow reveals that belief and practice mutually reinforce one another rather than one causing the other independently. Beyond the individual, ripple groups hope to effect *social transformation*. Organizations can target a variety of social contexts for change, such as those at the level of the institutional, interpersonal, legal, or cultural.[34] Although some ripple groups may have a more limited scope, JFM seeks a very comprehensive social transformation that includes relationships, structures, cultural mores, and so forth. Clearly, given the array of factors at play with any societal problem, it would be exceedingly difficult to measure the ways grads alone effectively ameliorate social ills. Churches, however, are a more contained system, making it possible to study the transformative effects of the program at the congregational level. By examining the ways Just-Faith changes churches, one can at the very least extend the analysis a ripple farther than the individual, discovering how an institution might transform via the ripple-group model.

For groups employing a ripple-group strategy, transformation is not simply a part of social outreach; it is also central to it. According to national data, people in religious small groups volunteer more time to every other sort of cause, from health to recreation to the arts, compared to those not in religious small groups.[35] When other factors are controlled for, a significant difference in volunteering remains between those in religious small groups and those not.[36] The difference does *not* correlate with holding specific theological beliefs, being more embedded in one's congregation, or simply from the fact that small group members are "joiners," that is, those who tend to get involved in groups and activities. *The factor that leads to civic involvement is having undergone a transformative religious experience.* The data suggest that this spiritual awakening causes people to think more deeply about the meaning of life and leads to a desire to help others.[37] Groups with explicit expectations of religious transformation, such as discipleship groups, should find it easier to instigate outreach among members. Ripple groups increase volunteer efforts by channeling this desire to help others to formal organizations and group endeavors.

What is most striking in the survey data are the strong similarities, with some notable exceptions, between the pre-JustFaith group and the grads, Catholics more so than Protestants. There is very little difference in the beliefs between these groups, yet grads describe JustFaith as transformational. There are two ways to reconcile these groups' similarity in belief with the grads' experience of transformation. First, JustFaith transforms people not by changing them so much as making their beliefs salient and equipping them with tools so that they might transform their co-religionists who *are* vastly different from them on a number of measures.[38] This explanation, with the evangelistic style it employs, is an important quality of ripple groups. The second, and perhaps stronger, explanation is that quantitative surveys—where these data come from—measure people's beliefs but cannot measure the depth, nuance, or salience of these beliefs. Many grads reconsider their priorities (religion-centering transformation), experience a deepening of their beliefs (intensification), or feel pushed to act on their beliefs (motivational transformation). When they begin JustFaith they already hold many of the programs' values—this is what drew them to JustFaith—but they do not grant these values a central place in their life. Interviews reveal that they have given a great deal of thought to their beliefs, much of this discernment because of JustFaith. Ziad Munson's study corroborates this, showing that pro-life activists and nonactivists who identify as pro-life have very similar survey responses.[39] However, when interviewed and given the opportunity to elaborate their beliefs, the activists, because of their ongoing engagement, are more articulate and certain than the non-activists. This demonstrates that although grads and those just beginning JustFaith might appear very similar on survey responses, those new to the program may not have the benefit of activism to strengthen, reason through, or make central these beliefs. Because the pre-JustFaith participants are only surveyed and not interviewed, one cannot conclude with certainty that the new JustFaith participants do not use these beliefs to organize their lives to the extent that the grads do. However, the similarities in beliefs coupled with the disparities in practices that enact those beliefs—discussed later as practical personal transformation—indicate that a phenomenon similar to that observed in Munson's study is occurring among those surveyed. The following discussion draws on survey data, illustrating the similarities and differences between three groups of people: American Christians broadly, JustFaith grads who participated in this study, and a small group of thirty-six people who had completed no more than three sessions of JustFaith.[40] Of this pre-JustFaith group, twelve were Protestants, and twenty-four were Catholic. Comparing these three groups will show the ways JustFaith transforms the participants as well as some of the predispositions of those who begin a program like JustFaith.

Cognitive Personal Transformation

JustFaith grads claim that the program significantly changed them. Two-thirds of grads describe their "experience in JustFaith as a conversion experience," demonstrating that a strong majority feel the program had a transformative effect. Likewise, just over three-quarters believe that they are a "significantly different person due to participation in Just-Faith." This is more than other Catholic small groups: just under half of Catholics in the "general" Christian communities of another study "had a religious experience."[41] Nearly all of the participants, 93 percent, believe that they are "a lot more knowledgeable of many issues due to JustFaith," and 91 percent say their "values are more firmly grounded in [their] faith thanks to JustFaith." Another 93 percent claim that JustFaith helped them "to find a greater sense of purpose in the world." As these numbers make clear, many grads feel transformed through JustFaith and even more find increased integrity and meaning in their lives because of the program.

Their political attitudes indicate a concern for poor and vulnerable groups as well (see table 3.2).

Among Catholics, 7 percent of grads agree that there should be a "stiffer enforcement of the death penalty," and 14 percent agree that there should be "further cutbacks in welfare programs," compared to 0 and 8 percent of those just beginning the program.[42] These stand in contrast to what William D'Antonio's team found of Catholics nationwide. For these Catholics, despite church teaching against the death penalty and in favor of public safety nets, a full 60 percent agree that there should be a stronger enforcement of capital punishment, and 53 percent agree that there should be further cutbacks in welfare programs.[43]

Protestant grads show similar attitudinal differences (table 3.3).

Unlike Catholics who have one denomination with a hierarchical polity, there is considerable disagreement among Protestant denominations on various political issues. National survey data illuminate a broad picture, with a mere 18 percent of Protestants believing that the federal

TABLE 3.2. Catholic Opinion on Social Policy

	Pre-JustFaith Catholics	Catholic Grads	American Catholics
Stiffer enforcement of the death penalty (agree)	0%	7%	60%
Further cutbacks in welfare programs (agree)	8%	14%	53%

TABLE 3.3. Protestant Opinion on Social Policy

	Pre-JustFaith Protestants	Protestant Grads	American Protestants
The federal government should end the death penalty (agree)	70%	95%	18%
Actively seek social and economic justice to be a good person ("very important")	64%	100%	40%
Those believing they pay too much in taxes	40%	5%	51%

government should abolish the death penalty and two in five saying that it is "very important" to "actively seek social and economic justice" in order to be a good person.[44] Protestant grads answered this with more concern for the downtrodden; 95 percent looked to end capital punishment, and *every* grad said a struggle for justice was very important to be a good person. Seventy percent of pre-JustFaith Protestants oppose the death penalty, and only 64 percent believe it is very important to seek justice. They also think differently of taxes, a monetary indicator of their willingness to contribute to the common good. Only 5 percent of grads think the amount they pay in taxes is "too high." Compare this nationally to the slight majority and the two-fifths of pre-JustFaith Protestants who believe they pay too much in taxes.[45] Among Protestants, the beliefs of those new to the program stand midway between the grads and their coreligionists more broadly. With Catholics, however, the grads' and new JustFaith participants' political beliefs are similar to one another and significantly different from Catholics not affiliated with the program.

Comparing those who believe that their small group altered their faith to those who do not reveals, by some measures, profound differences in their denominational affinity.[46] National data demonstrate that those who experience a religious transformation are less likely to regard their beliefs as private, less likely to say their faith does not depend on a religious organization, less likely to say churches are all alike, and vastly less likely to believe that it does not matter what one believes, so long as he or she is a good person. These findings appear counterintuitive as one might expect people going on a *personal* faith journey to separate from their *institutional* mores. Instead, being in a small faith-sharing group in their congregation colors participants' private beliefs with public significance and roots them more deeply in their religious tradition.

In addition to seeing religious relevance in their everyday lives, many JustFaith participants likewise develop a more robust affinity for their tradition. One woman said, "I think JustFaith is what keeps me [in the Catholic faith]. And you know, it wasn't a re-affirmation because it was really a totally new vision of what the Church is and what could be! So, you know, it's the reason I really strongly consider myself a Catholic." Grads claim that JustFaith drew them more deeply into the institutional manifestations of the church, many citing increased parish involvement and the study of magisterial teachings. Studying the church's social justice teachings, discussing the lives of contemporary Christians committed to poverty issues and sharing these experiences with fellow parishioners strengthens grads' concern for the poor as well as their denominational identity.

The survey data illustrate this, as well. Looking to Catholics first (table 3.4), parish registration rates indicate that grads and those who begin JustFaith are more committed to their parishes (both 91 percent) than are Catholics nationally (60 percent).[47]

The grads and those beginning JustFaith also found various items important to the Catholic faith to be "very important" to themselves personally, more so than Catholics nationally. These are the church's involvement in justice issues, having a regular daily prayer life and the church's teachings that oppose the death penalty.[48] These differences, centering on concern for the marginalized and prayer, show that grads and new participants embrace the JFM values of compassion, justice, and Christ-centeredness. The one exception to the similarities between the grads and those beginning the program is the percentage who believe helping the poor is very important, showing that this commitment

TABLE 3.4. Catholic Commitment to Church Institution and Teachings

	Pre-JustFaith Catholics	Catholic Grads	American Catholics
Registered at parish	91%	91%	60%
Church's involvement in justice issues ("very important")	79%	91%	34%
Having a regular daily prayer life ("very important")	71%	74%	47%
Church's teachings that oppose the death penalty ("very important")	75%	80%	30%
Helping the poor ("very important")	71%	94%	68%
Church's teachings that oppose abortion ("very important")	33%	38%	40%
Importance of church in life ("most" or "among the most" important part of one's life)	65%	61%	37%
Likelihood of leaving the church (least likely, answering 1 or 2)	67%	48%	57%
Scoring "highly committed" on index	44%	42%	19%

is significantly strengthened through JustFaith. There is little difference in the importance they place on the church's teachings that oppose abortion. Their stance on the abortion issue illustrates their firmly
Catholic sense of morality: despite the liberal/conservative dichotomy in
American politics and the strongly progressive attitudes among grads,
a concern for the unborn remains that approximates Catholics nationally. Further underscoring their institutional commitment, 61 percent of
grads and 65 percent of new participants say that the Catholic Church is
the most or among the most important parts of their lives whereas only
37 percent of Catholics nationally say this.[49] D'Antonio's team also asked
Catholics how likely they were to leave the church, with a 1 signifying
they "would never leave" and a 7 meaning they "might leave." Using this
scale, 57 percent of Catholics nationally chose a 1 or a 2, fewer than the
67 percent of new participants and a bit more than the 48 percent of
grads who chose this.[50] These last two items and Mass attendance form
a composite index of Catholic commitment. Requiring that highly committed Catholics attend Mass at least weekly, consider the church to be
the most or among the most important parts of their life, and select a

1 or 2 on the 7-point scale that estimates their likelihood of leaving the church, only 19 percent of Catholics nationwide are highly committed, 66 percent have a moderate level of commitment, and 14 percent have a low level of commitment.[51] Among JustFaith grads, however, an impressive 42 percent have a high level, 57 percent have a moderate level, and only 2 percent have a low level of commitment to Catholicism according to this index, with new participants nearly identical to grads. By most measures, JustFaith attracts those more deeply committed to their religion at both the parish and the institutional level. The rejuvenation some grads describe may demonstrate that JustFaith acts as a "pressure valve," giving Catholics committed to the poor a missionary outlet, despite the professionalization of many Catholic charitable endeavors.[52] These data demonstrate that Catholics who have a high level of commitment to Catholicism and progressive political values—save abortion— are attracted to JustFaith. Clearly, JustFaith programs are self-selected by those who have an attitudinal affinity to the programs, indicating that the transformative nature of the program does not impact beliefs as much as it refines beliefs, affects practices, or contributes to larger social transformation.

Like the Catholics, Protestants involved in JustFaith also have a stronger faith than Protestants nationally (table 3.5).

Sixty percent of Protestant grads consider themselves strong Protestants, and a mere 11 percent consider themselves not very strong. This shows more institutional commitment than the 33 percent of pre-JustFaith participants who identify as a strong Protestant and the 22 percent who say they are not very strong Protestants. Nationally, nearly half of Protestants consider themselves to be strongly Protestant, and a full 40 percent consider themselves not very strong.[53] In a similar vein, nine in ten grads think of themselves as very or moderately religious, compared to 67 percent of pre-JustFaith Protestants and 72 percent of Protestants in general.[54] Although none of the grads or new JustFaith participants thought that it was important to convert others to their faith in order to be "a good person" compared to one-third of their co-religionists, slightly more than the national average think that being a good person requires faith in God.[55] JustFaith brought these Protestants, by most measures, closer to the institutional manifestations of their faith.

TABLE 3.5. Protestant Commitment to Denominational Institution and Teachings

	Pre-JustFaith Protestants	Protestant Grads	American Protestants
Considering themselves a strong Protestant	33%	60%	49%
Claiming to be very or moderately religious	67%	90%	72%
Important to convert others to one's faith to be a good person (very or some-what important)	0%	0%	33%
Importance of faith in God in being a good person	82%	85%	75%

JustFaith appears to transform the beliefs of Protestant participants more readily than it does Catholics. Among Catholics, the program attracts those most committed to Catholicism and its social teaching. The Protestants, on the other hand, show change on more measures. An area that showed significant change for both is their assessment of their own political identity. New participants have a rather centrist political identity, with half identifying as moderate and 39 percent considering themselves liberal or very liberal. Only 9 percent of grads identify as moderate, and 85 percent call themselves liberal or very liberal.

Practical Personal Transformation

As a ripple group, JFM wants religious and moral transformation through a small group to affect beliefs as well as practices. Small-group data corroborate these hopes. Looking first to religious practices, those in "general" Catholic small groups engage in religious practices more frequently than those not in small groups, such as daily prayer, reconciliation within the last two years, retreat attendance, or attending a Catholic social justice meeting.[56] JustFaith grads and new participants are likewise much more religiously active than their coreligionists. The D'Antonio team found that 32 percent of Catholics nationally attend Mass weekly or more.[57] Seventy-two percent of grads attend at that rate, with an impressive subset of 13 percent who attend daily, which is

TABLE 3.6. Catholic Mass Attendance and Financial Giving

	Pre-JustFaith Catholics	Catholic Grads	American Catholics
Weekly Mass attendance	80%	72%	32%
Percentage of income donated to parish	4%	4.3%	1.5%
Percentage of income donated, all causes	8.7%	10.8%	3.7%[1]

[1] This figure is for regularly attending Catholics and is higher than for American Catholics generally.

TABLE 3.7. Protestant Financial Giving

	Pre-JustFaith Protestants	Protestant Grads	American Protestants
Percentage of income donated to congregation	4.9%	4.5%	2.5%
Percentage of income donated, all causes	8.0%	9.9%	7.4%[1]

[1] This figure is for Protestants who are regularly attending and is higher than for American Protestants generally.

slightly less than the 80 percent of new participants who attend weekly (table 3.6). American Catholics give roughly 1.5 percent of their annual income to their churches, and Protestants give 2.5 percent (table 3.7).[58] Catholic grads give 4.3 percent, and new participants give 4 percent. Protestant grads give 4.5 percent of their income to their church, and new participants give 4.9 percent.

Even for Christians nationally who regularly attend church, general charitable giving—church giving included—is quite low. Regularly attending Catholics give away 3.7 percent of their income, and Protestants double that at 7.4 percent.[59] New Catholic participants exceed this, donating 8.7 percent and the grads surpass them, donating 10.8 percent. New Protestant participants approximate their coreligionists nationally at 8 percent, and grads give considerably more at 9.9 percent.

Volunteer rates are appreciably higher among the grads. In her study on civic activism, sociologist Nina Eliasoph found that people claim not to care about an issue when they believe the problem is too difficult to solve.[60] By encouraging participants to care about specific issues and offering venues to address the problem, JustFaith groups make it more difficult for participants to avoid engaging an issue.[61] Of Americans who volunteer, most say they do so because of a "desire to help others" or to

TABLE 3.8. Catholic Volunteer Frequency

	Pre-JustFaith Catholics	Catholic Grads	American Catholics
Volunteer outside of church monthly or more	50%	80%	12%
Volunteer outside of church weekly or more	25%	35%	4%

TABLE 3.9. Protestant Volunteer Frequency

	Pre-JustFaith Protestants	Protestant Grads	American Protestants
Volunteer outside of church monthly or more	46%	90%	17%
Volunteer outside of church weekly or more	9%	35%	6%
Strongly agree that they try hard to carry their religious beliefs over into other dealings in life	10%	65%	37%
Very important to care for the sick and needy to be a good person	55%	95%	62%

"feel useful."[62] These demonstrate the connection between cognitive and practical transformation: people volunteer to satisfy an inner feeling, either that others need help or that they could be doing more. Yet, few Americans volunteer on a regular basis. Only 12 percent of Catholics and 17 percent of Protestants volunteer outside of church monthly or more (for Catholic data, see table 3.8; for Protestant data, table 3.9).[63]

Like congregational giving, new JustFaith participants outdo American Catholics, with 50 percent volunteering monthly or more. Although these new participants have high levels of volunteering, Catholic grads exceed them with 80 percent volunteering monthly or more. Similar patterns are found among Protestants, with 46 percent of pre-JustFaith participants and 90 percent of grads volunteering monthly or more. When one looks at those who volunteer weekly, only 4 percent of Catholics and 6 percent of Protestants nationally fall into this category. Yet one-quarter of the Catholics new to JustFaith, and more than one-third of the grads volunteer at this rate. Protestants follow this pattern more dramatically with 9 percent of pre-JustFaith participants and 35 percent

TABLE 3.10. Political and Civic Participation—Both Catholic and Protestant

	Pre-JustFaith Participants	All Grads	Americans Generally
Always vote in elections	75%	88%	62%[1]
Agree that despite all they do, they do not do enough	94%	88%	n/a

Note: n/a = not applicable; this was an original survey question.
[1] Obviously not all those voting in the 2012 presidential election would count themselves among those who "always" vote. Still, this illustrates that those in JustFaith, and even more so those who have completed JustFaith, are active citizens.

of grads volunteering weekly or more. Additionally, an astounding 88 percent of the grads claim they always vote in elections, higher than the 75 percent of new participants or the 62 percent of Americans who voted in the 2012 presidential election (table 3.10).[64] Looking for a moment to Protestant grads, 65 percent strongly agree that they "try hard to carry [their] religious beliefs over into all [their] other dealings in life" compared to 37 percent of Protestants generally and 10 percent of pre-JustFaith participants.[65] In their estimate of what one must do to be a good person, 95 percent of grads believe caring for the sick and needy is very important compared to just 62 percent of Protestants nationally and 55 percent of JustFaith beginners.[66]

Despite all this activity, 88 percent of all grads and 94 percent of new participants believe that they do not do enough, revealing the high priority they give to their activism (table 3.10). As the preceding shows, despite the similarities in beliefs, those just beginning JustFaith and those who have completed it are quite different from one another when one examines practices, with the general pattern being that the wider population is the least active, new participants more active, and grads the most active.

These cognitive and practical personal transformations raise the question: Does JustFaith transform its participants? This depends on how one defines transformation. If one means coming to an entirely new set of beliefs and practices, then the quantitative data suggest grads are not transformed. If, however, transformation means plumbing their beliefs, discovering which are most important, and organizing their commitments accordingly, then the feelings of transformation among grads makes sense. New participants and grads have very similar beliefs on many issues, but the disparity in practices reveals that the new participants have not incorporated these values into their definition of Christian living as fully as the grads.[67] JustFaith insists that beliefs can no longer be lukewarm, abstract, or glib. Instead, programs encourage participants to be passionate about their beliefs as well as provide opportunities and support for participants to act on these beliefs. This explains why grads' beliefs appear very similar to those of new participants, yet their practices are quite different. New participants are more active in their churches and communities than most Americans. Still, grads are even more active than those just beginning JustFaith, despite the reported similarities in belief. These survey data indicate that, by and large, JustFaith transforms participants by expanding and developing their extant commitments, channeling a revivified civic energy to organizations that, in turn, deepen their values. And the analysis does not stop here, as ripple groups contend that transformed people transform the world.

Social Transformation: The Transformation of the Parish

Small groups are not as self-centered as they are often depicted. Still, small contemporary Catholic groups are not hotbeds of charity and justice—even when the members say these values are personally important. With varying levels of support, participants in "general" Catholic communities say the following are "very important": helping others, the environment, and political issues.[68] When they break down "political issues," more than 80 percent name welfare policies and economic justice, and nearly as many say world peace.[69] Yet, participants do not engage these concerns. Among those in the general Catholic communities, 23 percent say the group assists fellow members, 16 percent say it helps nonmembers, and only 8 percent say it has addressed some social issue. This illustrates Jezreel's important distinction between what he calls "gathering and sending."[70] The members of these communities enjoy the prayer, joy, and fellowship their groups provide—that is, they enjoy the gathering. The groups do not, however, properly institutionalize the sending, failing to enact the church's mission in the world.

According to Jezreel, church communities—as parishes or where two or three people are gathered[71]—need to both gather and send.

One of the questions this ripple group strategy raises is its efficacy. Will the changed behaviors of the participants significantly affect the world around them? Jezreel claims that JustFaith has transformed many churches, explaining that as the number of grads reaches a critical mass, the ministries and parish culture begin to change. He believes his experience at the Church of the Epiphany is illustrative of this phenomenon:

> The prototypical experience in parishes is that the same five people are doing [social justice] work year after year after year, and who's going to be there and who's not. But that sense of, oh my gosh, every year that we do [JustFaith], we've got twelve or thirteen or fourteen or fifteen *new* people sitting at the table who bring all these gifts and enthusiasm . . . At some point, around after the third and the fourth year, suddenly the whole parish just seemed to [become involved]. And for about six consecutive years, the parish council president was a JustFaith grad, which had an enormous impact on the parish. I mean, the *kinds* of things that the parish council would talk about was in some ways substantively different than before JustFaith. And there's all these committees and suddenly, they've got these big projects and they're kind of attractive so the budget's getting bigger and bigger for our work . . . And it was influencing the liturgy, it was influencing the fifth-grade catechism classes and it was influencing the parish council. It was a very lively time.

Jezreel's argument is that if a parish runs a few sessions of JustFaith, the sense of mission of this small group of parishioners affects the parish as a whole. The thirty to forty people who have been through the program after three complete cycles is admittedly a relatively small number for the average Catholic parish of eleven hundred families.[72] Putting Jezreel's experience with the congregations that maintain a close relationship to JFM aside, does JustFaith tend to ripple out from the participants into the wider parish?

To determine this, I performed a content analysis on the weekly bulletins of four Bay Area congregations, three Catholic and one United Methodist. These bulletins advertise the ministry offerings of the congregations. Focusing on adult ministry offerings, I classified the events within

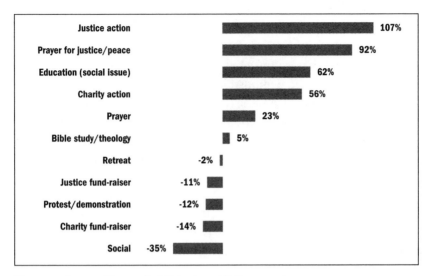

Figure 3.1. Average Changes in Ministries—All Congregations.

each church's bulletin into one of eleven categories: protest/demonstration, retreat, prayer for justice/peace, Bible study/theology, justice action, justice fund-raiser, charity fund-raiser, charity action, prayer, education (social issue), and social.[73] I compared the totals from the twelve months before the church offered JustFaith to the total after three groups completed the program. Because there are also other events within churches, such as a change in staff with different theological emphases, these data do not offer definitive conclusions of causality but are indicative of a general pattern. Yet, because the data come from four different churches, the findings are more robust than a single case study. In sum, the data from the four churches together at least partially demonstrate the ripple effects from participants into their churches as a whole. The congregations' total ministry offerings for the year were averaged with one another, and a percentage increase or decrease was calculated (see figure 3.1).

As figure 3.1 demonstrates, there was a substantial increase in many social ministries.[74] Justice actions and prayers for justice and peace roughly doubled while education on social issues and charitable actions saw increases of 50 percent or more. JustFaith grads sponsor or request these types of programs in their congregations, bringing their knowledge and activism to fellow congregants as well as elevating social ministry as a congregational priority. Ministries not related to mercy or justice—prayer and social events—also changed, with an increase in prayer and a decrease in social events. Bible studies, retreats, fund-raisers of any kind, and demonstrations showed little change.

As the rise in charity and justice projects is unsurprising, explaining these changes in social activities and prayer is in order. Beginning with prayer, JustFaith is grounded in prayer. Meetings include specific moments of prayer, which accustoms the participants to praying. Second, my field notes indicate that through JustFaith, participants came to believe either that they did not pray as much as they would like to or that prayer is an important religious grounding that would allow them to go out among the poor and marginalized; both of these beliefs would prompt an increase in prayer. Third, JustFaith also demonstrates to the participants the importance of both private and communal prayer. Graduates who may have before only prayed in the car or at home came to feel the need to pray among others, especially with those anchored in their church home.

As for the decrease in social events, JustFaith emphasizes both gathering and sending while treating them as two distinct phenomena. The data indicate that perhaps it is a bit more complicated than this. There are times when Christians are simultaneously gathered *and* sent. The more frequent opportunities to work together, such as sorting non-perishables, caroling at a senior home, and writing letters to lobby for greater food aid, both gather and send; people do not feel as strong a need to get together at a restaurant when they just saw good friends while they did yard work for a local senior. Or when they want to get together, they seek to do so in a way that is both sociable and altruistic.[75] Intimacy and civic engagement feed one another.[76] The church building is the primary place to gather, the community is the primary place to send, and transformed churches offer their members ample opportunities for both, sometimes even together.

This research cannot determine the impact JustFaith has on the wider society. Still, these congregational studies illustrate that the programs have rippled beyond the participants and changed the culture and priorities of their churches. Because these churches provide more educative events, more opportunities for works of charity and justice, and so forth, that the ripples go beyond the grads to other members of the parish who participate in these new ministry offerings is plausible. As a church devotes more resources to ameliorating poverty and, importantly, organizes this energy into something more lasting and collective, the influence of the program may ripple beyond the walls of the parish and into the wider society.

These findings show the ways small groups might instigate social transformation. Sociologists have cautioned against treating the small group as though it is a larger institution.[77] Small groups stand at the meso-level, mediating between individuals and institutions, supporting individuals in both their personal and social struggles, and encouraging them to act on their convictions. Small groups could prompt their members to work more fervently for social reforms, which they do very little of right now.[78] The hope of JFM is that grads continue the ripples beyond their respective congregations, transforming the wider society. The deliberate cultivation of leaders through a ripple-group program like JustFaith could help other Christian small groups find civic or political entry points even while the JustFaith program itself touches relatively few individuals. By drawing on the assets of the discipleship style, parish leaders can act as leavening, pulling their fellow Catholics more readily into the church's social mission.

Conclusion

This chapter has examined a form of social transformation called the ripple group, which seeks social change by focusing institutional resources on individual people. By transforming the way participants interpret and engage the world, ripple groups hope members will ameliorate social problems. Discipleship organizations, like JFM, adopt the ripple group as their organizational form. Discipleship groups change what participants care about and how they live their lives. These transformations fall into one of five motifs—religion-centering transformation, political transformation, religio-political transformation, intensification, and motivational transformation. If JFM is any indicator, these changed lives have an impact on the world around them, and other discipleship groups will also see their members change their beliefs and practices as these are formed and channeled through the organization.

Determining the greater social outcomes of JustFaith is exceedingly difficult. Yet there is compelling evidence that offering JustFaith groups over three or more years—directly affecting a relatively small percentage of the parish—can change the culture of a parish, giving it a greater sense of Christian mission. This shows that discipleship groups can be influential even when they do not saturate a population. Discipleship groups, then, will be more effective when they either target leaders or incorporate leadership development into the curriculum. These leaders can act as a leavening in their various communities, bringing the wider organizational mission to these groups.

Although not every grad experiences each transformation motif, all the grads discuss their conversion in terms of the religion-centering motif. In this motif, the grads make their religion the foundation of their lives, interpreting the other aspects of their lives through the lens of faith. After this transformation, their lives take on a greater meaning. For an organization that bases its entire mission on the religious transformation of individuals, it is worth exploring the theological moorings of the grads and JFM in greater detail. The next chapter explores these religious beliefs in the context of the social teachings of the Catholic Church.

4

Christ-Centered Discipleship

A Theology of Pragmatic Reverence

It is a surprisingly clear morning, a break from the typical "June Gloom" of the San Francisco Bay Area. Today is the Saturday that the East Bay JustFaith grads and several congregations gather for their monthly vigil outside a detention facility in Richmond. Inside are undocumented migrants, the vast majority from Mexico and Latin America. Given the fact that any of the people detained could be deported and separated from their family members—who are present—it is unexpected that people are smiling and passing crayons and coloring pages out to the children. Many mingle over homemade chocolate chip cookies as they wait for the vigil to begin. Three Protestant ministers call everyone together to introduce ourselves and say which church we attend (the woman speaking assumes everyone present attends church and all but one does). After hearing the names of their congregations, I discover that roughly three-fourths of the sixty or so attendees are Catholic, and I recognize several from other JustFaith events.

After introducing themselves, Bethlehem United Church of Christ leads the group in singing "Down by the Riverside." They use guitar accompaniment, and the pace is upbeat as those in the crowd nod their heads and sing along, "I ain't gonna study war no more . . ." The antiwar theme of the song seems a bit out of place at an event to show solidarity with immigrants, but no one seems to mind as they rhythmically sway to the music. The event is different from a typical protest or demonstration, more akin to an informal church gathering. The song is followed by six scripture readings, such as "You shall not oppress an immigrant . . . for you have been immigrants[1] . . . [Y]ou shall love the immigrant as yourself[2] . . . God has sent me . . . to proclaim liberty to the captives and release to the prisoners[3] . . . Do not neglect to show hospitality to strangers, for by doing that some have entertained angels without knowing it."[4] Some are read in Spanish and others in English, with translations of both provided in a leaflet. The readers are calm and measured in their speech, without any sign of anger or indignation.

Those present exchange a sign of peace with one another, hugging and shaking hands for several minutes. A woman calls the group back to their circle by singing "Go Down, Moses," every other line of which is "let my people go." Next, people give testimonies. A woman comes forward, a mother of a detainee. Breaking into tears several times, she speaks in Spanish about the heartache she feels having her son detained. Another comes forward and introduces himself as a former detainee. He continues: "It all comes down to faith. When I was in there, it was my faith that you were fighting a good fight in faith for me [that kept me going] . . . I have friends in there and this faith keeps them hanging on." The speaker uses *faith* in two ways. First, he uses it as faith in others, "my faith that you," as interpersonal trust. It helped him to get through his day to know that others were working to get him out. The second use, "a good fight in faith for me," is more ambiguous. It could refer to faith in him from others, but this does not make much sense; what sort of trust in him would those outside harbor? Another interpretation is more plausible: he believed those who were working for his sake were motivated by faith, that their fighting was happening in faith. That those present are religiously motivated is obvious. His double use of *faith*, first as faith in others and second as faith in God, is a faith that ties people to one another as well as connects this world to God's plan, giving humans responsibility for creation and placing those present in partnership with God.

The ministers invite everyone to offer a prayer for "a detainee, for his or her loved ones, for justice to be done," either silently or aloud. For those who verbally pray, a small bell is rung at the conclusion of each prayer. Some pray for particular people; others, more generally for the cause. Most of the prayers are in English; some are in Spanish. A man brings out his guitar again, and the group sings the refrain, "Lord, make me an instrument, make me an instrument, make me an instrument of your peace." The closing prayer includes "As we prepare to leave this place, we hold in our hearts those who are not free to leave." After a resounding "Amen," a minister invites the assembled to make as loud a noise as possible. He tells participants that this is a monthly tradition and that it is not done to disturb anyone; rather, it lets those inside know that we are here, that they are not forgotten. Most people yell, and a few bring out hand drums to beat. Children cover their ears and scream through wide grins. This continues for ten seconds or so. Following this joyous din, several people remain behind as most return to their cars in the lot twenty feet away.

Grads volunteer at sites that are both Catholic and nonreligious. For those at Catholic sites, the religious meaning in their activism is readily observable. Their day might begin and end with a shared prayer, or their shift could be peppered with glances at crucifixes and conversations of parish happenings or Lenten observances.[5] For those at secular sites—without prayer, religious symbols, or shared faith—the work is no less religiously meaningful because of the significance grads impart to it. JustFaith Ministries (JFM) communicates the value of Christ-centeredness to the grads who, in turn, weave "webs of significance" around their daily activities.[6] In his introduction to *Disruptive Religion*, sociologist Christian Smith argues that humans need purpose in their lives; religion, situated in the realm of the sacred, provides a more compelling meaning system due to its transcendent significance.[7] Smith also notes that religion is more often recognized for its role in contributing to social stability; the idea that religions offer values that can challenge the status quo has been underexplored in the social movement literature. This chapter helps fill this gap in the literature, illustrating the ways religious teachings and belief systems can challenge social realities.

Today's civically engaged Catholics understand their lives as a call to discipleship and this religious meaning in everyday life yields a "theology of pragmatic reverence," one of the hallmarks of the discipleship style. A theology of pragmatic reverence refers to the way discipleship-style Catholics strive to make God and their religion relevant to their everyday lives. Grads reveal this theology in their understandings of scripture and God, Catholic social teaching, and how they apply religious elements to everyday life. These themes together compose the religious worldview of discipleship-style Catholics and shape the ways they interpret and act on the world. A theology of pragmatic reverence was made culturally possible by the Second Vatican Council, which directed the attention of the laity to the needs of the world in a religiously grounded way and is critical to understanding the theology of discipleship-style Catholics.

The Significance of the Second Vatican Council

The Second Vatican Council was the twenty-first ecumenical council in the seventeen hundred years of the post–Constantine Church. These councils have become even less common recently, with only three occurring since 1545. As their rarity would imply, these ecumenical councils debate the most pressing issues of the church and, thus, can have a profound impact on Catholic teaching. The Second Vatican Council produced almost as many writings as all previous councils combined, and the impact was proportional to what it promulgated.[8] Pope John XXIII, the pope who called the council, wanted it to be an *aggiornamento*, an updating of the church. The church sought to hold fast to what it saw as timeless truths while reading the "signs of the times," that is, becoming more relevant to the modern world.[9] The most important council teaching for Catholic civic engagement was to affirm the role of the laity in the life and mission of the church, and it did so in two ways. First, the council declared that the laity were to become more active in bringing the church to the world. Second, the council developed new ecclesiologies, which included new missions and roles for the laity. These two teachings encouraged Catholics to understand their lives in religious terms.

The Post–Vatican II Laity: Bringing the Church to the World

One of the new teachings the Second Vatican Council offered was a theology of the laity. The leaders of the Second Vatican Council believed that the laity had the talent and initiative to bring the church into the world according to their own moral discernment:

> [T]he laity, by their very vocation, seek the kingdom of God by engaging in temporal affairs and by ordering them according to the plan of God. They live in the world, that is, in each and in all of the secular professions and occupations. They live in the ordinary circumstances of family and social life, from which the very web of their existence is woven. They are called there by God that by exercising their proper function and led by the spirit of the Gospel they may work for the sanctification of the world from within as a leaven. In this way they may make Christ known to others, especially by the testimony of a life resplendent in faith, hope and charity.[10]

Through intentional Christian living, the laity sanctify "the world from within as a leaven." They discern God's will and order their community and world according to God's plan. Their everyday lives are no longer mundane but a vocation. The council affirmed this new vision of the laity, illuminating the religious meaning in their lives.

The council likewise admonished laity who looked to eschew their obligations to the world: "Let there be no false opposition between professional and social activities on the one part, and religious life on the other. The Christian who neglects his temporal duties, neglects his duties toward his neighbor and even God, and jeopardizes his eternal salvation."[11] The council encouraged the laity to understand their religious and secular lives as one, integrating that which was previously separated. Furthermore, they wanted the laity to participate in service to the world as earnestly as they would any religious duty as these, too, have repercussions for their salvation. The church vested the laity's individual work in the world with a sense of holiness as well as charged them with a serious responsibility in the mission of the church.

The Post–Vatican II Church(es): New Ecclesiologies

There is some initial confusion when assessing the grads' relationship to their church, which displays both enthusiasm and frustration. Part of the reason for this ambiguity is that particular survey questions evoke different ecclesiologies—that is, church models—some of which are more favorable to the grads than others. As we have seen, the grads are deeply entrenched in Catholicism. On one hand, 42 percent of grads are highly committed to Catholicism compared to only 19 percent of Catholics nationwide; the latter figure has been steadily slipping since the study began in 1987.[12] The grads also show a stronger affiliation, with 93 percent agreeing that being Catholic is a very important part of their identity compared to 75 percent nationally.[13] On the other hand, only 26 percent of grads believe that Catholicism contains a greater share of truth than other religions do compared to 63 percent of Catholics nationally. Grads are a bit less likely to find it important that future generations of their family are Catholic[14] and a bit more likely to think that how people live is more important than whether they are Catholic.[15] There is no difference between grads and Catholics generally in the importance of the sacraments in their relationship to God.[16] These differences stem from the various ecclesiologies underlying the questions.

Immediately preceding and throughout the Council, new ecclesiologies were developing within Catholic thought for the first time in roughly four hundred years. Jesuit cardinal Avery Dulles has written a concise summary of each of the five contemporary Catholic models in his *Models of the Church*.[17] Claiming that the church is firstly and finally a mystery,[18] Dulles shows that ecclesiologies are attempts to approximate this mystery, but they always fall short.[19] Each emphasizes some aspect of God's communion with humanity at the expense of another aspect, yielding strengths and weaknesses to each model. He calls the models institution, mystical communion, sacrament, herald, and servant. The institutional model calls attention to visible structures, such as those with ministerial and teaching authority, and was the nearly exclusive model of the church from about 1600 through 1940. The model of church as mystical communion—or Mystical Body or People of God—calls attention to the intimate body of believers. Church as sacrament weaves the institution into the mystical body, bringing God's invisible grace to the world through the visible church. The fourth model, the church as herald, emphasizes scripture, with the church as the body that receives, proclaims, and spreads this message. The grads draw heavily on the fifth model, a servant ecclesiology.

The servant church exists to humbly serve and heal the world.[20] This model is an underlying theme in many council documents; Pope Francis, various theologians, and bishop conferences have developed this ecclesial model more fully.[21] When the church turns to itself and neglects the world, this model warns, it can fall into a "theological narcissism" that disengages the laity, costing the church the energy and public voice it once had.[22] This model of church is by far the most popular model among the grads, as Sharon Jones, a preschool teacher in her sixties, demonstrates: "I know parishes in the past have felt overwhelmed with what they have to do, but I'd love to see that leadership, where the social justice agenda is more on the parish agenda and the parishioners are all aware of it. Yes, you can't just come here and get fed week after week, you've got to go out too! Here's your opportunity, we're going to help organize that opportunity. We have some of that at our parish but it could be much, much, more." At the heart of the servant model is the idea that church must be more than a one-hour commitment on Sundays. The church must go into the world to heal what is broken. "Parishes in the past" could be a reference to the historical parish's niche as a religious institution as well as a social, ethnic, and relief institution. Vibrant outreach does not characterize most of today's parishes. Church, in the servant model, *must* have an outward element if it is to be church at all.

The elevation of this ecclesiology has social ramifications. To begin with its strengths, first, it offers Catholics a robust, energetic faith that brings them into the world. Second, it helps them understand the religious meaning in their everyday lives. Third, it builds social capital between parishioners, as collective service strengthens in-group bonds. A challenge that this model brings is that it alienates Catholics who have an affinity for a different ecclesial model. For Catholics who understand church as institution, community, sacrament, or herald, a servant ecclesiology appears to diminish the importance of gathering at church for shared worship.

Even in acknowledging the inadequacies in each of the models, and the ways that some are in direct tension, Dulles argues that they may be brought together through a "discipleship model," not to be confused with my use of discipleship style. Looking to ground his model in official statements, Dulles notes that the documents of Vatican II refer to church members as disciples over twenty times. Pope John Paul II refers to the church as a "community of disciples" in his encyclical *Redemptor hominis*,[23] and the American bishops use the phrase in their letters on peace and the economy. The discipleship model combines the strengths of each of the ecclesiologies into one: Catholics are gathered as community, under the spiritual leadership of clergy, and fed through the sacrament and Word so that they can be sent to bring good news to the world and healing to the least of these. Dulles's discipleship model incorporates the strengths of the five models in a way that responds to the grads' yearnings for a faith that embeds them in their historical community. It is also relevant to their contemporary lives without alienating Catholics of any ecclesiology.

This discipleship model most closely approximates that of official JFM materials. Jezreel often refers to the importance of "gathering and sending" in the life of the church. It is worth examining a large part of his September 14, 2013, address at the Catholic Charities USA conference as this outlines the foundations of JFM's ecclesiology:

> The narrative of the Gospels follows a pattern that gets repeated over and over—it's the drama of gathering and sending . . . Let me quickly define the terms: Gathering in the 21st century Church is the work of religious education, bible studies, catechesis, youth ministry, and spiritual formation [herald]. Gathering is the work of liturgy or worship—gathering the people of faith for prayer and sacrament [sacrament]. It is the stuff of retreats and conferences, like this one. Gathering is also fish fries, pot lucks and celebrations [community]. Most of the time gathering happens geographically, as you would guess, at the home base, the mother ship, that is parish property. Gathering happens at the parish [institutional]. And, at its best, "gathering" speaks to the sense of "Getting ready." Gathering is about nourishing faith, nourishing the community, about remembering our story, sharing in Eucharist, and being prepared for . . . the second part of the drama called . . . *sending*.
>
> Sending is about mission [servant]. Sending includes ministering in the slums, helping resettle refugees in our hometowns, serving meals at a soup kitchen. Sending is advocating for immigrants, the poor, women and the unborn. Sending is providing a safe place for battered women, extending care for battered soldiers, delivering care for the hurricane battered in Haiti or the tornado battered in Oklahoma. Sending is Jesuit Volunteer Corps and St. Vincent de Paul home visits. Sending is the work of community organizing and peacemaking. Sending is the work outlined and given a vocabulary by Catholic social teaching. The proclamation of the Reign of God is to embrace the gift of life and the gift of creation that God has given and to relish it, to share it, protect it.
>
> You see, the Gospel is a drama of gathering and sending. Gathering *and* sending. It cannot be one or the other. It is, by design, necessarily and unavoidably both [discipleship model].

Jezreel paints an ecclesiology that looks much like the discipleship model. However, although most churches are astute gatherers, making efforts to teach, pray, and so forth, he claims they overlook the sending aspect. This leads JFM to take a corrective approach in its curricula, as Jezreel continues:

And here is the problem. Parishes, as they are currently and routinely configured, are primarily or sometimes exclusively places of gathering. Period. If you look at the parish bulletin, the parish budget, the parish staff, the pastor's time, it's all about gathering. It's about gathering for Eucharist, gathering for prayer, gathering for education, gathering for fun, gathering for sacramental preparation (which amounts to gathering in preparation for more gathering). So often, the parish calendar is just one big list of gatherings. Let me be clear, I am *not* bashing gathering. I have dedicated my life to it—I am a teacher for goodness sakes. You can't teach unless people gather. *But*, gathering disconnected from sending ultimately mutates into something less than the Gospel and less than what is so very compelling about Jesus and the church he inspired.

Jezreel's emphasis on sending, propelled by his belief that many churches neglect service, has caused many of the grads to elevate the servant model at the expense of the others. JFM would attract more Catholics, especially those with a gather-centered ecclesial focus, if they were to make their discipleship ecclesiology more explicit in their materials.[24] Although there is some disparity between the ecclesiology of the grads and the ecclesiology of JFM, they both agree that the church must be active in the world to fully be church.

Vatican II offered new ways for the laity to understand their role in the world as well as new models of church, both of which invited the laity into new ways of being Catholic. With these new beliefs, laity could see the world around them and their individual work in religious terms. The cultural tools grads use to interpret their world fall into three broad themes: biblical and theological, Catholic social teaching, and reappropriating religious artifacts into daily life.

The Biblical and Theological Theme
Central Message of the Gospels: Love of God and Neighbor

The life and message of Jesus Christ are central to grads' understanding of discipleship. Beginning with the Gospel message, they do not believe that life as a Christian is easy given contemporary society. Time after time, grads laughed when asked if JustFaith made their life easier, indicating that it actually made life decidedly harder. An obvious question then follows: Why do you continue to practice things that make your life harder? Therese Brewer, a molecular virologist in her thirties, responds, "How could you not do them? Once you know, you can never un-know something. And it's conscience and responsibility, the community we're all a part of." Cathy Meyers from the Louisville office echoes this: "I think it is a challenged view of Christ that you walk away from our programs with. It isn't the comfy or 'aren't I swell' kind of Jesus out there. It is the challenging Jesus, it's the challenge of the Gospel, it's the challenge to be a disciple." Meyers also recognizes the temptation for many congregations to elevate a therapeutic image of God, which can undermine outreach efforts.[25] For grads, the central challenge of the Gospel is love of God and neighbor, giving them a mode of discipleship through which to understand and express their theology of pragmatic reverence.[26]

Love of God and neighbor can be interpreted in a variety of ways. Grads and JFM conceptualize love of God as doing God's will. Presbyterian staff member Christine Philips sees a potential conflict in what people may desire and what God desires for people: "There is always this sharp corrective to what we prioritize, which is not what God prioritizes." Grads are aware that a person's yearnings may be in opposition to God's intentions. Philips continues, relating it to love of neighbor: "Whether [God's priorities mean] explaining to people or getting our religion right, that we're constantly called back to how we treat each other." The lesson is that loving God and one's neighbor cannot remain only a private sentiment; these must manifest in the way we treat others.

Loving one's neighbor is a critical message of the Gospel for the grads and one of the ways they discuss this is through inclusivity.[27] The inclusivity required in loving one's neighbor continually recurs as central to the Gospels, as Marie Baker, who is trying to teach her three-year-old to be more inclusive, demonstrates: "[I do things that help her] see the world in a way that involves understanding, that involves care for other people, including strangers and people that are different and people that look different and smell different [laughs] and do things differently and treat people differently." If compiled, grads could collectively offer a long list of groups traditionally excluded that they want to see included. Underscoring this, the most commonly named negative traits were those they deemed exclusionary, as Samantha DeRouen, a retired business executive, states: "Traits I don't admire are the opposite of those [in-clusive ones]. Judgers, accusers, name-callers, especially in the name of righteousness."[28] Grads' concern for inclusion motivates them to ensure that the poor and vulnerable have what they need in order to fully par-ticipate in civic and political life.

Another way grads love their neighbor is by ensuring their material well-being. It is a unanimous consensus among the grads that loving others necessarily involves concern for their physical needs. This is such an obvious fact to them that otherwise garrulous grads become sud-denly terse, elaborating love of neighbor is simply as "Sharing." Lengthy explanations are unnecessary. The twenty-fifth chapter of the Gospel of Matthew is popular among grads looking to ground their claims in the Bible: "My favorite [biblical passage] is in Matthew's Gospel where Jesus says if you see somebody hungry and you feed him, and you see some-body thirsty and you give them something to drink, and you visit people in prison and you take care of the sick and if you do these in my name then you will spend eternity with me." Pete London claims here that love of neighbor cannot be grounded in sentiments alone. Those feelings must give rise to concrete works of mercy. Grads love their neighbors by attending to their needs or, on a larger scale, working to ensure that public policy attends to those in need.

Theology: The Transcendent in the Immanent

One of the things that allows grads to see religious meaning in their lives is their understanding of God. Whereas Catholicism contains both tran-scendent and immanent views of God, individual Catholics will often emphasize one over the other. The grads' primary orientation not only is toward immanence, as they also articulate a transcendent notion of God through an appreciation of mystery.[29] This "both/and" approach expresses their theology of pragmatic reverence.[30] The immanent piece gives their world spiritual relevance as they see God, especially Christ, in their daily lives. The transcendent piece gives them a notion of humility before God, which grounds their engagement in a sense of commitment and fidelity rather than a more voluntarist civic activism. This transcen-dent in the immanent manifests in five forms: mystery, humanity in partnership with God, vocation, miracles, and prayer.

Grads tie everyday experiences to the mystery of God. Helen Dalton, a graduate of the JWalking program, illustrates this: "I am talking to Adam, a paraplegic man in a day center for developmentally disabled folks, I am sitting there in the hustle and bustle and I am feeding him—he can't feed himself—and he grabs my hand he looks in my eyes and he says, 'You are a beautiful girl.' . . . I realized he is not saying that *I* am beautiful. He is saying that this moment of being present to one and another and honoring the sacredness there is what's beautiful, you just feel that. And that is the Christ-presence in the world for me." This experience is not only decidedly in the moment; it also points Dalton to an experience of the holy that is greater than the moment. For grads, religious experiences can happen in all times and places, allowing for an experience of the transcendent in the immanent.

Integrating immanent and the transcendent aspects of God also occurs in the grads' coupling of God and humanity. The grads understand themselves and others as co-creators in God's plan, as Jezreel demonstrates at the Social Action Summer Institute[31] 2012 convention in Louisville, Kentucky: "The bad news . . . is that human choices got us into this mess [of poverty]. The good news is that human choices can get us out. Human choices grounded in God's dream, grounded in God's goodness, can get us to where we want to go. The Good News is that the power of God can be unleashed in the apparatus of human effort." People are a part of God's plan. Grads believe that people must act to ameliorate the problems of the world rather than wait for God alone to intervene. However, simple human effort does not accomplish their ends. People participating with God—divine will and human efforts together—honors both human purpose and God's power.[32] Just as a prophet speaks on behalf of God, so should people act on behalf of God.

Understanding themselves as active participants in God's plan alters their sense of personal vocation. Grads are no more or less likely to believe in a God that is concerned with their personal well-being than Americans nationally (87 percent vs. 86 percent).[33] They are slightly more likely to understand God as a being with whom one can have a personal relationship (81 percent vs. 71 percent) and slightly less likely to see God as an impersonal force (22 percent vs. 29 percent).[34] Only 68 percent of Protestant grads have a view of God that is active in the world today, which is less than the 86 percent of Protestants across the country.[35] In sum, the grads' image of God is not extraordinarily different from that of the nation as a whole. However, the grads part company from Americans generally in their views of God's and their personal role in the world on several measures. First, while two-thirds of Protestant grads believe that God is active in the world, they do not have a vengeful image of God. A small minority of Americans, one in five, believe that God causes tragedies as a warning to sinners while one in four strongly disagrees with this.[36] Every one of the Protestant grads strongly disagrees with this. Second, the number of grads who feel "called by God to do something" is significantly higher than Christians generally: 93 percent of Catholic grads compared to 34 percent of Catholics nationally and 94 percent of Protestant grads versus 66 percent of Protestants generally.[37] The idea of receiving a vocation from an active, caring God reinforces their belief that people are in a covenantal relationship with God. In this scheme, people work in partnership with God and one another to enact God's will.

Grads' understanding of miracles illustrates another form of their transcendent in the immanent theology. A more immanent understanding of miracles draws upon the word's Latin root *miror*, "to wonder," and perceives all things awe-inspiring—from a child's birth to a brilliant sunset—to be miracles. A more transcendent understanding of miracles—the sort required for canonization to sainthood—necessitates that an event be of divine origin and unexplainable within the scope of the natural world. Grads take an approach midway between these when they contend that miracles occur through human effort. In this frame, people are God's instruments and divine intervention happens through compassionate individuals. Lucy Russell illustrates this when discussing the miracle of Jesus feeding the crowd of five thousand:

> How many people did you think actually *did* have food, but they didn't want to eat in front of anybody that didn't have food. Nobody had asked them, 'Does anybody have food? Is anyone willing to share?' Christ, yes, Jesus made the miracle happen, but it started with what they already had. And I love that story! Because it captured for me the responsibility of each one of us to give the little we have, and then Christ, the Creator, the Holy Spirit *makes* miracles happen with a phone call, a letter to our congressman, bringing food on Sundays for the collection for the

poor, spending three hours at [a ministry for migrant workers] so that a non-English speaking immigrant got their needs met that day! It's little things, but the miracle happens when you give what little you might feel like you *can* give or what seems like not enough, and whether it's impacting global problems, national problems, or local problems, or your own personal problems, the miracle comes from, "I'll give up my little fish here," and then they'll be twelve baskets left over. There was more than enough all along. The miracle was us working together under the guidance of Christ.

To Russell, the miracle of the loaves and fishes is no less miraculous when it involves human effort than if bread and fish were to descend from the sky. Furthermore, miracles, as God's action within the world, happen constantly through the actions of people who seek to do God's will through their work or other generosity. God's role in the miracle is to animate people's hearts to participate in God's plan. This middle-way approach is becoming part of official Catholicism. At the Angelus[38] on June 2, 2013, Pope Francis said of the loaves and fishes miracle, "This is the miracle: rather than a multiplication it is a sharing, inspired by faith and prayer." Sharing, people sacrificing for others, is itself a miracle—with or without a multiplication of loaves.

The final form of a transcendent and immanent perspective is grads' approach to prayer. There are three major types of Catholic prayer. The first are prayers of blessing and adoration, which is to worship God. The second are prayers of petition, for one's own needs or another's. The third are prayers of thanksgiving, acknowledging a blessing in one's life. Like many grads, Therese Brewer is uncomfortable with prayers of petition, troubled in praying for a specific outcome: "I don't think I would pray for [a specific outcome] . . . I think that what people are asking for is, 'Consider me, think of me. Take me in my suffering with you.' Which is something that I'm happy to do."[39] Grads prefer to spiritually accompany people rather than beseech God to intervene. This, again, acknowledges the role of human initiative in affecting the problems of the world. Prayer is less about affecting God or directly changing the world and more about drawing believers into God and discerning their role alongside God, as James O'Reilly, a retired homeless shelter director, explains. "I think lifting prayers to God is an important way for us to increase our understanding of what God is asking from us, because I think God hears all our prayers, but God doesn't need prayers, we need prayer. Prayer is for us. It's our way of—I hope—allowing God more deeply into our lives and who we are and what God is trying to do in the world through us." For grads, the primary end of prayer is to draw the believer closer to God.

The grads' central themes of the Gospel—love of God and neighbor—and a theology that brings together the transcendent and the immanent enable them to impart a deeper meaning to their daily lives. This allows them to not only understand reality through a lens of pragmatic reverence, but it also helps them integrate the various aspects of their lives, such as church, work, family, and so forth. Grads connect their faith to their everyday lives more overtly when they draw upon the social teachings of the Catholic Church.

Catholic Social Teaching

Catholic social teaching, which discusses both charity and justice, shapes grads' cultural understanding of their world. Although the Catholic Church has only formally articulated its social justice tradition since 1891, there is a long tradition that the rich *owe* the poor generosity. Almsgiving is not simply a way of fostering kindness and altruism in oneself and alleviating the suffering of others; it is also a matter of justice, giving back to the poor what is rightfully theirs. *The Catechism of the Catholic Church* recalls Pope Gregory the Great's (ca. 540–604) teachings on the justice of almsgiving: "When we attend to the needs of those in want, we give them what is theirs, not ours. More than performing works of mercy, we are paying a debt of justice."[40] In addition, countless Bible verses in both the Hebrew (e.g., Deut. 15:11) and Christian (e.g., Matt. 25:31–46) scriptures require the faithful to attend to the needs of the poor or marginalized. Pope Francis harkens back to the early church in an apostolic exhortation, quoting St. John Chrysostom (ca. 349–407) when he writes, "Not to share one's wealth with the poor is to steal from them and to take from them their livelihood. It is not our goods which we hold, but theirs."[41] These illustrate that the tradition of justice has existed since some of the earliest writings in scripture and that Catholicism has developed and formalized these teachings throughout history.

Catholics of discipleship-style organizations draw from this well of teachings and are well informed when discussing social doctrine. Each organization will, because of its particular mission, have its own unique set of Catholic social tools that it utilizes, emphasizing some principles over others. The grads and JFM have several tools from Catholic social teaching in their "cultural repertoire": the life and dignity of the human person, solidarity, subsidiarity, the preferential option for the poor, and structural sin.[42] These five tools allow grads to understand larger structural injustices through a framework of faith. These tools are also either antidotes to or a recognition of political theorist Iris Marion Young's "five faces of oppression," that is, five distinct manifestations of oppression: powerlessness, exploitation, cultural imperialism, marginalization, and violence.[43] The following section demonstrates the relationship between Young's work and grads' use of these elements of Catholic social teaching.

Life and Dignity of the Human Person

The Catholic understanding of the dignity of the human person is rooted in *imago Dei*, the belief that all persons are made in the image and likeness of God.[44] This means that people have transcendent worth that warrants careful treatment from individuals and society. Therese Brewer puts it simply when speaking about her impetus to help others who have less than she: "It's the value of the individual. The people that are in such situations [poverty] have value and worth." Catholic teaching says the dignity of the human person necessitates treating people with respect as well as ensuring that there is not excessive social or economic disparity within or between nations.[45] The whole of Catholic social teaching rests on this intrinsic worth of each and every human person and warrants concern for a variety of issues including abortion, subhuman living conditions, poor working conditions, and human trafficking. Furthermore, these are not mere offenses against a fellow human; they show "supreme dishonor to the Creator."[46]

From the dignity of the human person comes the importance of human conscience. *Gaudium et Spes*, one of the most important documents of Vatican II for the church today, was more of an afterthought, going through the committee and council with little controversy.

Archbishop Mark McGrath of Panama said that conservatives saw *Lumen Gentium* as the "heart and soul" of the Council and, once the issues of power and authority were settled, they allowed the liberals to put forth this document.[47] *Gaudium et Spes* emphasizes the role of personal conscience, calling it the "most secret core and sanctuary of a man."[48] Furthermore, the church has taught for centuries that the conscience, even when erring, is binding and that to *not* follow one's conscience—even when it is mistaken—is a sin.[49] Mark Bachman, a self-employed Bay Area grad, takes seriously his duty to discern the morally correct path in a given situation: "I think one of the things that I heard [my priest] say, is that if you really look hard, wrestle with your conscience, and pray about it, and you really think about it, hopefully you go with what your conscience says for you to do. I think that is important, and I think following your conscience is a part of living an ethical life."[50] Grads illustrate the importance of conscience when they struggle with church teaching and eventually decide that they must dissent from a particular teaching. They also show the importance of conscience when it causes them to agree with church teaching: serious discernment forces them to reconsider their own position in light of church teaching, at times coming to agree with the church's position. For example, several grads who were pro-choice said that they became pro-life after discerning church teachings on protecting the vulnerable and honoring the sanctity of life.

The dignity of the human person offers an important corrective to the way society treats populations that are powerless. Powerlessness for Young is an inability to fully participate—with creativity and autonomy—in the workplace. She notes the distinction within society between professionals and nonprofessionals: those who give orders and those who follow orders. The latter are additionally unable to fully develop their capacities or enjoy respectful treatment. When examining powerlessness within society at large, likewise, some have tremendous power over others, others possess power over their more immediate lives, and still others have very little power even in a mediated sense. Privileging the life and dignity of the human person recognizes the material rights of people as well as their civil and political rights. It protects and honors their claims to flourishing and self-determination, restoring power to those who have had it taken from them.

Solidarity

Pope John Paul II writes that solidarity "is not a feeling of vague compassion or shallow distress at the misfortunes of so many people, both near and far. On the contrary, it is a *firm and persevering determination* to commit oneself to the *common good*; that is to say, to the good of all and of each individual, because we are *all* really responsible for *all* [italics in original]."[51] Even when not named as such, grads continually express this interdependence and sense of being their brother's or sister's keeper. Megan Sims, a Louisville woman who regularly facilitates JWalking, juxtaposes what she sees as the typical volunteer attitude of assistance with one of solidarity:

> When I was in high school and in college I volunteered with Habitat. . . .
> I felt a deep sense of pride knowing that I had done something for someone. I don't feel that way at all anymore—my desire is not really to do *for* the poor but to do *with* and because most importantly the person who needs this the most is me; I need friends who will help teach me. Not to "appreciate what I have" because that is just ridiculous. If all we get is gratitude out of the suffering of the poor then we have disrespected another human being; it's ridiculous, it drives me absolutely crazy. But it's that we're in this together, we exist at the same point of history together that my heart should be breaking because people are homeless, because people are suffering, because people are hungry, because people are dying, because people are alone and I have this shift in desire from wanting to *fix* something—wanting to *build* houses and *cure* a problem—to this deep personal connection that has opened in me a limitless well of care and moving from that desire to this one, which makes me sadder and more heartbroken and more devastated and more, [nine-second pause] more *connected* with people.

Sims articulates the first of two aspects within solidarity that are important to grads. She discusses a new way to change society, a shift from doing things "for the poor" to "with the poor." For grads, doing things *for* the poor demonstrates a social hierarchy more than altruistic behavior, with those from above who come with their presumably superior knowledge to assist those beneath them.[52] Solidarity challenges this, allowing grads to follow the lead by working *with* the poor. This egalitarian approach creates a cultural space for grads to grow and benefit from these relationships as well. Working *for* the poor also invites criticism of what grads believe is a typical volunteer mentality: being around the scarcity of poverty makes people thankful for their middle-class blessings, which ultimately disrespects the seriousness of poverty and treats the poor as objects.

JFM staff member Mike Campbell turns this attitude on its head, making the poor subjects, "[The poor say,] 'We are precious to God. We are the subjects to this material [the Gospels] . . . either you're one of us or you're standing with us, to receive the blessing of God. Either you are poor in spirit, or you're thirsting for justice, you are mourning or you're humble in heart. So you get to either be one of us, or if you're not privileged enough to be poor, humble, mourning, you are standing with us.'" In seeing the poor as subjects, Campbell goes to the place of the poor and aligns himself with their values and suffering. Furthermore, not only are the poor subjects, but the nonpoor are also only made subjects of the good news through their intentional alliance with the poor.

Another important aspect of solidarity is a sense of unity and fellowship with others. This concern for all is a strong sentiment among grads and JFM, as Jezreel elaborates: "The reality is that almost all the world is crafted around the logic that some people are lovable and some people are not. And you're my people and you're not my people. What I think the Gospel tells us is everybody's my people. And everybody's my sister and my brother. And that, *that*, all you have to do is stop there and then you've got Catholic social teaching. Everybody's my sister and my brother. Go home. It's all done. You can read every encyclical. It all says the same thing." Solidarity offers an expanded notion of who is deserving of love and care.[53] Jezreel claims, and grads echo this, that we all are united in a human family and that those in need warrant special consideration from everyone. He also illustrates the primacy of solidarity when he argues that the whole of Catholic social teaching rests on it. Grads and the organization continually express this interconnectedness and interdependence among people.

These aspects of solidarity connect to Young's notion of exploitation. Young understands exploitation as taking advantage of people, usually their labor, for the sake of another's gain. However, she also notes that other social arrangements, such as rigid gender roles within marriage or a racialized understanding of "menial" labor, are exploitative. Through this social understanding of exploitation, solidarity provides an important corrective. If solidarity is not present, volunteers can exploit a beneficiary through participation in a charitable project to increase their own feelings of usefulness, gratitude, or being a "good person." Solidarity transforms the relationship here; beneficiaries shift from object to subject and, in gaining agency and autonomy, become cooperators in the project. Solidarity changes a potentially exploitative relationship into one of care and mutuality.

Subsidiarity

Subsidiarity means that the smallest social unit possible should handle any given problem. For example, if neighbors can come together to help a family who is experiencing financial difficulties, they should do so rather than lobby for a federal program to offer such assistance. If, however, the neighbors, churches, local charities, and state agencies are having similar budgetary problems and are unable to provide help to this family and similar families or communities, then federal intervention would be appropriate. The idea is to encourage individuals or smaller groups in "enterprise and industry" rather than absorb or usurp their agency.[54] Subsidiarity is in some tension with the idea of solidarity. The church attempts to reconcile this by showing that as larger organizations change norms or laws, this should enable smaller associations and individuals to seek and provide for their own ends.[55] In sum, the principle of subsidiarity says that the scope of the problem should correspond to the size or organizational level of the responding party, with a preference for the local.

Unlike the word solidarity, *subsidiarity* was rarely used by the grads. However, they showed the importance of the concept through granting a high priority to charitable involvement. Works of charity were important for putting a human face to the suffering that one was trying to alleviate. Works of justice are just as critical, but these often put grads in the company of politicians and advocates rather than with those in need of help. Charity is important not only because it meets a person's needs but also because it creates relationships. These relationships enable individuals and communities to come together on a small scale to solve social problems. Community organizing, one of the methods of engagement advocated by JFM, exemplifies many of the virtues of subsidiarity.[56] Community organizing addresses the problems that residents of lower-income neighborhoods identify, mobilizing local resources and altering public policy to offer solutions that empower the residents to be industrious and self-sufficient. For JFM, as an organization that recognizes the importance of intimacy, relationship, and the individual, subsidiarity is a natural tool for the grads.

Another face of oppression that Young identifies is cultural imperialism. Cultural imperialism is the hegemonic recognition of a set of values, experiences, and so forth as normative, with those outside of this understanding marked as "other." Although cultural imperialism is more about ideological dominance, subsidiarity provides an important contrast in cultural, material, or political contexts. Cultural imperialism comes from the top, "others" difference, and flattens particularities. Subsidiarity comes from the grassroots, requires sensitivity to difference, and thrives on particularities. In this way, subsidiarity brings previously peripheral voices to the table and respects the culture of local communities.

Preferential Option for the Poor

Church teaching rejects some parts of liberation theology[57] as it welcomes other contributions, with the preferential option for the poor an obvious example of its influence.[58] Discerning through a preferential option for the poor means considering the effects a decision—be it public policy or individual lifestyle—has on the poor, and to act with their interests particularly in mind. Due to the church's ambiguous relationship with liberation theology, both Pope John Paul II[59] and the American bishops[60] emphasized the continuity this option for the poor has with teachings of the past. This is one of several pieces of liberation theology that has become part of official Catholic social teaching. With Francis's papacy, there has been a heightened discussion of the centrality of the poor to Christian ethics. When critics described his teachings on the economy as communist, he responded, "I can only say that the communists have stolen our flag. The flag of the poor is Christian. Poverty is at the center of the Gospel."[61] The centrality of the poor within scripture demands their dignified treatment and the altering of structures that perpetuate poverty and exclude.[62]

This preferential option for the poor is central to the grads' and JFM's understanding of the Gospels. JFM claims that Catholics on both sides of the political spectrum criticize the organization for neglecting certain issues—liberals want them to address women's ordination and conservatives want more explicit attention to abortion. JFM, however, understands the Gospels as focused on poverty, and the staff ensure that the programs follow suit. As Jezreel says, "It's very hard to engage in the Jesus narrative and come out with anything less than an option for the poor and vulnerable. And the poor and vulnerable have become in some ways our *first* consideration. Not our only consideration, but one of the first considerations that whenever we look at a political piece of legislation or a political movement or a political agenda; that we're always looking at it through that lens." As Cathy Meyers says succinctly, "[t]here is only one bias that our programs come from and that is the bias of the poor."[63] Concern for the poor and vulnerable is a hallmark of Catholic social teaching, is the foundation of JFM, and is a central feature of progressive Christian activism.[64]

The grads also have an image of Christ that is in and with the poor. Eric Naughton, a Los Angeles–area retiree, cites scripture supporting this: "Matthew 25[65] says if you know the least of my brethren, it is where you are going to find the Lord . . . the ones that need the help are the ones where Christ is." This passage in the Gospel of Matthew does not indicate that Jesus merely appreciates such works of mercy or that serving people in need was *like* serving Christ. Rather, in serving them, they serve Christ himself in a mysterious, but actual, way.[66] The grads readily mention this presence of Jesus in the poor or the outcast. This is an echo of the "transcendent in the immanent" discussed earlier as well as a frame for the grads to understand their good works in a spiritual, rather than simply altruistic, sense.

A preferential option for the poor is a direct response to Young's notion of marginalization. Young writes that marginalization is arguably the most dangerous of the five faces of oppression. Concerns about marginalization as oppression go beyond material deprivation to include the invasive authority of benefactors as well as exclusion from full civic participation and social cooperation. A preferential option for the poor requires that people make the interests of the marginalized primary, for both personal decisions and public policies.

Structural Sin

Like the preferential option for the poor, social sin appears within Catholic social teaching and evolves in liberation theology and contemporary documents.[67] This phrase first appears in official Catholic documents in the Second Vatican Council's *Gaudium et Spes*[68] and is developed among liberation theologians and within Pope Paul VI's synodal document "Justice in the World." Social sin changes slightly in Pope John Paul II's encyclical *Sollicitudo Rei Socialis*. He maintains some of the previous elements, writing that "structures of sin" are cultural and legal patterns, making them more difficult to remove than a single personal sin.[69] John Paul II names rigid ideologies, different forms of imperialism and idolatry (e.g., money, class, and technology), and a quest for profit and power as examples of structural sins plaguing the modern world. These sins interfere with the common good, especially work for peace and development.[70] However, he adds a new aspect when he contends that these structures of sin have their roots in personal sin, that social sin is personal sin in the aggregate and that moral responsibility can be distributed. This relative newness and ambiguity of social sin has repercussions on grads and is examined more fully in chapter 6.

Only a handful of grads used the phrase "social sin" or "structural sin" to describe the phenomenon of injustices expressed through laws or customs. Yet, many allude to the concept and credit JustFaith with this new way of understanding culpability, as Margaret Wagner elaborates: "I think the idea of 'sin' isn't a very popular word, but a kind of institutional sin—structural sin—was really opened up to me through JustFaith." Grads might be tempted to inappropriately shoulder the responsibility of structural sin in their communities and nations. However, they understand their own role in structural sin without putting the full onus on themselves, as JWalker Helen Dalton explains: "And you realize those systemic issues that we have created—maybe not you or me—but like we-vaguely have created." Social sins are perpetuated through whole societies and their systems, so the moral burden is proportionally shared. This tool allows grads to identify both the individualist and the structural aspects of a problem.

Grads readily tie social problems to larger structural causes, rather than understand them merely as microlevel conflicts and causes. For example, 95 percent of grads believe that "poverty is structural and will not go away until major changes are made," and only 48 percent believe that poverty is a personal sin that could be eradicated if "some people weren't so greedy." Obviously, these are not mutually exclusive, with roughly half of grads understanding poverty as a result of both structural inequities and personal greed, yet nearly all perceive poverty as structural. John Lovett, a Southern California retiree, understands social problems as having structural roots. This leads him to underscore the necessity of both charitable- and justice-based approaches: "We need to give them a fish [charity] but I think simultaneously we need to be working on the structural change [justice]. In other words, teach them to fish or level the playing field so that they have the opportunity to fish. Otherwise, they are always going to need charity. But I think we should be trying to make the systemic changes so that people can provide for themselves." Charity is important for meeting the immediate needs of the poor. Justice, however, is a more stable, sustainable, and respectful solution. Grads prefer a "both/and" approach to problems, addressing immediate needs as well as directing efforts to root causes. The importance of both charity and justice are discussed in JustFaith materials as well.

Social sin provides a theological recognition of Young's use of violence. She acknowledges that misunderstanding violence as a purely microlevel act is easy; typically, violence is an act of aggression between individuals or groups. However, this reductionism misses that some acts of violence are not against a person for any rational (even if immoral) reason. Some people become victims of violence merely because they belong to a particular group, such as racial violence against people of color or sexual violence against women. Violence in this sense is oppressive of a whole group; even when not immediately under attack, a person is threatened by the possibility of violence simply through identity. Social sin lends a religious frame to understand and prophetically stand against these social practices and the attitudes that tacitly sanction violence, such as an acceptance of gang violence in low-income communities that would not be tolerated in more affluent neighborhoods. Social sin is also portable to situations besides physical threats and can be used to understand the social exclusion of the poor as social or political violence. In employing the religious language of social sin, the urgency and moral authority of a response are heightened for grads.

These five tools—the dignity of the human person, solidarity, subsidiarity, preferential option for the poor, and structural sin—compose the core of Catholic teachings that JFM and grads draw upon. This cultural repertoire allows them to live their everyday lives with spiritual meaning and provides a religious language to address the problems of the age. Although Young's faces of oppression provide helpful frames for translating grads' tools into nonreligious contexts, religious ideas carry much more moral authority for them. If JFM were to utilize more secular concepts—like Young's categories or brotherhood, autonomy, or others—grads would less readily understand their everyday lives in religious terms. Organizations of the discipleship style consistently draw on Catholic doctrine when constructing their cultural repertoire. By tapping into established religious constructs, grads bring divine authority to their moral positions, compelling participants with greater urgency to pursue their political and civic ends.

Reappropriating the Holy to Everyday Life

The third theme expressing grads' theology of pragmatic reverence is intentionally applying religious concepts to their lives in concrete ways. When asked whether creedal elements, like the Trinity and the resurrection, were more important than love for the poor, Pete London illustrates their interconnection: "If we're living according to the resurrection that would kind of lead to how we treat the poor, wouldn't it? It should." Kevin Patrickson, a Louisville doctor and father to a JWalker, said of Mary, "So in the Catholic Church we pray to Mary asking her to pray for us. And so I think little prayers that I learned along the way, like sort of a litany, kept coming back to me as mother of hope, mother of prisoners, mother of the homeless, mother of the dying, of the sick and so on."[71] James O'Reilly says of the saints:

I don't think you have to be dead to be a saint. I don't believe that's what God intends. You don't have to be perfect to be a saint. All we have to do is pay attention to the great saints of our Church and see that they were as fraught with issues and challenges and sinfulness as any of us are. So for me that's real, that's not something to be attained once I retire like a hall of fame thing. That's work that just is going on every day and in every moment. So I don't see a separation [of creedal elements and life] myself . . . I think actually a lot of Catholics probably do. And so again for me it gets back to the challenge of where do I see God at work in an instance, in a circumstance, where do I recognize Christ, who do I recognize Christ in.

From the resurrection emerges hope, love, and dignity for the poor. Mary becomes an advocate for the downtrodden. The saints demonstrate an attainable model for holy living. Grads readily ground their visions of justice and charity in some of the church's most important theological concepts. That not all grads expand doctrinal elements to give meaning to everyday life is important to note. Only those who were deeply involved in some sort of theological study—clergy, Rite of Christian Initiation of Adults instructors, retreat directors, campus ministers, and the like—appear to have the theological acumen to make such extensions. The lower frequency of reappropriation indicates that only the most theologically sophisticated Catholics within discipleship groups would employ this sort of lens.

Theologically central elements of Catholicism having "this-worldly" implications could trouble some Catholics as they might understand this reappropriation as devaluing the otherworldly aspect. An online article that had an unfavorable opinion of JustFaith read:

Week 25 "prayers" have other problems. The symbols of a crucifix and barbed wire, or perhaps a thorny branch, are held up and introduced, followed by the confusing "We, who are witnesses of God's loving-justice in a violent and divided world, see in the crucifix a symbol of solidarity . . ." Wait, wait, wait! This is a Catholic formation, containing a prayer to be said among Catholics who have much more to offer fellow sinners and sufferers than a "symbol of solidarity." How about the fact of salvation? Now, there's some good news.[72]

The author is upset about having a this-worldly understanding of the crucifix and limits legitimate interpretations of the crucifix to those of a salvific quality. However, symbols are often rich with meaning and lend themselves to multiple interpretations, as Pope Francis demonstrates when he preaches on the meaning of the crucifix: "As we contemplate Jesus in his Passion, we see reflected the suffering of humanity, and we discover the divine answer to the mystery of evil, suffering and death . . . This week it would benefit all of us to look at the crucifix, to kiss the wounds of Jesus, to kiss them on the crucifix. He took upon himself all human suffering, he clothed himself in this suffering."[73] Because maintaining a Catholic identity is central to JFM's culture, making a curriculum that can bring religious meaning to everyday life without contradicting other religious truths is important for the organization. As Pope Francis shows, the crucifix is not only a symbol of redemption; it is also a symbol of suffering and Christ's solidarity with the suffering of others. The pope has drawn similar connections with other Catholic artifacts.[74] Religious symbols are multifaceted and can offer otherworldly significance to the problems of this world even while staying within the bounds of orthodoxy. Grads most typically appropriate understandings of the Eucharist, the crucifixion and resurrection, and the incarnation.

The Eucharist is by far the most important sacrament for the grads. Many, especially those who attend daily Mass, claim the Eucharist provides spiritual sustenance and say it is the only reason they are able to be so civically engaged. In addition to being spiritual food, others say there are additional graces within the Eucharist. Dr. Emily Reese, a campus minister at a Catholic college, emphasizes the transformative aspect of the Eucharist: "It doesn't matter if you believe that the elements are transformed if you don't also believe we are supposed to be transformed at every Mass. And so that whole transformative piece is a constant! 'When did you become a Christian?' students would ask me, or 'When were you saved' and I'll say, 'Two thousand years ago. And every day.' So Eucharist, it's not just about communion on Sunday or weekday Mass. It's about all the time: How can you be Christ's hands, the body of Christ, to the world?" Just as Catholics believe that the bread and wine are changed into the Body and Blood of Christ, the communicant must likewise be transformed into something greater. And for grads, being transformed—as the last sentence indicates—means offering one's time and talents to others.

The crucifixion and resurrection symbolize suffering in the world and the hope that can arise in even the direst situations. The previous chapter noted the pieces of church teaching that grads emphasize compared to Catholics nationally. Fewer grads, however, say that the belief in Jesus's resurrection from the dead is "very important" to them.[75] Given the centrality of the resurrection in the grads' understanding of the world, this disparity may indicate that this particular doctrine is *relatively* less central than the other items on the survey, such as the church's social justice teachings or helping the poor. Robin Ingham, a retired director of faith formation, demonstrates grads' commitment to the crucifixion and resurrection when she expands these to describe the triumph of God and creation over the sin and suffering of the world: "[The crucifixion of Christ] is the worst thing in the world that could happen. It can turn out to be glorious. So that's a way to see the problems of the world, too, that there is hope that they can be completely turned around in ways that we can't imagine . . . But I think [St. Augustine] said to pray as if it's all up to God and act as if it's all up to you. So the resurrection, the glory that comes, it's totally dependent on God, but it's not going to happen without some participation on our part." The suffering of the crucifixion and the hope of the resurrection are real, historical events for Christians. Grads, however, do not limit these elements to singular occurrences and, instead, treat them as paradigms for understanding their contemporary world. This grad also illustrates that the resurrection is not some "pie in the sky" that lulls people into accepting unjust situations. Rather, similar to their understanding of miracles, people are instruments of God, with God acting through those who work to bring the resurrection to fruition on earth.

The final element grads use to bring a religious understanding to their world is the incarnation. The incarnation is the belief that Jesus is God made flesh, both fully human and fully divine. This allows grads to see themselves as participating in the incarnation through their baptismal call, imitating Christ in their daily lives. It also encourages them to see Christ in others, especially the marginalized, with Reese articulating both visions:

The Benedictine charism, "Treat every guest as Christ." You can look at that in two ways, in the way that it's phrased in English. You can treat [a guest] as if that guest is Christ. Or you can treat every guest as Christ would treat that guest. So you are Christ to them and they are Christ to you simultaneously. It's a double message. And to me that's the incarnational message of JustFaith. It's not me and them; it's us. And so the people who are on the margins are me and I am supposed to be making sure that they know they are connected to me.

The incarnation for the grads is a historical event that occurred two millennia ago as well as even more than that. The incarnation is also Christ dwelling among them now, both within those who need help and within those willing to sacrifice for others. Without minimizing the importance of the incarnation of God in Jesus Christ, grads more steeped in Catholic theology believe that God became flesh to "be our model of holiness" and "make us 'partakers of the divine nature.'"[76]

These elements—the Eucharist, the crucifixion and resurrection, and the incarnation—are essential to grads' Christian identity. They understand these elements as unique events in salvation history as well as events that continually occur in their everyday lives. Some Catholics might worry that expanding these theological elements undermines their otherworldly value. However, the opposite seems to be the case. As grads find ways to bring these elements to the world it elevates the significance of these in their lives, allowing grads to bring religion into the public sphere. The church has not developed a spirituality for the laity that brings Catholic social teaching, theology, prayer, liturgy, and daily living together into a coherent whole.[77] Theologically sophisticated grads are illustrating ways this could be done.

This also has implications for the religious and moral authority of the hierarchy. For the generation around the time of World War II, the magisterium articulated church teaching and instructed the laity in when and how to use this knowledge. The church was the source of faith and moral wisdom and the world was the place to employ this; active Catholics knew how to spend their Sundays and arrange family life. After the Second Vatican Council and with the rising professionalism among American Catholics, to be an active lay Catholic means to become more demanding as well as to engage in more advanced reasoning. The church is now *a* source of moral wisdom, and rather than the world merely being a place to put teachings to use, it is, likewise, a source of wisdom. Individual Catholics of discipleship organizations act as a nexus, bringing their faith, education, and experiences together in a way that is personally meaningful.

Catholics used to regard their hierarchy as the only authority in matters of faith and morals. Other spheres, like science and economics, also had their own experts within those realms. Now American society is shifting from this secular compartmentalization to a postsecular integration.[78] When there is an issue, like climate change, society no longer looks to a single voice. Ecologists report the devastation, sociologists analyze human practices, engineers research sustainable alternatives for energy, economists discuss financial impacts, ethicists offer principles and perspectives to consider, and theologians provide centuries-old insights from a living faith.

This new postsecular context of being a voice among others presents challenges and opportunities for Catholicism. The challenge is that the magisterium no longer enjoys the taken-for-granted authority it once had. No longer can it make a pronouncement and have this more or less accepted by the vast majority of Catholics. Now the hierarchy must present compelling and persuasive arguments; these will be accepted insofar as the arguments are logical and resonate with the experience of the faithful. But therein also lies the opportunity. When magisterial authority rested only on clerical rank, it was only the faithful who complied. As the hierarchy now pauses to consider the resources of the faith, the context of the society, and the giftedness of Catholics, it finds that it needs to rely more on cogency than office. And through cogency, Catholic positions and arguments find influence beyond Catholics themselves, within the wider society. In a postsecular context, Catholic teaching must have intrinsic merit if it is to appeal to Catholics or make a difference in the public square.

These discipleship Catholics also offer insights for healing the liberal/conservative divide in American Catholicism.[79] Although there is a significant political divide among American Catholics, they are quite united on matters of theological doctrine.[80] Discipleship-style Catholics illustrate how these theological doctrines, which are widely accepted by the faithful, are connected to Catholic social teaching. Clergy might alter the sentiments of Catholics who are ignorant of or who reject social teachings if they connect widely accepted theological frames, like the Eucharist, to issues of peace, justice, and poverty.

Conclusion

The Second Vatican Council developed new theologies and ecclesiologies that encouraged the laity to see the religious significance of their world. Catholics no longer needed to be in a Catholic context—such as a parish relief society—to act in the world as Catholics. Inspired and enabled by the council, new Catholic organizations emerged that engaged the public sphere with a new style, characterized by a theology of pragmatic reverence, imparting religious meaning to the everyday lives of Catholics. Three themes characterize the way discipleship organizations draw on religious teachings of the Catholic faith that encourage Catholics to understand their everyday lives in religious terms. The first theme is biblical and theological. Organizations, based on their particular mission, highlight the most significant scriptural passages, with JFM giving special place to the love of God and neighbor. They also draw on theological understandings of the transcendent in the immanent. The second theme is Catholic social teaching. Again, different organizations will emphasize different aspects of Catholic teaching depending on their missions. JFM focuses on poverty and justice, emphasizing the life and dignity of the human person, solidarity, subsidiarity, the preferential option for the poor, and structural sin. The third theme is an appropriation of otherworldly elements to this world. Bringing elements that Catholics typically understand as solely religious to real life circumstances imbues these situations with greater significance. Grads do this through their notions of the Eucharist, the crucifixion and resurrection, and the incarnation. Discipleship organizations will carefully articulate all these themes within the bounds of Catholic orthodoxy as their religious identity is foundational to their missionary thrust.

These themes allow grads to understand their lives as religiously significant. However, maintaining such a worldview on their own would be decidedly more difficult. Discipleship Catholics learn and maintain many of their values through the regular support of a discipleship community. These communities gather their members for formation, shaping one another's faith and sense of mission. With this new outlook, they go into their other communities of work, friendships, and among the impoverished to bring them good news. The next chapter explores the role of community for grads.

5

Transforming Community

Gathering and Sending American Catholics

It is Friday evening, and the St. Francis de Sales parish JustFaith group is beginning their opening retreat at a spacious home in the Oakland hills. After the last person arrives, they gather around a small, circular table. The table holds several items: a scarf-like cloth for decoration, a wooden cross with glossy white tiles, a simple paperback Bible, and a large, white pillar candle the group will use for the rest of its meetings. A facilitator reads, "We gather around the flame of wisdom's light and warmth to discover what gifts we have brought with us." Moving clockwise through the circle, participants read prompts from the retreat handout, concluding, "We thank each individual who has come to listen and to speak from the heart. Let us acknowledge the joy and strength we receive from this communion." The facilitators tell the group that this retreat is not going to educate anyone on a political issue, nor will it delve into any theology. Instead, the intent is for the members of the group to learn about each other, care more for each other, and become a community for one another. With this retreat, they warn, participants will only get as much as they are willing to put in. They ask that everything discussed in the group remain confidential and that no one share beyond what they are comfortable.

Later in the evening, a young woman with long sandy-blonde hair volunteers to read a passage from the Bible. The reading is from Ephesians,[1] and parts emphasize the importance of unity: "There is one body and one Spirit, just as you were called to the one hope of your calling, one Lord, one faith, one baptism, one God and Father of all, who is above all and through all and in all." Also, verses distinguish particular gifts and individuals: "The gifts he gave were that some would be apostles, some prophets, some evangelists, some pastors and teachers." There is another brief prayer and then another set of readings. This time there are four designated readers and between each of their passages, the group responds, "Where two or three are gathered in my name, there I am among you."

After some lighter sharing, the group now digs into heavier ideas. The participants consult their handouts to discern which stage of "human growth and spiritual development" they are each at. There are eight stages, with infants at the most primitive stage and particular philosophical systems at the final stage. After some time contemplating the various stages, a facilitator instructs them to each place a shoe in the center of the room. "A shoe?" someone quizzically verifies. After everyone does this, another facilitator randomly "pairs" the shoes to assign group members to one another. I am with Joan. We move to a place in the house that lends us some privacy, and she says that she does not really care for the stages, that they were too stark, and that she found aspects of herself in different stages, even down to the second level.

Joan tells me some of her recent struggles. She has a faith-based job that promotes economic justice in local communities and remembers hearing songwriter John Bell's "The Summons" and weeping in church, knowing that a lot of work lay ahead for her. Her husband just moved out to our area after work had separated them for roughly six months. He is currently looking for work, which can be difficult to come by in the Bay Area. "I just hope that we can make it in this window, I just have to have faith." She is crying as she adds, "But I don't know what to pray for." After some deep breaths and wiping the tears from her eyes, she smiles and says she was not sure when she was going to cry but that the retreat was probably a good bet! After the pairs had finished sharing stories, the group reconvened for an evening prayer that closed with "Your home, your heart, your humanness is treasure for others' poverty; be generous. And we will learn how community lives."

It is the next day, and the group has gathered in a small meeting room at St. Francis de Sales parish. At lunchtime, everyone unpacks their food. The conversation appears natural as people ask follow-up questions and add stories about a travel destination or the work they do. Following lunch is a more arduous task: members have a short period to journal about the pain they have experienced, which they will then share with the group. Several people cry during their sharing. Generally, the things members recount are concrete, personal sources of suffering, such as a death or alcoholism. Several members read reflections on community: "Humility and trust are more at the foundation of community life than perfection and devotion." Another proclaims, "It is only when we are conscious of who we are and who the others are, with all our wealth and weakness, and when we are conscious of the call of God and the life God gives us, that we can build something together." The participants journal about their understandings of community and their hopes for the coming weeks. Some say that they are thankful to be around like-minded individuals. Although the Bay Area is politically progressive and favors policies that improve the conditions of those in poverty, few residents ground these social concerns in their faith. These grads appreciate both the religiosity and the social convictions of the other members, with one crying as she laments that her husband is so different from her in these respects. Another participant says that this retreat has made her prouder to be Catholic.

The central theme of a lengthy reading is that we, like the first disciples, are called to follow Jesus. To celebrate their communal relationship to one another, the handbook suggests a bread and wine sharing, which the group modifies to bread and juice. The handbook calls this sharing of bread and wine "signs of companionship, signs of compassion." The bread and wine could be connected with the Eucharist. Perhaps intentionally distancing this sharing from the sacrament, a facilitator tells participants that sharing food and drink was traditionally used to "strengthen their communal lives," citing customs "from the days of Moses and Miriam . . . to the disciples who invited Jesus to dine with them after they traveled the road to Emmaus." After a reflection on Pentecost, a facilitator invites everyone to choose from a motley assortment of small candles—tealights and votives in a variety of colors—sitting on a table. She remarks that, at first, she was going to go out and buy new votive candles so that they would all match, but then she realized that each member of the group was different from the others. A few members agreed that this was a better representation of the group and the variety of folks that it encompasses. The group stands in a circle and a facilitator comes around to light each of the candles while everyone reads a call and response prayer. The group echoes the refrain, "Anoint us with Your Spirit; send us to proclaim the good news." There is a closing blessing, and everyone offers a sign of peace. People make a concerted effort to make sure that they do not overlook giving a hug to anyone before departing for their homes.

These excerpts from the JustFaith opening retreat show that establishing community early on is important to the JustFaith process. Community is a core value of JustFaith Ministries (JFM) as well as one of grads' most cherished parts of the JustFaith experience. Intimate discipleship groups are the central vehicle of formation within discipleship organizations, and these encourage participants to bring their strengthened religious commitments into public life. Organizations of the historical styles were unable to lend Catholics the cultural tools to understand themselves as both fully Catholic and fully American. Discipleship-style organizations encourage their members to cultivate both of these identities and to bring the values of their faith community to bear on their public communities.

The discipleship style is the first style to attempt to have a foot in both the American and Catholic world simultaneously. Republican-style Catholics were Americans in the public sphere, minimizing their Catholic identity there. Immigrant and evangelical style Catholics eschewed their Americanness and were distinctly Catholic in all things. These strategies resulted in what I call the dilemma of resistance, that is, how to be in the world enough to change it but not let the ills of the world change the actor. The historical styles were not able to effectively bring their religious values to the public sphere, weakening what could have been a more robustly Catholic civic engagement. Discipleship Catholics resolve this dilemma of resistance by fostering an identity that is simultaneously American and Catholic, emphasizing the importance of both their citizen and religious identity while privileging the latter over the former. After fostering value commitments among the participants, the members bring those values to their other communities in an attempt to make them more just or holy. This results in Catholics who are active in all spheres of social life—politics, leisure, the market, family—and understand these spheres through a religious lens. Chapter 3 studied the primacy of a religious worldview through religion-centering transformation. Chapter 4 explored the theological beliefs that JFM and grads bring into the world. This chapter examines the role of community— both the discipleship community and the grads' wider communities—as the grads bring religious beliefs to their everyday lives.

Religion as Practice

People bring religious meaning to their lives in a variety of ways, including to places and practices that that initially appear nonreligious.[2] In
his book on pro-life activists, Ziad Munson notes that social movement
theorists have conceptualized religion as "churches," emphasizing the
leadership, mass support, and other resources congregations provide.
This approach misses what is central to these organizations: they are
religious.[3] Social movement theorists miss critical sociocultural components of churches when they reduce them to organizations with
resources for a movement. Another way to understand religion, popular
among sociologists of religion, is as "belief," which emphasizes symbols,
worldview, language, and other cultural resources. One of the most
surprising findings in Munson's work is that nearly half of the pro-life
activists began their activism with either ambivalent or pro-choice sentiments about abortion.[4] Furthermore, his pro-life activists have nearly
the same religious beliefs as pro-life nonactivists.[5] Religion as beliefs,
therefore, only tells part of the story in terms of social activism. Munson contends that a more accurate conception of religion and activism
is religion as "practice." By *practice* he means activities that take place
outside institutional structures that have social meaning for those
involved.[6] Similarly, ethicist Alasdair MacIntyre argues that practices
reference moral excellence and conceptions of the good.[7] Conceiving
of religion as practice illuminates the need for scholars to look beyond
organizational resources or beliefs to include meaningful aspects of people's day-to-day lives.

The previous chapter's exploration of the beliefs of JFM and their
grads is only a part of the story. Understanding the significance they
impart to their communities and the activities they share with those
community members illuminates the ways grads live their religion in
everyday life. Matthew Collins, who helps create faith formation programs at his church, is purposeful in integrating his religious beliefs
with his daily practices: "There's a lot of people who are content to go
to church and put money in the basket . . . this is stopping your faith
formation at third grade and saying, 'Okay I got it, I'm good from here.'
There is much more. But not everyone wants to get more involved and
really have their faith kind of take over their lives. It's like a compartment

within our lives, I think." Rather than compartmentalizing his faith, Collins's faith permeates his daily life as a religious practice.[8] Elena Ross uses her denomination's language to bring faith and works together: "Our Methodist roots are in the personal holiness and social responsibility, so they always have gone together." Jezreel confirms that catechesis should have consequences in people's lives: "I know that ultimately what we're interested in as a church is not people who can quote encyclicals to each other, but people who live them, and are interested in them exactly because it's a living document in their hearts and in their lives instead of just something they can quote." The consensus among grads is that beliefs are critical to animating practices. To modify a verse from the Epistle of James, just as the body without the spirit is dead, so belief without practice is also dead.[9] These beliefs are nurtured into practices through grads' participation in their various communities. There are two main types of communities for grads. First are communities that gather. Grads recognize these as sources of formation, such as their churches. Second are the communities to which they are sent. Grads act on these communities and seek to transform them, and include their volunteer sites. This chapter examines the role of communities of gathering and communities of sending for discipleship Catholics.

Communities of Gathering: Community That Transforms the Individual

JFM believes authentic community both gathers and sends. Gathering includes study, worship, friendship, and general spiritual formation.[10] Yet, a community that only gathers, JFM believes, becomes stagnant and loses its vitality. JFM wants participants to take the love and insight they experience within the group setting to the world. The primary community for organizations of the discipleship style is the discipleship community. "Primary" is not to say that the most important community in grads' life is their JustFaith group. Rather, "primary" indicates that the discipleship community is the most explicit articulation of the virtues that grads hope to embody. Grads also claim that family and parish are likewise central communities in their lives, yet these communities also serve other functions (e.g., providing material goods) that do not necessarily undergird their commitment to public life. Family and parish do, in fact, influence grads' commitment to their wider community, so the impact of these communities are explored before examining the workings of the discipleship community.

Family as Gathered Community

Family is important to grads, yet it is a community that can either facilitate or hinder the commitments they have made in their discipleship groups. Families facilitate transformation when members take JFM programs together or when they simply support the grad's lifestyle changes. One Louisville couple appears especially close to their young adult daughter; the parents are both grads, the daughter was a JWalker, and they enjoy lively discussions about political and economic issues. Ron Stevenson, a retired accountant in the Los Angeles area, took JustFaith because he was impressed by his daughter's other-regarding commitments: "My daughter was kind of inspiring because she was in college and she was doing AIDS walks and projects for fair trade and these kinds of things. And so I was inspired by her." Couples at JustFaith information sessions—preliminary meetings, usually on church grounds, to answer questions of those interested in JustFaith—tell inquiring church members that JustFaith strengthened their marriage and faith life. That families who take JFM programs find that it strengthens their relationships is of little surprise.

The flip side of this is also often true: families in which only one member takes JustFaith can experience strain as a result. Sometimes it is simple, even an occasion for humor between spouses, as Matthew Collins says of his wife: "She just kind of shakes her head when I come home and say, 'Guess what I signed up for now?' [laughs]." Sally Armstrong, a Louisville grad, discusses instances that are more serious:

> Like running the water when he brushes his teeth. I mean, it drove me crazy. And I had to look at [it like] what's right for me may not be right for him. Does it bother me? A lot of things, yes, but I can't change the whole family. So, there's a tension in my own marriage. It's not a tension that causes—it's just that I'll think about it or I'll say something about, "[Use] the rags instead of the paper towels." I think it's a matter of not being a crusader for the cause and beating him over the head. It's a matter

of leading by example and maybe he would come along a little bit more. Because he said, "Well, I can't believe [what] you're going to give up. You want to sell the house and just give it all to the poor!" And I'm thinking, "Oh no, that's not exactly what I said!" But that's what he was feeling. I think he was feeling the pressure and the tension.

The lifestyle changes that this woman makes to lessen her environmental impact are in stark contrast with her husband's practices, leaving both of them frustrated. Consumption patterns are also the largest point of contention for Margaret Wagner and her husband: "That has always been an issue for me because I have a very loving relationship with my husband, but he is not anywhere where I am and so it's always a struggle for me to balance what I would like to do and his needs. So to downsize—Anthony has worked really hard to get where is and to get what he has got, so I struggle with that. I am so privileged that I just feel really feel guilty about that, but I am not in a position to do much about it." At first, this woman's feelings might simply be attributed to her belief that her husband has a greater say in the money his occupation earned than she does. However, male grads also express this wish to scale back more than their wives want, demonstrating that both male and female grads with spouses who did not go through the program find themselves in a bind when trying to bring their faith to their everyday lives. In sum, the family can be a place that fortifies or challenges JFM values, depending on the feelings of the grad's spouse.

The Parish as Gathered Community

The parish is a second key community for grads. Many grads mentioned the homily as important for their instruction, forming the listeners through the moral lessons it imparts, as Joyce Roberts, a Bay Area grad who has facilitated multiple sessions of JustFaith, says: "That particular church I go to has very relevant homilies. So, usually there's something important to take away from that. It's a way to hear the scriptures." Margaret Wagner underscores that preaching should challenge the listener: "I don't want someone to get up at the pulpit and tell me how to vote, but I want someone to be at the pulpit reminding me of the Gospel message, Catholic social teaching and that how I vote, how I spend my money, how I live my life is to speak to that. I want people to remind me not to just go home and be a good girl next week or whatever, which is basically what we're getting."[11] Grads attend parishes that provide theological instruction that helps form moral individuals.

Gathering at the parish also provides grads with a general group identity. The most common way grads experience this identity is simply through a group affinity as Wagner does, coupling it with the Eucharist: "The thing that holds me in the Church now is probably the Eucharist, that's probably—Eucharist and community." If grads struggle with the institutional church, they can still connect with institutional manifestations of the church through the parish community.[12] Eleanor Smythe needs the communal fellowship that her parish provides: "I pray, here, my car or wherever, but that doesn't give the community with anybody else. [Praying alone] doesn't provide the framework of reading the Scripture, listening to a homily. In some sense, I consider [my parish] 'community,' but sometimes I consider it family." For the purpose of group identity, the parish has affective meaning and is a place to feel a sense of belonging as a Catholic.[13]

Grads are also able to celebrate their sacramental life, especially the Eucharist, when they gather as a parish. As we saw earlier, the Eucharist is central to many Catholic grads' faith. Sacraments are an important part of Catholicism and are not celebrated alone—they require community for their ordinance. Nearly two-thirds of Catholic grads say that sacraments such as the Eucharist are "very important" to them. Many grads volunteer that Eucharist is their primary reason for attending Mass, with Joyce Roberts saying simply, "I love the Eucharist more than anything." As these sacraments are only available to them through the church, grads have a strong incentive to remain committed to their parish.[14]

Instruction, group identity and reception of sacraments sends them into other communities. Linda Tyson volunteers full-time as the director of a homeless shelter and does not think she could make it through the day without Mass:

One of the ways I feel it is that I am never burned out and . . . I will get up tomorrow and have another full day . . . and I find some people [who volunteer] tend to drop off, but I start every day with Mass . . . I start getting calls from the homeless saying the children need to ride to school or whatever. If I didn't make a point to come to Mass and just sort of close my eyes and thank God for letting me be His hands and His feet and His voice—it just sets the day in the tone I want it to be and then I can leave church with a peaceful heart and start handling the requests I am going to get.

Tyson shows that, like other Catholic small groups, JustFaith complements rather than replaces the traditional parish role.[15] Sharon Jones believes the parish is the most appropriate nexus for faith and action: "You can't just come here and get fed week after week; you've got to go out too! Here's your opportunity, [the parish is] going to help organize that opportunity." Some are critical of what they see as insufficient outreach on parish property.[16] Joe Vitale, a JFM board member, shows that major things can get done when a parish puts forth the effort: "[My wife] and I and four other people, we're on the steering committee to open a [fair-trade store] . . . my whole point is that's where the incubator was, the parish." This grad, along with several others from the parish, opened a fair-trade store in the summer of 2014. The parish connected members with one another, and they were able to build on their extant community and moral values to make this happen rather than having to begin from scratch with strangers.

The JustFaith Community

Both the JustFaith groups across the country and the headquarters in Louisville demonstrate the importance of community as a core value. The JFM staff are about the recommended size of a JustFaith group, and the organization takes advantage of this, with the employees enjoying more than a typical workday. The Louisville staff share the responsibility of beginning each day with prayer. Unless someone has extenuating circumstances, the staff takes their lunch together. They celebrate birthdays and other events together with a real intentionality in their time and presence for one another. JFM staff foster the same sort of community they ask of their small groups nationwide.

Small groups are a significant feature of the American landscape, with 40 percent in a small group.[17] Discipleship organizations have seized upon the popularity of the small-group model to create a faith community that dovetails with the current social ecology. JustFaith and other discipleship groups are ripple groups. From the perspective of community, ripple groups are similar to support groups in their fostering of *intimacy* and their encouragement of *personal growth*. They differ from support groups in ripple groups' ultimate goal of wider transformation, discussed here as *outreach*. According to the ripple-group model, intimacy, personal growth, and outreach provide three "formation opportunities," that is, experiences that invite reflection and are intended to transform participants and society. Although the formation opportunities of intimacy, personal growth, and outreach are distinct, they are mutually reinforcing. Unlike ripple groups broadly, for discipleship communities, these formation opportunities will be grounded in faith.

The first formation opportunity is intimacy. The geographic mobility that gives rise to organizations of the discipleship style also upsets traditional bonds. People seek new ways to build these same kinds of relationships.[18] Just over 40 percent of Catholics nationwide find parishes too big and impersonal, indicating that a large minority desire something more intimate.[19] Intimacy is a critical component to the formation of community in JustFaith groups. Before discussing political issues that might be divisive, JustFaith establishes intimacy among participants. Samantha DeRouen discusses the importance of this:

> I think the opening retreat is very important because when you're on a retreat with somebody all day and they are pouring out their inner most thoughts or hurts or you are getting to their raw vulnerability in such a way that engenders, if not love, sympathy. People would say in the beginning retreat, "I've never told anyone this. This is the first time I've ever said that." And it was in a retreat where they had never met any of these people before except for one or two sessions before. And suddenly everyone was in very deep sharing, very deep praying, very deep journaling. And so that sets the stage of mutual vulnerability and talking about things you don't normally talk about with anyone else because it's intimate space. That sets up that intimate space and that talking in a way that you don't talk with people at work, at the grocery store; you're talking about important things, important milestones in a

person's life. Deep reflection that sets up the start of community. There were no [social] issues in the retreat, it was deeply reflective.

The day-and-a-half opening retreat is meant to build community. Lifting up some particular elements, they begin simply by sharing the story of their name, how they got it and what they do or do not like about it. The sharing goes deeper, with participants offering a general "life map" of the major events in their life. Next, they focus on the delights of their life, followed by their sorrows. The last thing participants share is their thoughts on moving forward as a group. The whole experience is quite emotional, with both smiles and tears, and brings intimacy to the participants. These feelings of mutual care will act as a social lubricant, keeping the group together as it handles contentious social issues.

The groups establish intimacy early on and maintain it throughout the JustFaith sessions by engaging in shared ritual. Sociologist R. Stephen Warner contends that performing actions together, such as ritual, can be just as effective at creating group bonds as sharing values.[20] Ritual is an emotion-based means of creating community while shared values are rooted in the cognitive. Other scholars have expanded this, contending that ritual can build solidarity even in the absence of ideological agreement.[21] Ritual is an effective means of building solidarity precisely because it circumvents ideological divisions that can characterize a group of people. In drawing on ritual, group members build an emotion-based solidarity that masks, or at least diminishes, the importance of group like-mindedness. This is because the ambiguity of the symbols and the participation in the ritual itself designates them as part of the group.[22] For example, as JustFaith participants pass a map, the co-facilitator asks them to reflect on where they go as well as where they choose not to tread. One participant might feel challenged to enter lower-income neighborhoods, and another might regularly visit downtrodden areas and pray for those who live there. Yet, both will thoughtfully hold and pass the map, which creates solidarity and intimacy in the group, with or without consensus. Ritual fosters intimacy, building community in the small-group context.

Intimacy is not only important in establishing community; it is also critical in maintaining community. Among Catholic small groups, members claim that learning more about God or religion was the most important reason for initially joining.[23] However, affective ties are more often the reason one stays.[24] Eighty-seven percent of these grads continue to meet with friends from JustFaith monthly or more, an indication of the group bonds that developed.[25] This community of mutual care paves the way for a greater variety of ideological expression, fostering the participants' personal growth.

This personal growth is the second formation opportunity discipleship communities provide. The main reason people give for wanting to be in a small group is "the desire to grow as a person."[26] This illustrates that conversion is both active and social rather than something that happens to a person passively or in solitude.[27] After someone identifies a new reference group—that is, people recognized as having a shared affinity and considered peers—personal transformation can more readily happen as this reference group provides a script for feeling and action.[28] Samantha DeRouen, who spoke at length about the ways the retreat fosters intimacy, continues, showing that intimacy allows JustFaith participants to experience personal growth:

> And so I think that kind of [intimate] space, which is both prayerful and personal, starts to set up a journey-type of thing which then allows for the discussion of other things. Not to say that those discussions weren't difficult later on. Because I do think they were [laughs]. I think what it sets up is when you have a disagreement with someone on any topic, it's very easy to go to the demonization of the other person because you don't know them, so you can judge them, you can put them in a box you can say they are this or they are that and so you can judge them. But if you respect someone and then they disagree with you, that causes you to reevaluate and that is a harder thing to do. That can also be an emotional thing because they are challenging the core of who they are, too, when they are challenged by other people.

Intimacy is more than a social lubricant for difficult discussions. As the last sentences indicate, it also brings new people and their beliefs into another's life.[29] As participants orient themselves to the group, going beyond casual membership, they allow the group to influence their lives.[30] Through affection and intimacy, community facilitates personal transformation among its members.

Both support groups and ripple groups readily encourage their members to change. Typically for support groups, this change has a very specific focus of transformation, such as sobriety. Ripple groups are more general in their personal transformation, with feminist consciousness-raising groups working for the inclusion of women and women's values in society. Similarly, JustFaith grads have a more general notion of transformation, seeking a more caring, moral, and spiritual society. The JustFaith community has a crucial role in this personal growth. Grads use phrases like *challenged, pulled,* and *held accountable* to describe the encounters they have with their group. Jennifer Farrell, a Bay Area journalist in her thirties, draws a clear distinction between friends and community: "Community challenges you to be a better person. A lot of times, friends won't necessarily do that. If you're doing something wrong, [friends will] tell you, but they won't necessarily push you to volunteer or sacrifice." Friends are fun, but morally they hold each other only to a minimum. The community in JustFaith groups holds grads to their moral maximum, pushing them—as they understand it—to be better, holier people.

Religious virtuosity has a long tradition within the Catholic Church, fostered especially among communities of male and female religious. JustFaith groups, through both supporting and challenging, provide a similar formation opportunity for today's Catholics. Staff member Mike Campbell emphasizes the importance of growing through a community:

> They're going to *affirm* you and they're going to challenge you. And it's the balance of the two that makes it possible to grow. Too much affirmation is too easy, it's too sappy. Too much challenge is too hard. But in the middle somewhere, where you savor and the wonders of having people who genuinely care and care about you, but also who care about you enough to say, "That's not good enough [laughs]. That's just too narrow. That's just too easy." So I think that's what we try to ideally generate: a cultivated community that will both affirm and challenge us to stay on that journey together and hold us accountable to the kind of things we say we believe in.

The community is not free of judgment in a therapeutic sense. The group both loves and challenges, and JFM believes that this loving challenge allows personal growth to become a reality. The group expects that this personal growth will manifest in one another's practices, underscoring the importance of outreach for grads.

Outreach is the final formation opportunity that discipleship communities provide. Outreach is of peripheral importance to support groups. In contrast, ripple groups see this social transformation as their *raison d'être*. Only a handful of small groups nationally claim that community or political concern is their primary reason for gathering.[31] Still, surveys reveal that many people actually do help outside the group by dint of their membership as well as have more positive attitudes toward volunteering.[32] One of the explanations offered for increased activism among small-group members is that being part of a group makes significant action more feasible, as larger groups show more civic engagement than smaller groups.[33] The work of the many women's religious communities in American Catholic history—with their hospitals, schools, and orphanages—is a testimony to the capacity for small groups to create significant social changes. Some grads corroborate that efforts are simply easier with more people. In fact, sharing a ministry is the way some groups continue to meet after their commissioning at the end of JustFaith, as happened for Sharon Jones: "At the end of our last retreat we talked about next steps, and I said, 'I'm really interested in doing Family-to-Family.[34] Is anybody else interested in doing that?' Just about everybody said they were! So that's how we've continued on, around the Family-to-Family ministry." Group members sometimes pool their time and talents to continue meeting through a shared ministry.

However, other grads reflect a second and more robust explanation, which is that people often overthink ideas, rehashing their talents, desires, and availability indefinitely so that they never take action.[35] Group members encourage one another to go beyond inklings and to actually act. Miguel Cruz, an especially introspective grad who experienced considerable spiritual growth walking the Camino de Santiago,[36] pokes fun at himself: "I'm a fairly private person anyway, but finding these people, connecting with them, and knowing that I could get their support, or I could share with them my spiritual struggles, or my neuroses about whether to live a contemplative life or an active life [laughing] . . . Finally someone [said], 'Miguel, just do something! If you don't like it, then try something else, but just do something!'" JustFaith community members can help people turn their convictions, or even mullings, into actions. Compare Cruz to Joan Holland, a retiree who stopped meeting with her group at the end of the program:

> JH: After JustFaith, I [volunteered], but in my heart I've always thought I need to do something besides charity work. I need to do something more along the lines of social justice. I just haven't had time enough—
> MD: You don't have the time? [She had said earlier she was looking for something to get involved in.]
> JH: I have the time . . .
> MD: You don't have the opportunity?
> JH: [Thoughtful pause] I'm not sure if that's what I really want, but I know that there is a piece that's missing and something as drastic as joining the Peace Corps and going to Zimbabwe. But leaving my life, leaving my creature comforts, do I really want that?

Cruz and Holland are similar in their regular discernment and noble intentions. However, Holland does not have the community pushing her into outreach, and she flounders between volunteering and moving to Africa. Whether she discontinued meeting with her group because she did not want them to pressure her to act or if the lack of group puts her in a state of perpetual discernment is unclear. This desire without action was otherwise absent among grads and illustrates that sustained commitment is easier when one has a community that reinforces those values.[37]

Coming together in their JustFaith group sets and reinforces tacit expectations of service, compelling them to increase their own engagement. Grads' transformation cannot be sustained without maintenance, as the competing pulls for their time and money remain at the end of the program.[38] The grads who continue to meet with friends from their JustFaith group "almost weekly" or more frequently are significantly more likely to volunteer. For example, roughly three-fourths of grads volunteer in a charitable activity monthly or more. Yet, of the twenty-five grads who meet with friends from JustFaith almost weekly or more, twenty-three of them—92 percent—volunteer in a charitable activity monthly or more. Political activity shows a similar but less dramatic increase. There is no significant difference for either type of volunteering among those who meet with JustFaith friends less often. Whether meeting with one's friends causes an increase in volunteering or if volunteering raises one's interest in being around others with shared values is unclear, yet it shows the connection that community and activism have for the grads.[39] Sociologist Christian Smith found the same in Witness for Peace, an organization that transformed the lives of forty-two hundred people in the 1980s through immersion trips to war-torn Central American countries.[40] After one to three weeks of tears, education, and a personal commitment to end the war, these changed individuals were put back into their totally untransformed social networks.[41] People would call the main office and ask what to do and, after roughly six months, would find their energy had dissipated and their interests were elsewhere. This illustrates that moral isolation and a lack of community can undermine or nullify personal commitments.

Grads' efforts are not simply altruistic good deeds. Because of the intimate coupling of prayerful community and public action, participants believe their outreach has religious significance. As grads engage their world—civil society, the workplace, and their various ministries—they understand these practices as a religious engagement. They bring the values of the communities that gather them to the communities to which they are "sent."

Communities of Sending: Communities the Individual Transforms

Helen Dalton, a Louisvillian JWalker, remembers her first encounters with those in poverty: "I knew that when I placed myself in close proximity to people who suffered my heart broke. I knew that there was something behind the words that happen in those encounters. I knew that the actions of my daily life impacted others. But I didn't know how to integrate all that into a daily practice." JWalking and other JFM programs transform or deepen participants' beliefs and channel them toward concrete practices. Some of these practices, as outlined earlier, involve gathering. Yet the organization emphasizes, as do all ripple groups, sending. Grads are encouraged, unlike some of the more sectarian organizations of the past styles, to remain involved in their old communities, as staff member Cathy Meyers illustrates: "[JustFaith] isn't prescriptive. It isn't telling you to leave your job . . . in their job and in their own circle, whatever that is, make it better. Make it better and call people to join you in making your community." A closer look at some of the most significant of these communities of sending illustrates the importance of mission and outreach for discipleship groups.

The Community of Civil Society: Transforming Greed into Generosity

Grads see the wider world as a place that needs their efforts and attention. From neighborhoods and families to American culture more generally, grads are disturbed by the lack of care and vitality in many institutions. When offering their assessment of the health of civil society, the first reaction by many is a negative one, as Caroline Dunn, a long-time facilitator of JustFaith, shows:

> Christmas we were at my brother's house. And they had bowls of candy sitting out all over, you know how you have at Christmas, and three or four different kinds of desserts. And then they went down in the basement. They had a piñata . . . Anyway, Ellie came up—she's the [daughter] that went to Nicaragua—and she said, "Mother, you should be *so* ashamed of your grandchildren." . . . And she said when they broke the piñata, everybody ran and got candy and put their arms around it so their neighbors, their cousins, couldn't get any. In Nicaragua they broke the piñata, they got the candy, and then they came and gave it to you, the guest. So I thought: That's our culture. We're trying to get as much as we—we've got so much. But we've got our arms around [it]. And then they're looking to see that nobody gets theirs. And in other cultures, they're taking it and giving it away.

As grads evaluate civil society, greed is a recurring theme in their assessment. Other common critiques are a hectic and fast-paced lifestyle, an obsession with technology and gadgets and an arrogance that blinds fellow citizens to the needs of others.

After their initial criticisms, these same grads are also generous in their view of the wider society, with Lucy Russell saying, "If you think about any disasters, Americans *pour out* resources and volunteer hours to meet natural disasters over and over. Yes, we have horror stories where they don't—[Hurricane] Katrina—but the American spirit is *based on* helping others. That's a wonderful spirit that not everybody in other countries sees. Needs are met by the individuals helping other people." Grads perceive a "greedy America" in the day-to-day and a "generous America" in crises, the latter responding quickly to discrete and concrete events or people in immediate trouble.

Because grads believe that society is generally greedy but capable of immense generosity, many claim that the best strategy is to raise awareness, as Louisvillian Marie Baker says:

> I think, for many, education is a helpful solution because when you talk to someone in depth about a social issue, sometimes their eyes open up so widely because you've taken the time to tell them about it, to explain it, to help them understand. I feel like some of my friends, if I sat down and talked with them, like I had lunch with some friends today, that they would be like "Wow, really? Oh, okay, whoa!" You know, "It shouldn't be that way." Maybe not like, "Let's go out and do something," but at least broaden their understanding and acceptance of this issue and why it's wrong. So I think education is a big solution because it gets people moving.

In telling friends what they have learned, grads evangelize the wider culture, spreading the good news in a way that will ripple out to others. This is why, unlike Catholics of the evangelical style, discipleship organizations encourage participants to maintain their old ties to other communities. That the majority of the grads' closer friends already share many of their political and spiritual values is true. Yet many, especially those outside the San Francisco Bay Area where progressive attitudes are less prevalent, claim that they have close ties to people they differ from spiritually or politically. Among California grads, 38 percent strongly agree that most of their closer friends share their political values compared to only 16 percent of the Louisville grads. Likewise, 29 percent of California grads strongly agree that most of their closer friends share their spiritual values, and only 5 percent of the Kentucky grads say the same. In a place with many politically and theologically progressive people, one happens to have closer friends of that ilk. In the relatively more conservative climate of Louisville, grads have like-minded others through JustFaith but are less able to saturate their friendships with such people and will more readily include others whose opinions differ from their own.[42] The political situation in Louisville is more representative of the nation than California, indicating that JustFaith grads as a whole probably mingle with a variety of people. Having friends who differ from them allows the grads to affect their friends' values and have a larger impact on the world.

Community of the Workplace: Vocation or Means to Living

Roughly half of the grads are employed and many bring their JustFaith values to their workplace. Over half of the grads work or have worked in medicine, education, or ministry. These grads see their work as a vocation, as Lucy Russell passionately explains: "I would *hate* it if any of my work, as a *teacher* was disrespected, because it was holy work! It wasn't a Catholic school, but no matter where it was, that was *holy* work. My mothering at home was *holy* work!" A fair number of grads in these helping fields, such as Therese Brewer, are "double helping," according to grads' standards, in that they employ their already-beneficial skills for lower-income populations:

> And basically the purpose of our work, although it's also to understand virology and evolution and pathogenesis and how it causes disease, but it's also to bring sustainable science to the third world as a means of supporting the third world. So we're not going there and taking samples, we work in collaboration with trained scientists there. And they offer and we offer and they grow and we grow and they get publications and we get publications, et cetera, et cetera. It's truly the best model that I have found on the macro-scale about how to support the third world in a way that's sustainable for oneself, or a lab in this case. But also in a way that supports them out of poverty. But it's also something that I struggle with because of so many years of living and just working with the poorest of the poor people [she spent six years alternating between a Catholic Worker and a community in Chiapas, Mexico]. That's not what I do now. I work with trained scientists. But I still feel, I think, that my work is equally significant. Managua is now a center of excellence for molecular virology, and it's not because we've gone there, it's because we've developed programs with them.

Although Brewer has some ambivalence about being so removed from the poor, she sees the impact of her work and takes pride in its principles of reciprocity and solidarity. Additionally, some of the grads not in traditional helping professions employ their skills to aid the poor, such as the accountant who works at a nonprofit or the journalist who covers stories on violence and education problems in inner-city neighborhoods. Grads who work in professions that help others believe that their job sends them into the world to transform it in a socially and religiously significant way.

Another way grads think of work, especially those whose work benefits low-income populations, is that their colleagues and sometimes their clients are communities of both gathering and sending, as former shelter employee James O'Reilly says: "[The shelter clients] didn't have a secure place to live or enough food to eat often and there were other kinds of life issues that we would get involved with and try to help, so that transformation was already planted and growing when I encountered JustFaith . . . And I found that sharing some of those stories of the people that I have to shelter was really transformational for others and they began to see 'Oh, so just being homeless isn't a category that means this and this and this and this.'" Before going through JustFaith, this grad had close relationships with people experiencing homelessness that transformed him, just as a community of gathering in the discipleship style is intended to. He then was sent into his other communities to transform their way of understanding homelessness. This is an awareness of work as a community that both gathers and sends.

A handful of grads think of work simply as a way to pay the bills. Some retired grads feel this way about work that they did before Just-Faith, claiming they would have gone into a different line of work if they had known then what they know now. Others are currently in a job that they do not feel is an expression of their faith but that they continue in to support their families, as Miguel Cruz does, who works in information technology:

I've struggled with my job and with my career for *years* because I would rather be doing something that was more directly involved with the common good. I would rather be working with a non-profit, but non-profits don't make a lot of profit [laughing]. I've got a mortgage and two

daughters to send to college. I know that even that is a choice, I understand that. But if I'm going to make that choice, I'm going to do something else with my other choices so that that part of my life is aligned with
my faith. Those hours, the forty hours I spend at work, are not aligned,
are not allowing me to manifest my faith. That's okay, but I've got other
time, other opportunities where I can do that, and I need to do that.

Cruz's work gives him significant spiritual dissonance. It is not that he
is not involved in things and his guilt causes him to blame his job; he
sits on his parish council as well as the board of Catholic Charities and
is involved with Habitat for Humanity. He feels his work is a community
of neither sending nor gathering; it simply pays the bills. Not being able
to have one's faith in such a time-intensive part of one's life as work is
a problem that only the male grads mention. This may be because hus-
bands feel more pressure to seek high-wage jobs—which are often more
profit- than helping-driven.[43] It could also simply be that men are less
likely to pursue service professions.[44]

Ministries as Communities of Sending: Bringing Light to the Darkness

The main communities of sending the grads belong to are the ministries
they are involved in. As discussed in chapter 3, grads volunteer at a much
higher rate than the national average, with Catholic grads seven times
more likely to volunteer monthly than their co-religionists and Protestant grads five times more likely than typical Protestants. Although there
are a few cooperative endeavors, such as building raised garden beds at
the Catholic Worker or organizing medical supplies for shipments to the
global South, most grads engage society as individual volunteers and in
a variety of settings.

The first theme in grads' understanding of their sending is an acceptance of diversity among the various ministries in which they are
involved. Megan Simms, a retreat director in her thirties, says, "How
you express it looks really different from the way Martin Luther King
expressed it, which looks different from the way Dorothy Day expressed
it." The grads bring Eucharist to the homebound, tutor at learning centers, run shelters, lobby at Catholic Advocacy Day, promote fair trade

products within their parishes, organize their congregation to write letters for Bread for the World, walk in pro-life marches, serve and eat with homeless seniors, and engage in any number of activities that benefit those experiencing poverty and vulnerability. As they are typically sent forth as individuals, grads find projects that suit their interests and talents, unbothered that their own ministry is different from others in their group.

This is because, although their ministries take on many forms and serve different populations, grads see these as sharing a common element, namely that these serve the poor and vulnerable. Miguel Cruz elaborates: "Our shared belief, going to that of my perception of community, our shared belief is that Jesus represented something. What that something is may not have always aligned, but there were common threads, such as ministering to the poor and the needy. How each of us decided to manifest that in our lives might have been different, but we all believe that Jesus's life meant something and he was trying to teach us to minster to the needy and the poor." Some grads add that there are ministries their community members engage that are difficult or unsuited for themselves but that they nonetheless appreciate their efforts. Grads believe that all their ministries are grounded in a response to a personal yet universal call to follow Christ. Unity coheres their diversity.

Their service is also animated by the conviction that service is a necessary part of faithful living. James O'Reilly believes outreach is a fundamental part of being Catholic: "I think the message we most miss every Sunday at Mass is 'The mass is ended, go forth to proclaim the good news in the world.' That's what we're called to. We are called to do that. Being Catholic is not a spectator sport. We just don't show up for an hour and listen and stand up and sit down and kneel and receive the Eucharist and then just stick that on the shelf 'til next week." O'Reilly illustrates two things. The first is that people's religion must manifest in their daily practices. The other is a critique of Catholics whose idea of practicing their faith is limited to an hour on Sundays. Religion as practice must permeate daily life, which explains the angst of grads who do not find religious meaning in their paid work.

This demonstrates the other-regarding aspect of ministry for the grads. For a person to be uninvolved in improving the world is akin to not being a Christian at all. Grads continually speak of Christians' obligations to others, rather than viewing their ministries as "something extra." A theologian who speaks on a video in the GoodNewsPeople program criticizes a self-centered attitude:

> Living for others, living for others, altruism, does it make sense in the world that we live in today? No, no. If you think that the world we live in today operates on purely rational lines then no, living for others is not a rational pursuit. It is a super-rational pursuit. It is calling individuals— human beings—to live to their potential, not just to live at a rational level. If I simply want to live at a rational level, I'll look out for myself and I'll say, "I can manage on my own, you can manage on your own. You look after yourself and I'll look after myself. I won't get in your face, you don't get in my face." But the Christian Gospel is not just a piece of rational-political behavior. The Christian Gospel is a call to transcendence. It is a call to go beyond. It's a call to deliberately reach out. [Voiceover:] And in reaching out, we find the challenge of discipleship.

In a criticism of the wider culture, the speaker grounds Christians firmly in a calling higher than that which society extends. The Gospel, he contends, demands more than the self-interested or prosocial rational actor predominant in society.[45] The Gospel calls Christians to reach out for others, recognizing altruism as a "super-rational" part of the Christian faith.[46] Grads understand these ministry opportunities as religious practices. In ministry they act on the communities they are sent to.

Communities of Sending: The Problem of Solidarity

With few exceptions, grads have communities that gather them and separate communities to which they are sent. The discipleship style faces the same tension the historical styles faced: how to be in the world enough to change it without letting it change them. This challenge yields the dilemma of resistance; they resolve it by placing their communities that gather above those to which they are sent. The discipleship community, for example, is a place of moral and religious instruction that forms and encourages grads to act in the world.[47] The (moral) discipleship community acts *on* grads, and grads act *on* the (less moral) world.[48] This schema, while it resolves the dilemma, is in direct conflict with another important value for grads: solidarity. Solidarity warrants that grads work *with* the world.

There are two obvious options in this dilemma. The first is to privilege solidarity, abandoning the bifurcation between communities of gathering and sending, allowing religion and the world to shape one another. This risks the world corrupting discipleship Catholics' faith. The second is to privilege the sanctity of the communities that gather, forming volunteers who believe themselves to be morally superior to the world they serve.[49] This risks creating a paternalistic model of engagement.[50] JFM and the grads have found a creative third approach. They continue to divide the world into categories of gathering (more moral) and sending (less moral) at the same time that they enter into intense solidarity with those they serve. They do this by privileging their communities of gathering over the *world* at the same time that they enter into a relationship of solidarity with the *particular person* in need. They continue to see the *world* as a place of brokenness and darkness in need of their healing and light. They believe that the *world* that they go out into is inferior to the justice, mercy, and love of God they experience within their group. Yet the *individual people* who suffer offer wisdom and relationship to grads as they cooperate in the repairing of their shared world.

Resolving the Dilemma of Resistance: Relationship with the Poor

The importance of relationships for grads cannot be understated, with Helen Dalton explaining, "We're born into the world in connection—we were literally linked to another human being physically. And our first breath is only possible because of the trees that have provided oxygen and we are birthed into a web of relationships." Seeing relationships as an intrinsic part of being human reflects their notion of the human person as a socially embedded individual, drawing on both communitarian and individualist elements. The communitarian piece necessitates they pay special attention to solidarity, and the individualist lens affects the way they live out solidarity. Rather than aligning grads with a class of people—a more traditional approach to solidarity—the individualist aspects cause them to live in solidarity with particular individuals of a marginalized group. There are few opportunities for interclass relationships in the contemporary United States, and that grads are trying to foster these is significant.[51] By creating relationships with the poor, JustFaith resolves the dilemma of resistance, enabling grads to enter into solidarity with a person or a small group of people at the same time that they keep some moral distance from the world. These friendships are extraordinarily important to grads, the vast majority citing these as the foundation of their engagement.[52] Megan Sims implies that the relationship is more important than the actual helping:

> But it's that we're in this together, we exist at the same point of history together that my heart should be breaking because people are homeless, because people are suffering, because people are hungry, because people are dying, because people are alone and I have this shift in desire from wanting to *fix* something—wanting to *build* houses and *cure* a problem—to this deep personal connection that has opened in me a limitless well of care and moving from that desire to this one which makes me sadder and more heartbroken and more devastated and more [nine-second pause] more *connected*. It makes me in the muck with people . . . Somehow through relationships people are lifted up. [previously quoted]

This JWalking facilitator once measured her "success" in terms of how many houses she helped construct for her campus's Habitat for Humanity chapter. Now she, like many grads, concentrates on building relationships rather than houses. Some grads mention an absence of a relationship between other volunteers and clients, with volunteering being a good but not a complete investment of oneself for another. The safety behind the counter at a soup kitchen allows volunteers to see themselves as those who make an impact instead of being personally impacted.[53] Without friendship and affection, volunteers are people doing favors for recipients rather than friends engaging in mutual care or a more robust understanding of charity.[54]

This focus on relationship does not mean grads believe relationships need not yield concrete acts of care. Because religion is a practice, they believe that acknowledging the humanity of another necessarily yields acts of care, albeit with a different motivation than the typical volunteer. Helen Dalton exemplifies this idea when she says, "Eventually you might do something just because now you are friends but you don't do [it] with a sense of obligation—because you have and they have not. You go with a sense of, 'These are people I care about. These are people I know and I know their children and I know their story, and it sounds lot like mine.'" For grads, relationships cannot help but build solidarity and will naturally lead to practices that support the needs of the poor. They also believe solidarity is grounded in perceiving similarities between oneself and another rather than distinguishing between people as the volunteer model does.[55] Relationship, in sum, allows grads to reconcile the dilemma of resistance while maintaining solidarity.[56] Relationship also gives them, they believe, a more meaningful foundation for their engagement. That grads place so much value on their relationships is no coincidence. JFM intentionally cultivates relationships between grads and those less well-off through specific elements within their programs.

Strategies to Foster Relationships: Immersion and Reciprocity

The first strategy JFM employs is a formation program that encourages immersion while omitting service and a second is the framing of the relationship in terms of reciprocity and mutuality. Beginning with immersion, most JFM programs require participants to engage in immersion experiences, which are very different from service projects, as this grad shows: "So it was a huge group of young people who are all really, really engaged and interested in asking questions . . . at St. Vincent de Paul, which was like a transition housing/overnight emergency shelter. They just had a chance to hang out with them. There was no going to serve anybody. We weren't doing any service. We were just sitting and talking and we didn't serve at the kitchen, we just ate there." To have a service project distracts the participants from the purpose of the event, which is to hear stories of suffering or injustice and to be transformed by them. This transformation cannot happen, they believe, without relationship. Relationships with those on the margins cause participants to care differently, as well as fuel their desire to alleviate suffering.

Reciprocity helps both grads and those they become friends with feel as though there is a mutual give-and-take in their relationship, preventing the paternalism that many grads consciously avoid. Mike Campbell describes this: "You have empty bellies and you have empty lives. You may have full bellies, but the lives are empty. You may have full lives, but the bellies are empty. The only way to resolve one is to connect it with the other. Because each help each other. Because that engagement gives us purpose when our lives are empty . . . And it's that mutuality and relationship that brings us into wholeness." All people possess some type of wealth. Likewise, all have a hunger. By serving others, grads and the poor satisfy the poverty of each other. Megan Sims, who has facilitated numerous JWalking groups, illustrates this through an immersion experience:

> I take a group of generally rich, upper middle-class, white, Catholic school girls. Take twenty-four of them into [a community center] where there are refugee kids screaming and running around because it's so radically different and then give them the invitation to just get to know someone, just hanging out with them like you would with friends and just don't be afraid. And then in 30 minutes I come back in and it's like—so many times I felt myself laugh with tears because they were all playing a basketball game or something. Or here is this child who has lived through a civil war or something climbing in the lap of this girl who has had everything handed to her on this silver platter. And I don't know which one is having more fun. And it sounds so simple but I think that that's the radical nature of it. That's what causes people to care. Just to have space to. Because then when you know someone, you [care] and it only takes knowing a few people.

Grads believe that as those in poverty and the privileged get to know each other, they are likely to become friends. This is not unfounded as familiarity leads to friendship more often than it does not.[57] An encounter is even more likely to bring about friendship when people are explicitly seeking this and believe the relationship has a profound role in their life, as grads do. In emphasizing immersion and reciprocity, grads look for friendship with those on the margins and grant these relationships special meaning.

It is important to add that the quality of these relationships varies greatly. Some of the grads describe real friendships, in which they meet their less affluent friends regularly and include them in their social lives. For others, the relationship is more of a spiritual nature. For these latter grads, they may have met someone on an immersion trip and been touched deeply by his or her story. This experience might be a significant part of their personal transformation and inspire them to act for a specific social issue. These latter types of relationships are not friendships, yet they have real significance in the grads' ongoing formation.

Conclusion

Discipleship-style organizations deal with the dilemma of resistance in a particular way. They "gather" the faithful into community for important teaching and formation experiences, necessarily including intimacy and personal growth. Ideally, parishes and family members will promote the values of the discipleship community, but this is not necessary. Discipleship groups are the primary socializing agent, acting on participants to spiritually form them and reinforcing these values through regular meetings. As discipleship groups follow the ripple-group model, they differ from support groups with their expectation that members engage in outreach, bringing the values of the group into public life. The group "sends" members to act on their communities of the world: civil society, the workplace, and their ministries. Regarding the dilemma of resistance, JFM and grads have one foot in the church and the other in the world yet privilege their religious identity. Grads allow the discipleship community to have special influence in their lives, recognizing them as people worth emulating. They give a subordinate place to the world and perceive it as a place in need of healing through their service.

This schema puts JFM, as well as other discipleship organizations, in a precarious position as it is in direct conflict with a concept that is central to both JFM and grads: solidarity. As discipleship organizations resolve the American–Catholic tension, they create a new problem for living out solidarity as they conceive of the world as a place and people to act *on* rather than as a place and people to act *with*, as solidarity would recommend. This new tension can undermine these organizations' ability to instill a way of acting that both benefits society and promotes solidarity. The grads must choose to either be in solidarity with the world or understand themselves as coming from an enlightened position to assist those on the margins. Grads, however, circumvent this binary by amplifying another aspect of the style: the emphasis on relationship with individuals. The *world* is a place of darkness and suffering in need of light and healing that they, nourished by their communities, can bring. Yet the *people* they encounter are made in the image and likeness of God, possessing human dignity and goodness. These individual people allow grads to both form and be formed, offering relationships of equality and reciprocity even if there are considerable social differences separating them. By keeping their service commitments focused on the level of the individual, grads are able to be both American and Catholic, nourished by both their discipleship communities and those they serve.

This examination of community provides insight into the ways contemporary Catholics are interacting with civil society, including families, parishes, and other voluntary groups. This examination of community demonstrates that Catholics' engagement as individuals is a break from traditional bloc engagement, and it points them toward individual-level solutions. The other realms of society—the state and market—are not as directly related to community for the grads, yet this individualist focus remains. Grads seek to understand and interact with the state and market through the lens of justice. The core value of justice is discussed in the next chapter.

6

The State, the Market, and Poverty

Seeking Justice

It is warm and sunny for a February morning in Oakland. Most days, St. Lawrence Catholic School is bustling with the laughter and smiles of youth, 95 percent of whom are from low-income families of color. Being a Saturday, the grounds are quiet until the JustFaith groups from two parishes arrive for their Journey to Justice Day. Soon enough, laughter and smiles fill the grounds again, with the JustFaith participants sharing pastries and doughnuts and greeting their community members with hugs as they arrive.

At nine o'clock, the groups fill a third-grade classroom to hear from several people affiliated with St. Lawrence. The president of the school speaks first, explaining that typically she is involved in fund-raising and administration. However, owing to the high crime rates in the neighborhood, this is not always the case. She remembers trying to write a grant and suddenly hearing over a dozen rapid shots from an assault weapon. It was the end of the school day, and most children were waiting outside. She dashed out to the children; they knew what to do and were running into the gym. Once everyone's safety was established, she went back to her office. She juxtaposes her urgent response to the violence with the quotidian nature of grant writing, recognizing that both tasks are important in their own way and fundamental to her job. Next, the principal discusses Catholic identity within the school, evident in the classroom's prominent crucifix. She does not "water this down" for the non-Catholics as Catholicism is "the core" of St. Lawrence. A mother, Nellie, tells listeners that the school is an incredible blessing for her children. She was homeless and did not know how to provide her children what they needed. Nellie met a woman who helped watch her children, and this caretaker came to love them as her own. She became their godmother and encouraged Nellie to send the daughters to St.

Lawrence. Her children excelled there, they are now on the honor roll, and the oldest is doing very well at a local Catholic high school.

Participants gather into two groups for a short discussion of the parable of the Good Samaritan. A woman from one of the parishes that sponsors St. Lawrence gives a reflection on this passage, tying it to social sin. She paraphrases Martin Luther King when claiming, "What affects me directly affects all others indirectly." She follows this by asking, "What do we as a community do to others?" Thinking of social sin was, for this speaker, to consider how we harm others in ways that we do not realize, in ways that can be traced back to personal sin generations ago, such as contemporary inequality between black and white Americans stemming from a history of slavery. As she elaborates social sin in practical terms, her understanding is less about social patterns, culture, or law and more about individuals going along with or breaking established conventions.

After a fifteen-minute break, two groups funded by the Catholic Campaign for Human Development speak. The first is a child-care advocacy group that began as a small group of low-income mothers forced to choose between low-income jobs that cannot cover child care or paltry welfare benefits. They creatively chose a third way, forming a babysitting cooperative. From these humble beginnings emerged a whole legislative group. They initiated serious change, including overturning California governor Arnold Schwarzenegger's line-item veto of Stage Three child care, the last stage of child-care assistance before financial independence. The second organization is a faith-based community organizing group that is currently working on getting free bus passes for all Alameda County youth. Helping to represent them, a 13-year-old—who begins shy but quickly becomes more self-assured—explains the benefits these bus passes would bring her and her classmates, many of whom miss school when their family is short on money. A JustFaith participant asks these groups how they understand charity and justice. A woman from the community organizing group responds that traditional mercy ministries are very popular in parishes, but charity can prevent people from seeing things through a justice lens. She adds that too often, if politics becomes involved, parishioners will say that church is not the place for politics. A woman from the childcare advocacy group disagrees with the first part of the organizer's answer, saying that mercy and justice go hand in hand and that people must do both to get things done properly. Another woman from the community organizing group dovetails this, claiming that mercy is often a stepping-stone to justice work. After a pause, she adds that mercy without justice or justice without mercy are *both* empty and that they need each other to be truly Christian.

After two speakers from the diocese outline the local social ministry opportunities available to Catholics, the local JustFaith board member leads the group in a closing prayer. Bringing the group back to the Good Samaritan passage discussed earlier, she takes excerpts from the final speech of Martin Luther King before his assassination. In his speech, King speculates that perhaps the priest and the Levite thought the victim was faking his injuries to ambush them. They asked themselves, "If I stop to help this man, what will happen to me?" But the Good Samaritan reversed the focus: "If I do not stop to help this man, what will happen to him?" She asks the participants not to consider "If I stop to help, what will happen to me?" But rather, "If I do not stop to help, what will happen to *them*?" This is the question the participants wrestle with as they head home at the end of the day.

Contemporary society is characterized by highly specialized spheres, such as government, science, economics, family, and religion. Many assume that each of these independent spheres has its own logic and expertise. In this conception, religion should operate according to its own otherworldly logic, with little external regulation from or influence on the other spheres and affecting mainly personal matters.[1] Indeed, there are stronger correlations between religious beliefs and private matters than between religious beliefs and public opinions.[2] Religion-centering transformation, discussed in the third chapter, challenges these boundaries. Granted, grads value the country's religious pluralism and do not want any church body to legislate for the nation. Yet, they do not believe that the morality of scripture is to be limited to Sunday sermons or strictly personal choices, such as theft or adultery. Instead, the moral tenets of one's religion should be made primary and organize all the other spheres. This chapter examines the ways grads' religious beliefs shape their political and economic attitudes and practices.

Poverty is not a compelling issue for many Americans. This is demonstrated in the 2016 presidential debates, in which Hillary Clinton and Donald Trump used the words *poverty*, *poor*, or *low income* only seven times over the three debates. If the candidates were hoping to resonate with the voters, their choice of words reveals their priorities as well as those of the American people. This erasure of the poor from political life is a central concern for both grads and JustFaith Ministries (JFM). This chapter investigates grads' attitudes about justice through their understanding of the state and market.

Catholics in the Political Sphere: Contextualizing Contemporary Engagement

The Catholic vote has shifted considerably since its post–World War II days. Of white, non-Hispanic Catholics, in 1952, two-thirds were Democrats, and one-fourth were Republicans.[3] With the exception of their coalescing in the Kennedy election, Catholics gradually defected to the Republican Party until 1988. Along with a political fissure, Catholics developed progressive and conservative ways of understanding women, work, and family life.[4] Since *Roe v. Wade*, liberal causes have virtually abandoned religious rhetoric and conservatives display a corresponding increase. Americans of all stripes perceive the Republican Party to be "friendly" toward religion, and the Democrats, neutral.[5] As far as the religiosity of the two parties goes, Republicans are far more churched than Democrats, with 55 percent of Republicans attending church weekly or more and over half of Democrats attending several times a year or less.[6] However, this correlation between attendance and Republican identification is not present among Catholics. Among Catholics who attend Mass weekly, 34 percent are Republicans, and 29 percent are Democrats.[7] This negligible difference persists at all frequencies of Mass attendance. Catholics are one of the few larger Christian groups in which greater measures of religiosity do not correlate with increased conservatism.[8]

The inability of either party to woo the Catholic vote illustrates the poor match of the Republican and Democratic platforms with Catholic doctrine. Bay Area grad Michael Collins is unequivocal in his frustration:

I tended to vote Republican because they had a stance against abortion and I had a hard time feeling I could vote for someone who didn't have that viewpoint. But, there are just so many different issues and you can't just pick one and say, "Okay, because of that I am going to vote this way," if everything else you disagree with, and so there has been a struggle. I truly believe that I did not follow either the Democrat or the Republican political party completely 100 percent. There are elements of both that I agree with and there are elements of both that I disagree with and it's kind of frustrating as a Catholic Christian.

To outline some of these religio-political conflicts, the Democratic platform attracts Catholics insofar that it advocates for increased social spending for public goods like education, social security, and programs that directly aid the poor. Democrats are more welcoming of immigrants, are against the death penalty and are in favor of some sort of national health care scheme. They part company with church teaching when they argue in favor of abortion, same-sex marriage, and euthanasia. Republicans are in step with the church's stance on these latter issues; however, they advocate downsizing or completely eliminating various federal programs that serve the poor, marginalized, or public generally—often claiming that private associations or vouchers could handle the vast majority of issues. They also are more inclined to accept the death penalty and more restrictive immigration legislation. Both parties support fantastically high spending for the military, with the United States spending \$611 billion on defense in 2016.[9] This is more than the next eight countries *combined* and accounts for 36 percent of the *world's* total military budget. The *Catechism of the Catholic Church* and major leaders, while allowing for the possibility of a just war, have made it clear that with the sort of weapons that are used in modern warfare, it seems difficult, if not impossible, to execute a just war.[10] Furthermore, the United States Conference of Catholic Bishops has challenged US involvement in some of its more recent military attacks.[11] The issues that the church opposes and supports demonstrate that with American political lines drawn as they are, it is difficult for Catholics to enter the political system as Catholics.

Political attitudes among Catholics are complex. Holding demographic variables constant, white Catholics are 8 to 12 percent more progressive than white Protestants.[12] On nearly every issue—military spending, homelessness, welfare, and equal rights for women, minorities,

and those identifying as lesbian, gay, bisexual, transgender, and queer—
Catholics are more liberal than Protestants and usually more liberal than
every denomination of Protestantism.[13] However, many Catholics' political attitudes more often reflect those of their party, such as attitudes
on same-sex marriage or welfare spending.[14] Determining the effects
of Catholics' religion on their political beliefs is difficult. On one hand,
Catholics of both parties show large support for their bishops' call for
a more welcoming immigration policy, more government monies for
health care for poor children, and reduced spending on nuclear weapons.[15] On the other hand, Catholics of both parties dissent from the
church's opposition to the death penalty, with 68 percent of Republicans and 58 percent of Democrats favoring stricter enforcement. In sum,
Catholics embrace church teaching on some issues and are less warm on
others, indicating that the church, as well as general American political
ideology, influences Catholics' political attitudes.

Bringing Faith to Politics: The Role of Government

The relationship between church and state has a long and complicated
history in the United States and the grads have their opinions on the
proper relationship of these spheres.[16] Miguel Cruz wants to keep the
institutions of church and state distinct at the same time that he makes
sure his faith informs his political beliefs: "We don't live in a theocracy,
so I don't think we can expect our government to base their legislation on their religious beliefs. But, we allow our religious beliefs to
seep into the political discourse." Only 45 percent of grads, compared
to 68 percent of Americans generally, believe that the federal government should allow the display of religious symbols in public places,
reflecting grads' reluctance to bring these spheres to such close proximity.[17] However, they did not hesitate to bring their personal religious
beliefs to bear on their political values, with nine grads in ten disagreeing with the statement that their faith has very little to do with
how they vote and more than two-thirds strongly disagreeing. JFM
believes bringing faith to all spheres of life, including the political, is
very important. Religion-centering and religio-political transformation
facilitate this. Religion-centering transformation reorganizes grads' lives
so that all aspects are informed by faith. Religio-political transformation

illuminates the religious significance of political life. These transformations shape their notions of the role of government in ensuring justice.

The purpose of bringing faith and politics together is, according to grads, to build a more just, holier world. This hope propels their efforts to make policies that benefit the common good. Grads are remarkably similar to one another in their visions of the just and holy society, universally attentive to securing material needs and often including affective needs. Even Jeffrey Swimme, who wonders if, at times, some of the JFM messages are too idealistic, describes a just society as a place where "everybody would have enough to take care of themselves, would have a decent living with food, shelter, peace, harmony, compassion. I sound like a total bleeding-heart liberal!" Laughing at himself, he continues: "With a government in place that was willing to share those values and to help people achieve those things that everybody needs, or should have." Grads have criticisms of their government at the same time that they believe the state effectively promotes the common good.

Government: Special Efficacy for Systemic Problems

Grads describe social problems as enormous, structural and not easily fixed, as Jennifer Farrell of the Bay Area summarizes: "I feel like our system is set up to be that way. Like our whole system. I don't really know. We need people to work at the [drugstore], but you can't work at the [drugstore] and feed your family and yourself at the same time. You can't be below the poverty level, especially in California. We need people to work these low-wage jobs, but we make it impossible to live here and raise a family." Social problems are not simply a few families who need temporary shelter or a handful of children who need some extra tutoring. Instead, this grad argues, the structure of the American economy exploits and underpays significant segments of the population. At these employees' current level of pay, they are unable to secure even basic goods, let alone the education that might help them move to a different occupation. Additionally, even if that individual moves into a more financially secure position, the disadvantaged position remains. *Somebody* needs to work at the drugstore. Securing meaningful, dignified, and well-paid employment for all human beings is something that must be addressed at the structural level.

When people understand problems as systemic, they look to social institutions to address them. Political conservatives have criticized too strong a role for government, asserting that citizens and private associations can handle the problems of the day without governmental involvement. However, Methodist pastor Luke Dowell believes it is the responsibility of both governments and private individuals to work for the common good as best as they are able: "I think the strengths of political solutions are they can be so broad-reaching and they're a little more enforceable sometimes. And I think it's the safety net thing; they can cast a wider safety net. I think the faith-based thing, one of the advantages of that is it involves people and you engage your heart . . . in a political solution, you're not necessarily engaging your heart, you are enacting laws and that program and that kind of thing. So, I think there's a place for both [government and private initiatives]." Members of discipleship-style organizations reach out as individuals in fulfilling ways that make use of their talents. They also work within the political process to bring benefits to all those in need, as this strategy ensures that fewer people slip through the cracks. From free school lunches to health care, grads recognize the massive scope of some problems and believe that state provision ensures a fairer distribution of goods than a private initiative would. By assigning the state systemic or large-scale responsibilities, grads simultaneously carve out a social space where they can "engage their heart," as civil society is intimate and without the bureaucracy of the state.

The Common Good: A Cooperation between Government and Citizens

Grads imagine the common good as a cooperative project that state and citizens shape together in a collective moral enterprise. Martha Evans, who occasionally hosts Latina mothers and their children transitioning into independent housing as well as teaches at a Catholic middle school, emphasizes the necessity for cooperation between citizens and government: "There are good parts to government, bad parts, of course. I just think when we are all working together for the common good, I just think that's us at our best." Far from the caricature of the liberal promoting big government, JustFaith grads seek a participatory democracy.

Concern for the common good is one of the ways that Louisvillian Chris Miller brings religious values to the political realm: "I am looking at [the values of the Gospel] perhaps from the governmental perspective. We have a government, of the people, by the people, and for the people. And so, we all are focused on what we can do for the least of our brothers." Miller contends that the government, at its best, is not an impersonal, unwieldy bureaucracy. Government can and should be an articulation of its people's highest principles. This also reflects JFM's belief that the common good is not a secular, political concept with little import for one's faith. For grads, the common good is a religious concept that requires Christian citizens to take an active role in shaping society. Rather than a theocracy, it is government and citizens actively cooperating for the good of the community.

Grads see their personal good embedded in the common good. Although higher income is associated with a greater likelihood of Republican affiliation and half the grads make $90,000 a year or more, only 6 percent of grads are Republicans. This makes sense given the amenability of grads toward government assistance. Mike Campbell, creator of JWalking, uses the metaphor of a cookie to explain the ways the wealthier also benefit by providing public goods: "The one who got the smallest bite of the cookie is the one who wants things to be reorganized. Here's a way to reorganize that cookie so you get a little bit more. Well, that's great for [the one with less]. That's good news! But what about the person with the big half of the cookie? Is it good news for [the other] person? *Yes.* Because now you get to share and that's a good thing." Wealthy people might be materially worse off when they pay more taxes, yet spiritually they benefit knowing that their contributions allow a wider sharing of goods and improve the lives of others. And spiritual goods, he implies, are far greater than material goods. Matthew Collins presents his priest's teaching on the reciprocity in working for the common good: "I like what one of our priests said at the end of one of his homilies. He said that the poor need the rich so they don't starve to death and the rich need the poor so they don't go to hell. I think we need to be taking action to help people, but it's not so we don't go to hell, but for our own souls, our own growth, to be doing that." Collins appreciates his priest's concern for the poor, albeit transforming the warning of damnation into an opportunity to sanctify one's soul. Some admit that voting in a way that adversely affects one's finances is sometimes difficult, but even these people believe that providing for the common good is not a true sacrifice as it benefits all involved.

Criticisms of the State

Grads see the great potential of the state as well as its problems. At their most cynical, government—when it is poorly run—is the body creating the problems. Eleanor Smythe, whose experience as a high-ranking employee for the Centers for Disease Control and Prevention gave her much insight on American public policy, claims, "Our public policy is actually increasing poverty by the *dramatic* increase in inequality in this country. So, to *not* look at the government's role in either exacerbating or hopefully alleviating poverty is just futile." Smythe believes that bad public policy is contributing to the nation's problems at the same time that she sees government as holding the best solutions, capturing the frustration, as well as the paradox, in discipleship organizations' understanding of the state. Louisvillian Jeffrey Swimme believes that most of those with political power use it to further the interests of the wealthy: "Government should be responsible to fill the needs of those who have needs, that are hurting and need help. Give tax breaks to the people who need them as opposed to those who don't need them." In short, despite grads' view of the necessity of the state, they believe that government is fraught with problems.

Grads believe that both politicians and the public are more concerned with their party than the common good. More than three-fourths of grads are registered Democrat, and 85 percent identify as liberal or very liberal. However, they do not blame the problems in Washington exclusively on the Republican Party. Rather, they typically fault the politicians of both sides and Americans generally, saying most are too caught up in party platforms to seek compromise and the common good. Mark Bachman exemplifies this perspective in saying, "I think the whole divisiveness in the world today, that there is not room for much compromise for the two political parties. I don't think about it all the time, but if you really do think about it, it seems like we're not pulling together." Bachman, encouraged in JustFaith to sincerely consider differing views, is upset by the current state of political antagonism. This illuminates the importance of religion-centering transformation for the grads. JFM believes that when grads make their other identities—income level, political party, race, sex—secondary and their religious identity primary, they can reconstruct their political values on the basis of that faith, as Jezreel explains:

> We're very deliberate about insisting that we look through the lens of faith and then make our way to political choices . . . Let's start with Jesus, let's look at the Scriptures. Then let's look at the Church teaching and look at the lives of the saints. And look at the agencies that have evolved over time and *then* form political commitments, as opposed to carrying our political inclination like a football into the arena and looking for ways to make our *pre-existing* political commitment look more Christian by putting on sort of the veneer or the label related to that. And I insist that that's not for one political camp or another. It should be the way we enter into that dialogue between faith and politics.

By letting the values of the Gospels guide their political commitments, JFM believes grads will favor policies that alleviate the sufferings of the poor and vulnerable. Furthermore, despite the dominance of registered Democrats, grads do not believe that partisan loyalty will do much to solve the problem. Many criticize Republican policies even as they try to avoid demonizing any group, as Vicky Fuller, a Methodist lay minister, demonstrates when asked about her feelings toward conservatives who claim that Jesus is on their side: "Well, Jesus is on everyone's side, that would be my answer, but how we interpret is different whether it's judgmental and fear-based or whether it is really, truly love-based and acceptance-based." Rather than claiming that Jesus is on the side of political liberals, she brings Jesus to everyone, albeit asserting that any message from Jesus must be grounded in love, which may have political assumptions for her.

Another problem grads see in relying solely on the political arena is that the government is unequipped to handle certain types of problems. It is not a matter so much of bureaucracy or inefficiency—although many grads cite this—so much as they perceive some problems to be fundamentally personal. Grads believe that government can secure certain goods for its citizens, but it cannot change the minds and hearts of people, with Megan Sims saying, "Political solutions, they won't fix it. I'm talking about a real shift in consciousness." Discipleship groups take a ripple group strategy, transforming individuals so that they will transform society. Having experienced this transformation themselves, grads believe that more people must have a similar shift in moral worldview to enjoy a moral society. Although the government can raise the minimum wage, secure extra funding for low-income schools and families, and provide health care, it cannot, grads believe, change cultural attitudes or make the citizens more virtuous. Individual immorality and a disregard for the common good, even with the provision of basic goods, will still linger as a social problem unless people take intentional steps to change themselves and others.

Militarism: Regrettable at Best, Grossly Immoral at Worst

Grads are well aware of the vast amount of resources spent on the US military. They are correct in assuming there is strong public support for the military, as well.[18] Even with the teachings on peace that the Catholic Church proclaims, the American bishops are less vociferous here than are many other episcopal bodies worldwide, as this European-born staff member indicates: "In other countries there are not seven [social justice] themes. There are twelve or nine. And of course, the biggest one when I came to this country, I couldn't believe that *peace* wasn't one of the seven themes that bishops identified. And I know why they didn't, because it's the most militarized country in the history of the human race." Many grads believe that being entrenched in what they perceive to be a bellicose culture has hampered the ability of the church and individual Catholics to adequately challenge attitudes and policies on war.

Both pacifist and just-war stances are affirmed by the Vatican as legitimate moral positions.[19] Although a handful of grads are pacifist, the large majority articulate the just-war position, claiming that war can be a recourse if used rarely, generally reserving it for humanitarian intervention. Brian Dunn, a retired Louisvillian judge, says, "It'd be a beautiful world, a utopia, if we never had wars. And I think if you see some other nation just putting to death millions of people, I think you have to step in and do something, whether it's a war or some other means. I think you have to step in and do it. As a human being and as a nation you have to help other nations." War, in this scheme, is a regrettable decision that Dunn permits only when innocent lives are being lost and diplomatic means have been exhausted. Grads are, however, extremely dubious that most wars are waged to defend the innocent.

Instead, they believe that the vast majority of wars serve the interests of the wealthy and powerful. Janet Bolls, a Bay Area retiree who entered the Peace Corps after college, is angered by the greed she sees fueling wars:

> Our society is very strange in its adoration of the military; we thank every soldier for his service. Why is he there? Because he's serving the interest of some very rich people who are making more profits because *he's* willing to put his life on the line because he thinks he's doing it to save our country. He's doing it to save that rich guy's ass! It's the Halliburtons of this world that are the true evil people because really, they are sacrificing people's lives not only overseas, but our own young people's lives for their own benefit. And then couching it in terms of patriotism. I fail to see it as patriotic. If it's patriotic to serve your country, do you ever hear someone say thank you to a Peace Corps volunteer?! They have probably done more to engender good feelings overseas for Americans than any soldier ever has!

Bolls is representative of the others when she criticizes militarism and depicts the soldiers themselves as being deceived and taken advantage of. Wars, she claims, are not generally waged to prevent genocide or the oppression of a people. Governments levy wars because they, either directly or indirectly, will profit from them. To kill people in other countries or risk American lives for profit is a moral evil. Bolls also points out the intimate connection many Americans have drawn with the military and patriotism, claiming that we should instead laud peaceful efforts as a more authentic service to the nation.

These grads illustrate the ways power, structural issues, foreign and domestic policy, partisan conflict, and others share important relationships and overlap with one another. JFM programs, while they focus on poverty, do an excellent job of demonstrating the ways other issues are also connected to poverty and with each other.[20] The next section explores the ways grads connect poverty to other issues.

Politics and Poverty: Connecting the Dots

Grads and JFM care deeply about poverty. Yet, JustFaith grads are also enthusiastic participants in the JustMatters modules, which cover a variety of topics, such as prison reform, climate change, and life issues. They see these other issues as interconnected with poverty. Martha Evans, who teaches her Catholic school students Catholic social teaching, claims that issues like the environment and unemployment are felt most acutely by the poor: "I think people aren't getting their basic needs met: food, employment and then the environment. Because with climate change, I think it's affecting poor people first and foremost because those of us who are all better off had ways of dealing with it, whereas those who were very poor don't have ways to deal with it. And they bear the brunt of it." Wealthier people can use their economic advantages to secure goods and services in difficult times while the poor are left to cope with everything from unsanitary and distant water to inadequate education. This section demonstrates the ways grads learn to see connections between various political issues, beginning with poverty and then illustrating this interconnection through the abortion issue.

Poverty

Grads believe issues relate to poverty in both a structural and a personal context. Beginning with the structural context, Helen Dalton believes that there are systemic problems that keep the poor impoverished: "When you start to know someone who is homeless and realize he is disabled and so he can't work, so he can't pay the child support that he owes, so he can't get his criminal record expunged, so he can't get a job, so he can't make money, so he is going to stay on the streets." A person who cares about those experiencing homelessness, she argues, should also understand and work to change the social and legal barriers that they face, which are not only numerous but also perpetuate their poverty. This realization widens grads' and JFM's lens of focus to include a variety of issues that may not at first appear to be related to poverty.

Grads also believe that their personal practices affect the poor, with Lucy Russell explaining why she conserves energy: "When I got into JustFaith, there's a *huge* section on simple living . . . You're burning coal

to get that [electricity], which somebody mined, okay?! So, that connectedness on, where did it come from? Who needs it? Who's going to use it,
too?" Russell believes that using fewer resources honors the people who
produced and harvested the product as well as the others who need it.
Grads also are willing to pay more for fair-trade goods as they believe
this business model pays a living wage to the workers and encourages
environmentally sensitive agricultural techniques, creating a more just
and sustainable economy.

Issue Intersection and Abortion

Grads' understanding of abortion demonstrates the ways they connect
poverty to other issues. When abortion first became a major political
issue with *Roe v. Wade*, Democrats were more likely to oppose abortion
than Republicans due to the large numbers of economically liberal and
pro-life Catholic Democrats.[21] Since then, Catholic political activity has
been most prominent in the abortion issue with implicit—and sometimes explicit—support for the Republican party.[22] Although clergy
preach on a variety of issues, they have only been able to consistently
mobilize their parishes in the abortion issue.[23] The Protestant survey
did not contain a question that directly asked grads about abortion,
but the Catholic survey reveals that these grads have strong feelings on
abortion. One might expect them to be pro-choice, given the fact that
80 percent consider themselves liberal or very liberal and that they are
willing to part ways with church teaching—91 percent say that same-sex
couples should have the right to marry one another compared to just
under half of Catholics nationally.[24] Yet 81 percent of Catholic grads,
compared to 70 percent of Catholics nationally, say that the church's
teaching on abortion is somewhat or very important to them.[25] Despite
being progressive on many issues, the vast majority of Catholic grads
are pro-life. These progressive grads' pro-life tendencies might be counterintuitive, but they are unsurprising as other studies of progressive
Catholics demonstrate similar findings.[26] This is because grads, like
many Catholics, understand the abortion issue as a life or justice issue.[27]
JFM shows its concern for abortion when staff help authors revise books
used in JustFaith to make them more inclusive of the topic.[28] The way
grads understand abortion and other issues create a "moral context" for

grads; that is, they situate the specific issue within a larger political and religious frame. These moral contexts require that grads do three things: they frame the issue in social terms, connect the issue to others, and understand the issue through a consistent ethic of life. This example of abortion offers a specific and in-depth look at the moral context grads bring to political concerns more generally.

Grads view the abortion issue like they do many political issues: as something that is more a social issue than a personal issue. Abortion activists in the United States frame the abortion problem as one of rights: pro-choice groups emphasize women's rights and autonomy, and pro-life groups frame the debate in terms of the rights of the fetus.[29] The dominant frames do not resonate with grads as it forces them, in their estimation, to pit two vulnerable groups—unborn children and predominantly young and unwed mothers—against one another. They instead approach the issue socially, questioning the larger forces that give rise to unwanted pregnancies and the lack of support offered mothers postnatally. Margaret Wagner, a Southern California grad, illustrates the social frame grads use to understand abortion:

> I'm against abortion period. I think there is a legislative role to be played in the issue of abortion, but I don't think we can legislate abortion out of existence. And then the other side of it is that if we're going to have laws prohibiting abortion we need to have social programs in place to support the women who we insist should have these babies, bring them to full term. How are we going to help them out? What are we going to put in place to support that? So that's where I see the role of government. I believe abortion is taking a life and I think we should call it that. So when we call it a women's "choice" about her own body I think that's very misleading, I don't think it's the truth of the matter. But I see the complexity of it and I see the dilemma that's facing a woman who can't afford, doesn't have the skills, the facility, that support system, whatever, to bring this child into the world and so I think it's another very complicated issue.

Wagner frames the abortion issue as a structural issue. This allows her to see both women and the unborn as victims in a tragic situation, a situation that society can improve through the provision of material and affective support to women and children in need.

Grads also express their pro-life stance through their refusal to take a single-issue approach to abortion. They believe the abortion issue is connected to many other concerns, with preschool teacher Sharon Jones framing her pro-life stance as against racism: "[At a pro-life demonstration] there were a lot of women of color, especially Hispanic women, protesting when abortion was made legal. Because we said, 'We want education, we want health care for our kids,' and you say, 'Here's an abortion, we'll even pay for it.' They see it as outright genocide for people who are down and out." She claims marginalized groups—and those who stand in solidarity with them—believe an abortion-on-demand policy allows the state to justify not providing social services for children and families, disproportionally affecting those of lower income and people of color.

Seeing abortion as connected to a variety of other issues makes these Catholics—who want to support all vulnerable groups—frustrated when they enter the political arena. They vote for politicians based on all the issues they represent, making it exceedingly difficult to find a candidate that supports life from conception to natural death and every point along the way, as Pete London expresses:

> I had a real tough choice when Dukakis was running in '88 against Bush . . . And I really thought about voting for Bush because of the abortion thing. Finally, after a lot of time and thought and prayer, I decided I couldn't vote for the one issue. I could make a case to vote on the one issue, but I'd be saying no to a lot of things I really believed in what Dukakis was in favor of, [things like] helping out the marginalized. So I ended up voting for Dukakis even though I was not happy with his position on abortion. And I'm afraid I've had to do that a number of times since then. I think Obama's pretty soft on it, if I take a look at what he's going to give us versus what the Republicans offer.

London weighs the candidates very carefully, discerning which candidate's platform best supports life issues, and he is usually disappointed with aspects of each. Mike Campbell is just as frustrated with his fellow Catholics, including many bishops, who understand abortion only as a personal issue and do not see its connection to other issues: "So to the degree that you can be a pro-gun, anti-environment, pro–death penalty, anti-abortion Catholic legislator and get voted and get endorsed by, largely *passively* endorsed by, the Church institution because of that last one. And all those other things don't count." He argues that divorcing a candidate's position on abortion from other political concerns warps or diminishes the full scope of Catholic social teaching, inadvertently promoting numerous social ills.

Grads also express their pro-life position when they advocate for a "culture of life." The notion of a culture of life appears in the *Didache*, some of the earliest nonbiblical Christian writings.[30] The church's promotion of life in the fabric of personal and social existence is reiterated in contemporary church documents.[31] Father Ryan Delaney, who has participated in JustFaith, illustrates the pastoral frustrations of bringing American Catholics divided by party lines to a consistent ethic of life:

> I used to have a lot of people who went to school in the '60s and early '70s, were anti-war, anti–Vietnam war, and yet were very pro-abortion. Then other people were pro-war, bomb-the-hell-out-of-whoever-it-is, but anti-abortion. And they're not being consistent. But both of those issues are connected and I think Cardinal Bernardin's[32] great gift to the Church—that seems now to be not paid attention to—is the consistent ethic of life. And it's from womb to tomb and all of those issues are important and the womb is not more important than euthanasia is, but how do we deal with those.

Fr. Delaney knows firsthand the difficulties in pointing Catholics to a culture of life, here discussed as a "consistent ethic of life," given the extant political ideologies of the country. A culture of life will permeate the social and political landscape, necessitating a multi-issue approach to the abortion problem as James O'Reilly learned when he worked at the family homeless shelter:

> The great gift of meeting people in the [family homeless] shelter is that I think as a society we fail women as girls, we fail men as boys and then we get all up in arms once they're in a predicament where a birth is imminent and a decision about abortion is imminent. And in all of the debate, we don't ever go back and say but what were we doing to help those children grow up in a healthy family and get a great education, have enough

food to eat, have a stable place to live, their parents have the support they needed to have meaningful employment, all of those things. So, when I look at right to life, those are also rights to life that we have to own. So, it's bigger than just a narrow piece of it and I think that when I get caught up in debate with that, that's where I go.

When society promotes a complete culture of life, according to O'Reilly, it promotes the whole panoply of issues and policies that ensure individuals will flourish and grow to their greatest potential. A consistent ethic of life is both personal and structural, both material and psychosocial. It is a concern for the whole society and the whole person from conception to death. It is demanding, yet grads believe it is attainable. These three expressions of their pro-life stance—that issues have structural implications, that issues are connected to one another and the promotion of a culture of life—constitute the grads' moral contexts, which situates the concern or policy in a wider cultural and religious frame.

JFM, the Market, and the Dilemma of Efficacy: Focusing on Consumption

In chapter 5, we examined the role of community in the grads' life, illustrating their understandings of the various communities that comprise civil society. The discussion in the first part of this chapter explored their understandings of the state. This chapter finishes by examining the final component of society, the market. Numerous Catholic documents critique capitalist markets.[33] Grads have ambivalent feelings about the market and wealth. The individualist focus of discipleship-style organizations shapes their understandings of the economy, emphasizing consumption and lifestyle changes over production and structural changes. This is at loggerheads with the priority both JFM and grads grant justice. This individualist focus also gives rise to the dilemma of efficacy: Should one remove oneself from places of social and economic power to more deeply live in solidarity with those excluded from power or should one remain in these positions and use one's power for the excluded? This poses a serious difficulty for grads, as we will see after first defining their understandings of the economy as a sphere of both production and consumption.

The Economy: Disparity

An important theme many grads bring up when discussing the economy is disparity. Socioeconomic disparity prevents people of different backgrounds from having equal access to goods that have significant impacts on their life outcomes.[34] This economic gap has been steadily growing in the United States since the 1950s, when the middle class was strongest. Then the top 1 percent earned 13 percent of household income, compared to 2015 when they earned just over 20 percent of household income.[35] Sharon Jones believes this income gap makes it difficult, if not impossible, for the poor to live a decent existence: "I think the gap between the rich and the poor is *huge* and getting bigger! I think that's the biggest [problem], I think there are so many more problems. I would sure like to see a little shift there—at least the super-wealthy pay their fair share of taxes so that the poor can have a decent life. Even the middle class is getting slammed." Some believe that this material disparity leads to political or social disparity, with the poor having less time and money and therefore less able to advocate for their interests. Others claim that the tireless pursuit of wealth has caused Americans to instrumentalize and disregard the poor while other countries have a greater appreciation of life, with Janet Bolls saying, "It isn't just the poverty that exists in third-world countries where they make less than a dollar a day—although that is terrible—sometimes they're not as poor as the people in the inner city right here in Oakland. A lot of those folks [living in a poorer country] live in a culture that is life-affirming and people are not discarded; they're taken care of to the best of the society's ability. We discard people here. The grinding poverty that exists in this country is in relation to the *obscene* riches that these people can see and not touch." Bolls claims disparity is an even bigger problem in the United States because of both cultural reasons—that Americans and their government neither value nor care for the poor—and material reasons—the poor in America, unlike those in a village in a poor country, are continually reminded of what they lack. This concern with disparity demonstrates that it is not just poverty that is a problem for grads; it is also the immense wealth flaunted so near to the poor.

Critiquing Production: Profits and Alternatives

Grads have relatively little to say about the sphere of production. The most common criticism is that the sphere of production has become so profit-driven that it ignores the rules of morality. Lucy Russell critiques the primacy of profit grads believe pervades large-scale businesses today: "You don't take God's mountaintops off because you want the coal underneath, then you don't pay your miners a living wage! . . . Church brought us the message, 'I am my brother's keeper' . . . And then, we find from the statehouse that this is a *national* problem created by national conglomerates coming into Kentucky, grabbing all our coal, cheap coal, going out, and *hauling* it off to other metropolitan areas for creating electricity for them. And they're raping our land!" Russell illustrates a common theme in grads' assessment of the sphere of production: large corporations are usually willing to do whatever it takes to make the most profit. This is not to say that generating profit and growing the economy are bad, far from it. The problem, as grads see it, is that when the bottom line is profit, this overrides justice, costing people their livelihoods or lives. Many grads support fair-trade items when possible—as mentioned earlier, one group of grads opened a fair-trade store—in order to circumvent this profit-at-the-expense-of-justice model.

A handful of grads attempt to rethink how they participate in the economy. The Gospels, the book of Acts, and religious and lay communities all offer alternatives to a conventional economy. Jezreel, likewise, says that his experience in the Catholic Worker Movement challenged dominant ways of understanding the economy: "Everything about the Worker is meant to be personalist. So how do you personalize things that sometimes we industrialize? The Amish may have the best health care system in the world. First of kin takes care of the elderly, for example. There's no negotiating, that's what it is. But it makes it personal instead of institutional, industrial." Some grads sell their homes to live in community with one another, and one grad says that she and her Just-Faith group acted as a member's primary caregivers in the last months of his life. These alternative economies happen, but they are the exception. Grads, when considering the production of wealth, tend to take for granted the economy they criticize—even as they participate in it.

Critiquing the "Culture of Consumption": Lifestyle Changes

While only a handful of grads criticize production, they vociferously object to what they identify as a culture of consumption in American society, as Sister Ruth Bosco of Louisville illustrates: "That it's all just a matter of buying, buying, buying and purchasing and it is—it's that false thing of how much you need in order to be happy, whereas I think all of us know that doesn't make us happy. I think we all know that, but we keep getting sucked in by it, that same message and it's there, so much trappings of—we are such victims of it." This culture of consumption has material, ethical, and spiritual consequences.

Sociologists corroborate this culture of consumption.[36] If one compares spending habits of Americans between 1959 and 2000, there is a marked increase in spending on oneself of nonessentials, such as dining out, toys, live entertainment, and travel, at the same time that charitable giving decreases.[37] Some of the noteworthy expenditures are that Americans spent $92.9 billion on nonalcoholic beverages in 2004, more than $100 billion per year on fast food in the early part of the century, and $288.7 billion on domestic travel and tourism. This indicates that people have discretionary income; it is simply that they would rather spend it on themselves than make charitable donations.

One danger grads identify in this culture of consumption is the ease with which it creates greedy people. Laura Dowell, a Methodist lay minister who helped produce a major play that promoted social justice, claims that this culture of consumption makes selfish behavior the default among Americans: "The other reason I think people don't get involved is because I think ultimately just a lot of people, even where they don't want to be, are really selfish. They'll say, 'Let me give at the end of the day when I was living to standards I want to live [by]. When I was able to go get my third latte for the day and go out to a nice dinner and this, we'll see what's left then.' So it's all about throwing the scraps to the dogs." Dowell claims American culture condones and encourages self-centered behavior, leaving people very little money or spirit with which to be generous. Greed also has material repercussions as spending on oneself causes there to be less money to share with others. Poverty is not a matter of absolute scarcity; it is a problem of greed or a lack of awareness. Greed hurts everyone, both the materially poor and the spiritually poor.

This hefty consuming also stresses the environment. Bay Area resident Mark Bachman believes American consumption monopolizes resources, which is taxing on the planet: "It frustrates me when there are people who feel like God gives us this Earth to exploit to a certain extent. Like we're here to eat cows, build places for our own . . . I think we should be good stewards of the Earth." To *take* goods from the earth is different from cultivating it and accepting what it yields, and grads worry that Americans have long crossed the line, pulling resources from the planet at an unsustainable pace. Episcopalian deacon Diana Stewart argues that not only does this mass-consumption result in scarcity for some but that it also damages the environment through excessive waste: "We have had the great American dream that you can be successful and buy, buy, buy and get everything you want. And people did that and we're destroying the world and taking more than our fair share. The amount of trash and it just goes on and on and on what our lifestyle has done to the world. And we need to wake up and redream." As people opt for the convenience of disposable goods or the markdown of poorly made furniture and electronics, they are opting for quickly consumed, rather than durable, goods. This generates larger amounts of waste, even more so when one accounts for the energy required to build and ship items. In sum, consuming at an American pace, grads aver, has devastating effects on the environment.

Grads also bemoan that this culture of consumption has become so normal to Americans that it seems almost heretical to abstain from it through voluntary poverty, a centuries-old Catholic discipline. Living in actual poverty was rare among grads, with only one grad living below the poverty line[38] and 88 percent with household incomes of $50,000 or more.[39] Only a handful of grads go so far as Eddie Brown does to recommend poverty as a Christian rule: "It's almost like an unwritten, unspoken interpretation—stewardship—that you give your 10 percent of time, talent, and treasure, and you can do whatever you want to with the 90 percent. It ought to be you give 100 percent of your excess, 100 percent of your excess, 10 percent of your need to those who have more need than you until you can't find anyone that has more need than you. And then we've all got what we need and we're all happy and it's one big community." Even Brown, while he extolled the virtues of poverty, mentioned his own comfortable living and wished he were not so worried about money. Grads often found themselves in a difficult tension, admiring Catholics such as St. Francis of Assisi and Dorothy Day while they sheepishly admitted that they were not able to embrace poverty in the same way. The taken-for-grantedness of "stuff" has affected even those who enter professed religious life and take vows of poverty, as Sister Ruth Bosco can attest to: "We are extremely middle-class believe it or not. I do live with three other sisters, we do live in a neighborhood that is not considered the finest in the city, a lot of poverty. So I think we face that same struggle. I look around my bedroom in my house and I have a bedroom. I'm not sharing it with anyone else, which people in poverty would be doing that. And yes, I have a computer and so there are many things that I have that people in poverty don't have." Although Bosco's material indulgences consist of her own room and a computer, her point is that this is not truly poverty and is more akin to simple living. Simple living was a typical option for grads, forgoing total poverty and instead reducing their consumption.

A final consequence of a culture of consumption, according to the grads, is that it makes life more complicated than it should be, distracting one from the things that matter most. Grads believe they have significantly cut back on their use of resources since JustFaith, with 90 percent of Protestant grads indicating on their survey that it is "very" or "somewhat" important to consume fewer goods in order to be a good person compared to 61 percent of mainline Protestants nationally.[40] Grads are deliberate in weighing the necessity of an item before purchasing it, as Tammy Czap of the Bay Area asks herself, "Do I need it? How many do I already have? Is there anything I already own that I could substitute for it?" She is very careful in her assessment of needs and wants and strives to forego unnecessary things. Megan Sims is aware of the comforts in her life and reduces them without eliminating them: "I know how many pairs of shoes I have; I know how many shirts I have; I know how much I have. And that's not so that I have this crazy attachment to it, but it's so that I keep myself in check so that I don't have too much. I do have too much, let me restate that, of course, I have too much." Simple living poses a precarious tension for grads, with Sims demonstrating this in real time, as they attempt to navigate their own wants and needs with the wants and needs of others.

This insight offers an important caveat for simple living in the lives of grads: simple living is not an end in itself. Simple living for grads ensures that resources are spread more evenly. The importance of this motive cannot be understated, and an outside speaker at a JustFaith meeting illustrates this. The speaker was an accomplished author and radio-show host and advocated simple living for the benefits it brought the individual rather than others. He said people may direct their saved time or money toward others, for travel, for learning an instrument, or for participating in community theater, each option listed as morally equal to the others. The moral division was revealed early on when the speaker suggested that people should buy clothes as cheaply as possible to save money. When JustFaith participants asked about unfair wages or environmentally damaging practices that some companies allow in order to reduce costs, the speaker said it sounded "jingoistic" and that third-world workers are better off with low-wage jobs than none at all and did not address the environmental concerns. This began a series of escalating political and ideological disagreements—most pointed when a participant asked him to stop speaking poorly of unions—that culminated in the speaker's abrupt departure. Other instances of the other-regarding motivations for simple living are far less dramatic, with Caroline Dunn saying, "And it used to be I'd get so many catalogs and just a few requests for money. And now I get *way* more requests for money than catalogs. I think that's a really good sign." Dunn and other grads, in sum, practice simple living in the hope that these sacrifices will have a positive impact on the world around them. It also serves as both an involvement and abandonment mechanism, signaling to themselves and others that they have rejected part of their former lives and embrace a new alternative.[41]

It should be noted that simple living is much more ambiguous than a vow of poverty, causing grads to continually discern their choices and clarify their needs and wants. This constant examination leads them to question how they can be most effective with their material possessions. Should Christians take seriously the vow of poverty and work for little money, living on bare necessities, with little to share? Or should they remain in their careers, working—as some do—in fields that have little to do with poverty or justice yet give them the social or economic power to foment change? I call this problem the dilemma of efficacy.

The Dilemma of Efficacy: Downward Mobility or Reform and Generosity

Grads learn two mutually exclusive life practices in the JustFaith program. The first practice is "downward mobility," and the second is "reform and generosity." Downward mobility is akin to voluntary poverty but typically less extreme. Those who practice downward mobility usually work in nonprofits full- or part-time and live in low-income areas of their city. They shop at thrift stores and give large portions of their income away. This is a typical evangelical-style arrangement, exemplified by a Catholic Worker, but individuals or families can practice these without living in intentional community. Reform and generosity is a two-part practice.[42] Reform means challenging the social and economic structures that compose one's world.[43] Rather than leaving their for-profit tech job, for example, they seek to push the company to become more centered on the common good. Even when this strategy is not effective, their lucrative careers set them up for the second part of the practice: generosity. Generosity compels grads to use their personal wealth or influence to transform the situation of the poor rather than reserve it for their personal benefit. There are many examples of downward mobility in JFM programs and significantly fewer with a message of reform and generosity, illustrating the organizational bias toward the former. Grads also hold downward mobility in high esteem—the Catholics more intensely so than the Protestants—yet most feel resigned to practicing reform and generosity. Grads navigate this dilemma by emphasizing the importance of simple living and claiming that by remaining within their position of economic or social power, they are better able to help the poor than they could if they abandoned their post.

JFM demonstrates their organizational preference for downward mobility within their various materials. For example, one of the books features biographies of contemporary Christians active in peace and justice issues.[44] Here the participants read about Dorothy Day, Fannie Lou Hamer, and others who committed their lives to tirelessly work for the welfare of others. Some made great sacrifices of popularity or comfort when they began working with marginalized groups. In Engaging Spirituality, JFM provides confidential letters to be read each session. The vast majority of these "bearings letters" are written by people who work in occupations that are directly related to peace or justice, and many live in intentional communities that practice voluntary poverty. Grads have an affective preference for this practice, with many saying they admire those in Catholic Workers and claiming they are not personally brave enough or ready to embark on that ministry. A JFM staff member is concerned that those who work in conventional jobs rationalize their positions: "The grads who are struggling with downward mobility, and probably what is my judgmental take on that, which is it sounds like justification—and that totally could just be me being judgmental. But I do those same justifications. Not that I have $50,000 dollars to give, but my small things. Like I want to go on a vacation this year. Could I do something else with that money? Yes, so I tend to think that those kinds of struggles would be redefined if they were in a group with people who need more in order to have enough." This staff member worries that those who remain in their previous occupations compromise too much, with large donations distracting them from the fact that they also spend large amounts on luxuries, a problem she admits to struggling with as well. Although a handful of grads echo these concerns, the dominant practice is a reluctant approach of reform and generosity.

As for reform, this is more difficult than its partner of generosity as it requires the transformation of one's company or field. Rather than direct reform, which requires considerable effort, grads bring their skills from their jobs to serve the marginalized, either in a paid or volunteer context. A lawyer engages in *pro bono* work to help refugees gain asylum, a retired accountant manages the books for a Catholic school in inner-city Los Angeles, and Therese Brewer, a medical researcher, finds ways to support poorer countries: "This just spoke to my faith directly, how to support the third world in the best way that you're able to. Not a lot of people know how to do molecular virology and I do. So I think I ought to stop hanging out at homeless shelters and making meals for people. That's kind of how I came to it, although I miss it very much." Brewer lived in a Catholic Worker for six years and has practiced voluntary poverty; during that time a suitcase and a filing cabinet held all her possessions. Although she was doing necessary work—feeding the hungry and housing the homeless—she knew other people could do that and that few are competent in molecular virology, pushing her to pursue the latter. Grads vary in their evaluation of their work's impact on the poor. All of them, however, make poverty a high priority, and this shapes the way they work and spend their time and money.

Generosity is a very important practice among grads, but some struggle with this idea more than others. Part of the difficulty with ideas like "simple living" and "generosity" is that they are not as clear as "downward mobility." That is, generosity requires serious discernment from grads, leaving them unsure as to whether they are being adequately magnanimous. Many worry that some of their comforts are excessive or selfish as Caroline Dunn of Louisville demonstrates: "It's partly rationalization because I remember going to a JustFaith meeting and coming down our street looking at our house, and I thought 'Oh, we oughta sell this house and get a little apartment.' I thought, 'Oh, no. My cousin from Cambodia lives here and we have all these priests coming for dinner all the time.' So, you can justify why you're doing it." Grads use Dunn's words *rationalization* and *justify* many times when talking out this tension. They recognize the value and importance of money at the same time that they worry they are justifying the comfort they enjoy. Generosity is important, but they are generous through their economic and social privilege. Simultaneously, these grads put forth reasons for remaining in positions of wealth or power that they believe ultimately aid the poor. This ambiguity leaves many grads unsure if they are living as simply and generously as they would like.

Some grads worry less about their own or others' wealth. Wealth and fortune are fine so long as they are used abundantly for others, as Methodist lay minister Laura Dowell claims: "If I was making six figures and sitting on a board and that was giving away six figures and blah, blah, blah, would I sit? Absolutely, because compassion is huge but money needs to be there, too. I think to pretend you go into this place of poverty and living in a simple poverty sort of thing so you're in tune with God more . . . but people can't live on my compassion. They can feel it, but their stomach still hurts at the end of the day when they don't have food in their mouth. There's nothing that makes me happier than taking money and giving it to people who need because that can make a difference." Dowell values wealth and believes that Christians can engage in holy living by making large sums of money and sharing it equitably.

If JFM hopes to instill a practice of downward mobility among grads, then they have failed. Grads embrace—some tentatively and others enthusiastically—a practice of reform and generosity. And perhaps this failure is actually a huge success for the organization. Remaining in positions of wealth and prestige grants grads greater social influence. Working in lucrative jobs while living simply allows them to share financial resources with organizations that promote the common good—organizations, incidentally, such as JFM. Balancing their lifestyles with the needs of the world is a serious dilemma for grads. This dilemma of efficacy may characterize many organizations of the discipleship style. As Catholics rise in socioeconomic status, they have more wealth to offer a variety of social causes. Having a tradition that is more suspicious of wealth than many Protestant denominations, Catholics are unsure how to reconcile their wealth with others' needs. A practice of reform and generosity allows them to go about their daily lives as Catholics in a way that reflects their commitments to the poor.

Charity, Justice, and the Dilemma of Volunteerism

When there is a social problem—be it in the realm of the state, civil society, or market—it can be approached with a strategy of charity, justice, or both. Charity meets specific, immediate needs, and justice works to reform social structures. The difference between charity and justice is akin to, as the saying goes, giving a person a fish versus teaching a person to fish (and providing a fishing pole and lake access). The upsides to charity and justice are that the former satisfies needs right away and the latter makes future provision unnecessary. The drawback to charity is that it requires a constant stream of resources and the downside to justice is that it can take considerable resources to achieve reform. Both are expressed in American Christianity. Social expressions of charity include food pantries, homeless shelters, and the underground railroad. People can express a justice-based approach to the problems of hunger, homelessness, and slavery by setting aside land for community gardens, advocating for subsidized housing, and becoming an abolitionist. JFM encourages their participants to utilize both these strategies as they ameliorate social problems.[45] However, despite the encouragement from the readings and the speakers, grads generally pursue works of mercy rather than justice. This is the dilemma of volunteerism, and it is faced by grads, JFM, and justice-based discipleship organizations.

The Greatest of These Is Charity: The Value and Limits of Charity

Grads believe that charity is an essential Christian virtue. The Catholic Church defines charity as the virtue by which Christians love God and neighbor and that charity brings joy, peace, mercy, and a desire to serve one another.[46] Staff member Cathy Meyers believes that churches are doing well on the charity front: "I think the Catholic Church and most churches get an A-plus for getting people involved in direct service and we will always need to have that. We always need to feed hungry people. You don't go out lecturing about, 'Why is there hunger?' when there are people in front of you starving to death. You need to feed them." From Catholic Charities to Catholic Relief Services to St. Vincent de Paul societies, grads are pleased with the charitable endeavors of the churches. Most say that they would like to see even more activities, especially at the parish level. Charity, in and of itself, is a worthwhile endeavor that JFM promotes and grads embrace.

Despite this esteem for charitable endeavors, retiree Matthew Collins recognizes the practical limits of charity: "I feel that churches and me as an individual also have an obligation to contribute and do whatever we can, but my feeling is that it is just going to be like a drop in the bucket." Collins says that with all the need that is out there, the impact of his efforts, or even that of his parish, will be negligible. This is a reasonable assessment as, on average, only 4 percent of a church's budget goes to direct assistance or outside organizations.[47] Joyce Roberts, a San Francisco–area grad, claims the state is better able to bring about social change: "I remembered as a kid you would never see an African American as a clerk in a store or a postman, obviously not a doctor or lawyer. Then there was a change in the law and suddenly it was just very normal for African Americans to have good jobs, we thought, 'Oh, it's just the way it is,' because the structure had changed, the law changed. There's no way that churches can do that." Roberts recognizes the ways wider social forces, in this case, law, constrain or enable individual actors, giving rise to cultural patterns. Later, Roberts is more pointed in her concerns over charity: "There's no way, that with the amount of poverty, even in our country, the church working day and night on the thing, the church is really going to have a—okay, let me put it this way: we have to change structures." The scope of the social problems is so enormous that individual or congregational generosity will not meet those needs.[48] Instead, the very structure of society must change. The practical limits of charity direct grads to justice.

Justice: The Little-Known Solution

Justice is a core value of JFM. The attention JFM and grads give to justice specifically sets them apart from discipleship organizations that opt for a more charitable approach to outreach. Because they see social problems as structural, they believe that lasting solutions must change structures, with JFM staff member Cathy Meyers saying, "And for the majority of people who are starving to death, it isn't because they're lazier than I am and they don't have the same work ethic that I do, or that they aren't just as good of a human being as I am; it was circumstance. I was born into a middle-class family, in a small town with a great public school system— all the advantages I had that people who were born in poverty don't have." Meyers contends that when people have the proper tools and opportunities for growth throughout life, they will succeed. The question as grads see it is, How does one create a just and equitable society that will foster the well-being of its members? This socio-ethical frame prompts grads to solve social problems at their roots, encouraging them to educate fellow citizens on the importance of justice-based strategies.

They also believe that Americans have a myopic view of social outreach and need education on the importance of justice-based approaches to social problems, summarized by board member Claire Sullivan: "I truly feel we are stuck in the charity mode." Sullivan's blunt assessment is not unfounded as many other people associate "volunteers" with words like "caring, kind-hearted, and unity" and "activists"—those who engage in policy and justice work—with words like "anger, corruption, unhappy, and hippie," in addition to a few positive words like "transform, awareness, and challenge."[49] This sentimentalism toward volunteers and adverse ambivalence toward activists has skewed civic activism in the United States: a quarter of Americans say they engaged in civic associations or community service several times or more in the last twelve months, and only 5 percent say the same for participation in political parties or organizations.[50] Furthermore, Catholics' embrace of charity has masked the fact that some are not accepting of their church's teachings on justice, complicating the practical relationship of justice and charity.[51] JFM contends that charity and justice are both necessary responses to human suffering, as Jezreel states: "Charity, or mercy, that sort of one-on-one flavor, that *has to* morph into a justice perspective because they are twins ... And they're joined at the hip. You *really* can't do one without the other. If you don't care enough about me to care about whether my kids have an opportunity, then you really don't care about me. You're doing something else." True love and concern for the plight of those who suffer must give rise to meeting a person's immediate needs as well as a commitment to structuring society in such a way that allows people access to the goods and opportunities they need to flourish. Any charity that does not point the volunteer toward justice is "something else."

Grads also believe that justice is more effective, as charitable approaches only alleviate immediate problems momentarily. Staff member Ronald Jelenic highlights the efficiency of justice over the long term: "We have to write checks. That's part of the deal ... And you begin to understand what systemic change is about so that, 'We gotta do this other thing or we're not gonna ever stop writing checks. We're not gonna ever stop carrying signs if we don't get to the systemic issues involved in stopping war, stopping poverty, ending trafficking, whatever it may be.' And then roll-up-your-sleeves, hard work that takes sustaining, strategic, long-haul kind of things." Jelenic points out that the needs are endless if society only takes a charitable approach to an issue. He acknowledges that charity is important, as there are pressing needs that must be handled today. Still, he argues, people must also engage in systemic change if the problem is to be truly solved. Given grads' strong support of justice one would assume that they regularly engage in structural-level activism. However, this is not the case. There are important individualist elements in the program that frustrate JFM's mission of justice in partnership with charity. This conflict that grads feel toward involvement in structural change and individual charity is the dilemma of volunteerism.

The Dilemma of Volunteerism: Where One Dilemma Closes, Another Opens

We saw earlier the sophisticated way that grads reconcile the dilemma of resistance: they privilege their communities of gathering over their communities of sending and yet remain in solidarity with, rather than patronize, the poor through an emphasis on individual relationships. This focus on individual relationships, individual transformation, the lone civic actor, and so forth undermines one of the core values of JFM: justice. As the grads focus on relationships and micro-interactions, they give less attention to justice.[52] Granted, grads could, as Jezreel suggests, participate in both charitable and justice-based endeavors. However, 80 percent of grads participate in a charitable activity monthly or more, and only one-fourth of grads pursue justice-based activities that often. Because of these individualist aspects within the program, grads, while they cognitively assent to justice, are deeply concerned with individual persons, leading to much-higher participation in charity activities.[53] This concern for individuals turns grads' attention away from justice toward personal charity.

One way this manifests is through grads' perception of the individual as the primary locus of social change. Historically, American Catholics have banded together to form relief societies and the like to address social needs. Today's Catholics have a far more individualist view of themselves and others, as Bay Area resident Mark Bachman's reading of the Good Samaritan parable illustrates: "There's another good example about the underdog. In a sense, somebody doing something that you wouldn't expect. They were just a good person, they weren't a priest, or a Pharisee, they weren't some high-up person. In fact, if I understand correctly, [Samaritans] were looked down upon by most people . . . This guy was not of the same community, not of anything other than the fact that he looked into his heart and told himself that this person needs help and helped him." From the earliest teachings through the Middle Ages, church leaders used the parable of the Good Samaritan to remind listeners of the support the church community offered in the image of the inn, which is omitted in Bachman's account.[54] His interpretation demonstrates the privileging of the individual within JFM—and among Americans more broadly— understanding this parable as instructing listeners to be compassionate individuals.[55] Understanding social change as occurring through individual actors legitimates grads' strategy for social change as independent volunteers rather than the coordinated aid societies of the past styles.

Megan Sims is one of many grads who contend that social ills can be handled through the steadfast commitment of individuals:

> We begin by letting our lives speak to it. So if you want a place where everybody is welcome, start welcoming everybody. If you want to have a table where there is always room for more, then make sure you've got plenty of seats and make sure the invitations are going out. If you want people to listen, then you have to be a good listener. If you want people to care, you have to care and then encourage others to do it. And speak out against what is wrong—it's not just about reclaiming the possible, but about really renouncing the wrong and saying when things are unjust that they are unjust.

Just as grads change their consumption habits in an attempt to create a more just market, they believe that social change happens through changes in their own life. Although this grad qualifies her statement that this is only how one *begins* social change, others, like Jeffrey Swimme, are far more optimistic about the ability of individuals to foment large-scale change: "Haiti or India or wherever, there's so much injustice, and injustice in the world, but it's hard to imagine how it would ever get better. It's hard when we're hearing about it, reading about it, you figure having people continue to treat other people like that, people need to change their heart, their mindset. Being realistic, that ain't gonna happen any time soon." This grad is not the consummate idealist who imagines that people change easily, as his last sentence indicates. Yet he oversimplifies injustice when he states that it can be ameliorated by changing people's hearts and minds. Grads hold two mutually exclusive beliefs—the practical limits of charity and the primacy of individual effort in social change—in a precarious balance. Part of what cognitively supports this balance is their definition of *structure*.

Many grads have an individualist notion of structure that undermines their pursuit of justice. JFM programs embed political, civic, and moral issues within a structural framework without carefully unpacking what *structure* means. Sociology discusses the structure and agency duality in a myriad of ways. Karl Marx writes that people make their own history, albeit limited by the circumstances in which they find themselves.[56] Max Weber contends that ideal and material interests create metaphorical

tracks to guide beliefs and behaviors, yet ideas act as switchmen to determine which tracks are taken.[57] Contemporary theorist Michel Foucault focuses on a diffuse, omnipresent power—which he maintains is
not a structure—and is far more complicated than simple binaries of
oppressor and oppressed.[58] Within these sociological definitions there
is an emphasis on institutions, customs, norms, laws, and so forth that
constrain and enable social interaction on the micro- and macro-level.
Furthermore, these structures both shape and are shaped by individual
actors, organizations, social groups, states, and so on.

Yet, many grads discussed structure as merely an aggregate of individuals.[59] That is, there are no "structures" in the sense of institutions or
customs; there are only actors cooperating, wittingly or not, in moral or
immoral ways, as Southern California resident John Lovett says simply:
"[Structural change] begins with changing people's hearts." He continues: "Because it's not a physical structure at all. Yeah, it was a system of
laws and rules and regulations in place, but the bottom of all that, what
allows it to work and to continue or to change is the belief system and
practices of all the people, of all the components." If one can change
"people's hearts" or the beliefs and practices of "all the components,"
the structure will naturally shift as it is nothing more than the collective
mores and behaviors of the individuals. This notion of structures as ag-
gregates of individuals is present in their political strategies (e.g., quan-
tities of letters to Congress) and strategies to change the market (e.g.,
recruiting people to purchase fair-trade coffee).[60] The idea of changing
structures is reduced to changing the beliefs and practices of large numbers of individuals. In not providing participants with a more macro-
level notion of structure, grads finish with a simplistic understanding
of this, frustrating JFM's hope for grads to engage in justice work that
results in lasting social reform.

Before turning away from this dilemma, that this intimate, individualist experience pushed a small but significant number of grads into a
serious commitment to justice work is important to note, as Megan Sim's
account of her immersion encounter at a soup kitchen makes clear:

> The first friend I ever made who was poor, his name is Carl French . . .
> I sit down with Carl French and I found that he was the middle child of
> three, he had an older brother and a younger sister and I'm the middle

child of three I have an older brother and a younger sister. And Carl French was from Atlanta, he lived right off of the street called Peachtree and, I'm not lying to you, the week before I had been in Atlanta I'm visiting my friend who lived off the same street that Carl French lived off of. And Carl French was really interested in the violin. If I could learn an instrument, I would play the violin. Carl had been listening to a CD that I had just been listening to and he was reading a book that I had finished. And I recognized that myself and Carl French who on the surface could not have looked more different . . . we were very much alike in a lot of particular ways. I made a friend and Carl and I ate lunch together at the soup kitchen for weeks and weeks and weeks which turned into months which turned into probably about a half year and then he got housing. And we stayed in touch, which was great. And all of the sudden I started caring about people who are homeless in a different way because Carl was homeless, because my friend was homeless. So I started talking with other people about homelessness. I wanted to learn more about homelessness so that what started really as like a personal thing—this is where I met someone, he was my friend—I wanted to then learn as much as I possibly could about data like . . . 40 percent of Louisville's homeless population is employed and 25 percent of that 40 percent are employed full-time so then all of a sudden I became aware that like not only do we have problem with housing we have a problem with wage issues. So I started talking to people about living wage . . . And I was writing to Congress people, I'd write to representatives, I'd let them know what's going on here.

What began as a simple one-on-one friendship propelled her into serious activism. Sociologist Stephen Hart believes that the decoupling of civil society and politics is at the root of many social problems.[61] Clearly, some participants have been pushed into justice engagement because of their relationship with particular individuals, relationships that make connections between civil society and politics, individual, and structure. But these grads are the exception rather than the rule. By and large, relationships with marginalized individuals distract grads from, rather than focus them on, justice issues. JFM would be more successful in its mission if it were to teach participants to place these relationships in a larger sociopolitical frame, as this grad does.[62]

Saying that JFM fails in its mission to lead its grads to justice would certainly be too strong a statement. That they engage in acts of mercy far more often than acts of justice is true. Still they engage in acts of justice at a much higher rate than the typical American. Most Americans, 84 percent, have not been involved in a political party or organization in the last year, and only 2 percent have been involved in the last month compared to 25 percent of grads who are involved in justice activities on a monthly basis.[63] Granted, some of this discrepancy might come from the variation in the question, with grads' responses not limited to organizations—"justice activities" could include writing a letter to a politician or other individual actions. Most of this discrepancy, however, is probably due to real differences in life activity, with the grads seeking opportunities to make their world a more equitable place. Saying that JustFaith plants a seed of justice in their grads that starts them on a path to justice and will grow to the extent that individuals and communities cultivate it is accurate.

This question of failing in justice also brings to mind Jezreel's earlier words: "You *really* can't do [charity without justice]. If you don't care enough about me to care about whether my kids have an opportunity, then you really don't care about me. You're doing something else." Discussing JFM's success in fomenting justice when its grads lean toward charity should give us pause: What about the countless civic associations that engage *only* in charity and in no justice? Are these actually even doing charity, or are they doing "something else," such as easing their volunteers' consciences? Can we say that they are exercising true charity when they numb the effects of social problems without any efforts at reform? These are questions organizations must seriously consider.

Conclusion

This chapter examined important elements of grads' beliefs and practices having to do with the state and market. JFM, like other discipleship-style organizations, encourages the participants to approach all aspects of life, including government and the market, from a position of faith. Discipleship-style Catholics are tentatively engaged with the state, aware of both its potential and its shortcomings. Grads are very critical of war, with the Catholics articulating their church's teaching on just war and suspicious that many wars are motivated by profit. Grads believe poverty is connected to a host of issues, and this involves them in a variety of causes, from the environment to prison reform to abortion. Discipleship groups will vary according to their modification of consumption habits, yet many will live more simply as this allows them to be more generous with their personal resources, facilitating outreach. JFM encourages participants to make serious changes in their consumption habits through the model of voluntary poverty. This presents the dilemma of efficacy, with grads ultimately believing that they are more effective in alleviating poverty and other ills by remaining in conventional positions that offer them more social and economic power. Grads' attitudes about and strategies for the state and market reveal their understandings of justice and charity. JFM differs from some discipleship organizations in its specific attention to justice, rather than exclusively charity, as its form of outreach. The individualist factors inherent in discipleship-style organizations pit grads' desire to serve individuals against their strong convictions on the necessity of justice, yielding the dilemma of volunteerism. The individualist factors win out, with grads often choosing participation in charitable ministries over those involving justice.

JFM does not foment justice activism in grads as much as one would expect given the organization's stated mission. After JustFaith, grads care about the well-being of others more deeply and prefer the personal relationships that direct service offers. Transforming grads' field of care is a central enterprise of JFM as they hope to push grads into civic engagement, as Jezreel explains: "I'm not gonna care about the structure unless I care. Where does caring happen? We start with a book like *Compassion*, or *Tattoos on the Heart*, which is about all these one-on-one interactions." JFM does not get the results in justice that it hopes for because grads are so moved by the one-on-one experiences they have in JustFaith. For what grads lack in justice, they compensate for with compassion, the core value of the final chapter.

7

Compassion

Knowledge through Stories

Louisville staff member Mike Campbell is experiencing a bout with allergies. His coughing and sneezing are frequent, but they do not interfere with his story. He has a strong theological background, having been a Xaverian missionary who studied and lived in a variety of countries and contexts. He was a transitional deacon for just over two years before deciding that he did not want to become a priest. He has since married and has two grown children and a teen. As he reflects on his numerous joys, hardships, and epiphanies, he tells a story of a time in the Amazon rainforest when he grew in his own sense of compassion:

> But what I learned was that there's a way of seeing the Gospel as integral to our lives. And I'll give you an example. We would go to these Christian communities and they had fifty-five islands. It's called Nossa Senhora das Ilhas, Our Lady of the Islands, that was our parish. There were fifty-five island communities scattered across the estuary of the Amazon and it was at least fifty to sixty miles wide, the Amazon estuary. It was hundreds of miles of islands and it's a hundred miles wide at its mouth. There's an island in the middle called Marajá and it's the size of Switzerland; the river goes around it. So, we were just dealing with one side of Marajá and the island there. And the only island between thousands of islands, the fluvial islands with communities on them, people who were called *caboclos*, or backwoods people. [The equivalent of] "rednecks" or "peasants." Most of them didn't read or write. But they had these communities there, and they couldn't come to the mainland, so we went to them. And they got Mass once a year, when we came. And the pastoral team would generally navigate the stormy, incredibly *dangerous* waters; the Amazon's rushing out *billions* of gallons of water into the sea. For over a hundred miles the sea is fresh water. And then the sea pushes back and it takes you, and

the Amazon comes up. Trees are a hundred feet long with animals on them. Just going five knots, just right out to sea. And one time we got stuck in the tides, because there's tremendous tides there. Our boat was stuck in the mud and we were trying to dislodge the boat. We got to the island at nine o'clock at night and they had already started without us because that was the one time a year to get Mass. There was a big feast prepared and we were going to have all the things. We married people; we baptized babies; other people who were just married, they'd give first communion to people who were being baptized. It was all done in the one day. And then we walked in on this delegate of the Word. A woman was leading the service and we decided that since we had gotten there so late we were not gonna have Mass, we're just gonna carry on with the service. They were doing this; she was having them read the Gospel. And if you can just imagine. They didn't get a generator set up. They were having Coca-Cola cans with a Brazil nut on top lit. That was the candle. Because the Brazil nut will light like a flame. And they were reading The Gospel of Matthew. And I don't remember the citation but it was the story of the cure of the paralytic. And so, they read the gospel and the woman approached me and she said, "So, where are we, in this gospel? Where are we?" And then, somebody said, "Well, I know where we are. We're the people carrying the paralyzed person." And she said, "Well, why are we the people carrying the para—" [and somebody responded,] "Well, because we're the poor." And the person said, "And the paralyzed person is the rich world. And the rich world can't get to Jesus. There's just too much in the way. And the poor have to pick them up and carry them to Jesus." And somebody else said, "And you know what, there's nothing wrong with that, because *that's our job*. And you know what Jesus says when the rich person gets to Jesus; Jesus says, 'Get up. All these things you're guilty about, they're all forgiven. Pick up that mat and walk.'" And, and nobody even talks about that, that *it was the poor that got them there*. And that's their job. And, my heart is full and I'm thinking, "I've never heard this before. Why?" Now you can see how this is good news to these people, because it didn't give them the answer, but it said to them, "We are precious to God. We are the subjects of this material. And if you want to be subjects of this material, then be with us."

One of the core values of JustFaith Ministries (JFM) is compassion. JFM holds this virtue in high esteem, reasoning that there cannot be a just society without compassion, with Jezreel saying, "We use the word *compassion* because we feel like in some ways that's the building block for everything related to social mission, the Catholic social teaching or ultimately even the Gospel." As discipleship groups transform Catholics using the ripple-group model of social change, participants care about new things, widening their sphere of compassion. Compassion is not ameliorating an unjust situation or feeling sorry for someone in unfortunate circumstances. *Compassion* is from the Latin "to suffer with" and happens when a person or party feels some degree of the pain experienced by another. JFM and other discipleship organizations reason that as people come to care more broadly and more deeply, they will bring positive change to their world. Thus, compassion is a key personal quality that JFM programs and other discipleship organizations attempt to deepen or foster among the participants.

JustFaith and other JFM programs attempt to widen participants' field of care by expanding their knowledge through new information and experiences. The most vivid and effective way that programs transmit this new knowledge is through storytelling. Knowledge as experience shared through stories offers JFM participants a personalist account of suffering, transforming their field of care.

Knowledge as Facts and Experiences

JustFaith and other JFM programs use two types of knowledge to facilitate transformation in their participants: fact and experience. The word *fact* is intellectually troubling in the postmodern age. It implies an air of truth in and of itself, absolutely correct, objective, exact, and without error. Thinkers from philosophy to science are challenging this notion of fact, arguing—to put it very briefly—that observations, no matter how reliably assessed or measured, are taken from a particular perspective, a perspective that influences the object of study and the interpretation of the observations, and have little difference from what is colloquially called experience.[1] Without entering this debate, fact and experience are defined here with a sociological—rather than a philosophical or empirical—bias, that is, as that which is colloquially meant by fact and experience. Here facts are knowledge generally understood in a way that privileges the observable qualities over the moral or affective qualities, emphasizing the objective aspects. In contrast, experience is knowledge that people interpret through a lens that privileges its moral and affective qualities over its observable qualities, emphasizing the subjective aspects.[2] The sociological difference between fact and experience is the way people understand such knowledge, both individually and collectively.[3] Using these understandings, as people experience another's suffering, they experience compassion as an emotion and a drive as well as a form of knowledge.

Knowledge as Facts: Role and Limits in Bringing about Compassion

Facts have a distinct role in the formation process of grads: facts corroborate extant beliefs. New facts motivate them to engage society and help them to understand the scope of a problem or to help them find an effective solution. Learning the unemployment or poverty rate in one's city, for example, strengthens a grad's convictions that unemployment or poverty is a problem. Grads expand their notions of justice as they learn about movements and heroes of the poor, as Adam Rousseve, an Episcopalian from Louisville, explains: "I hadn't heard of Dorothy Day, I didn't know much about her and Catholic Workers—I knew that as a lefty paper newspaper from the '60s in New York. So, when I think that, I really got exposed [through JustFaith] to a much wider or broader [political reality] and also to be aware that this justice can be sought in many different areas of one's life." The new participant surveys confirm that most have some exposure to social justice, sympathies for the poor or even simply an affiliation with the Democratic Party prior to Just-Faith. These preexisting beliefs lead them to JustFaith and later grow more intense and extend to new causes as they learn more about poverty and related issues during JustFaith.

Grads do not suggest, however, that new facts caused them to *change* their feelings toward the poor, the environment, countries torn by war, and so forth. Jezreel acknowledges the limits of facts in actually bringing about personal transformation through a story he heard on public radio:

In the Great Plains, there were native tribes that had three-poled teepees and there were native tribes that had four-poled teepees. And the question was: How did that evolve? And in terms of functionality, the three-poled teepee was by far the superior design. It stood easier; it was stronger against the wind; everything about it was superior. So, the guy [on the radio show] asked the question, "So why was it that some tribes used only the four-pole design?" And he said, "Because their parents did it." And that's the only answer. There is no other answer that can be given, except that people sometimes believe what their parents believed because their parents believed it. And even though the four-poled teepee was *clearly* an inadequate design, culture and even sort of sacred language became part of continuing to do the four-poled teepee. And the conversation was fabulous because it demonstrated, and the author goes on to explain, that even while you can make the case, and some did, that the three-poled teepee would be the better design, it's not what holds the day. The *truth* is not what will convince people. It's what their parents told them. Or what their people told them. So, for example, if you hang out in an environment in which everybody thinks poor people are lazy, then no matter what data you put in front of people, there will be the inclination for people to believe that poor people are lazy because the environment in which they were in kept repeating it and repeating it and repeating it until it becomes part of your loyalty. And your loyalty will actually trump hard-and-fast facts.

A closer look at the participants who are more politically conservative helps illuminate the limits of knowledge as facts.

A handful of grads began as loyal Republicans and became more centrist or progressive on poverty issues, even as they continued with their party affiliation. Ron Stevenson discusses his negative feelings toward the homeless before JustFaith: "I'm a much different person. I was always very skeptical. I would see homeless people and, 'Oh geez, if they wanted a job they could have a job. They're just lazy!' Just as an example and very non-tolerant . . . And then after going down and feeding the hungry and getting exposure to a lot of these types of people that are just really victims maybe of just wrong place at the wrong time or illness or whatever, abuse and realize yeah, there is a lot of other stories that are out there, too. So, it softened me." It was not facts—as sociological data of the causes of homelessness—that changed his beliefs about homelessness. Instead, it was immersion experiences with people experiencing homelessness that altered his worldview, leaving him, according to his own account, more compassionate.[4] Not all the programs use immersion experiences, and Stevenson does not have the same enthusiasm for the JustMatters modules:

> So, [the module on the federal budget] is how much we're spending on the war and here is how much we're spending on the poor and you keep drawing these conclusions. So, if you weren't paying attention—and not that I'm maybe smarter than anybody else—you sit back and say, "How come we're doing this? We've got to stop the war and give all the money to the poor." Well, you can't do that either. You have to take care of certain necessities. So those were just a couple of examples of things that I thought the agenda was there and it was just under the surface and you are kind of getting led down that path. And again, not that I'm maybe smarter than anybody else, but if you didn't pay attention you could only draw that conclusion at the end.

This grad illustrates the limits of facts alone in bringing about a change in what one cares about. JustMatters modules, due to their brevity, do not have opportunities for immersion experiences. His experience working in finances as an accountant trumps the facts of poverty as he understands the federal budget. He continues by saying that he is suspicious of the *facts* in the module: "You can come up with stats to prove anything. Literally, you can . . . And if you're just going to hit one side of the story then you're led to a conclusion that you may not have been led to had you been presented with the other side." Life is complex, and social issues can be viewed from multiple perspectives. There are groups and individuals who differ as to which governmental strategy will best serve the common good. This grad believes that the module presents only "one side" of the facts, leading to only one possible conclusion. In sum, the programs transform participants through experience, rather than facts, illustrating the efficacy of the former in changing participants' field of compassion.[5]

Knowledge as Experience

Experience is a type of knowledge in which people generally emphasize the affective and moral dimensions over the tangible dimensions.

To clarify, there are both objective and subjective elements to an event. Here, what people *feel* is experience and what they *observe* is fact. Obviously, these two bleed together, but these differences are culturally important as they distinguish the ways people understand their world. Facts reinforce grads' beliefs but do not change them. Experience, as knowledge that emphasizes the moral evaluation and affective qualities to an event, succeeds in both transforming and deepening the grads' sense of compassion. Returning to Jezreel's teepee analogy:

> I think Jesus was saying, "The three-poled teepee lifestyle is the way to go! A love like the three-poled teepee is where we're gonna go, but all of you have been training for a four-poled teepee." If you're a southern white man, convinced that whites are superior to blacks, the fact that your mommy and daddy said that every day of your life is unfortunate, but it's not true. But that transition is very difficult. So, what JustFaith is trying to do is to say, "Here's the facts on the ground, here's the faith tradition. Go, go see for yourself." I mean really what the immersion experiences [say] are, "Go see for yourself! Go have the conversation yourself!" And with any luck—it doesn't always work out perfectly—but with any luck or with the Holy Spirit's presence, when people go on these immersion experiences they're shocked! What are they shocked about? The world didn't change. It's just they didn't see it. And now they see it! It's like, "Oh, my gosh! Everything I thought about this was wrong!" . . . And on one hand, it's troubling. But then on the other hand, it's liberating.

Jezreel believes that many have embraced lies as though they were truths and no amount of reason or study allows them to let go of these lies. He claims only after *encountering* the truth through a person living it can one view the world through a more compassionate lens.[6] Ron Stevenson, the Republican discussed earlier, illustrates this in a significant shift in his perception of homelessness and countless other grads echo his sentiments in smaller ways as they recall the experiences that opened their eyes to what they now see as the truth. This rings true with Fr. Ryan Delaney's experience with JustFaith:

> [On immersion experiences] you experience other people. And I think in the JustFaith groups hearing other people, hear their stories, and that's

where, "Oh! Well, you're thinking the same way. I know your fears are the same as my fears and we're kind of going on this together." But I think so often you can talk head-wise until you're blue in the face about rights, African American/Caucasian American issues. But when you get to know an African American and they can tell you their real story, and you begin to feel their story, then it becomes real . . . ultimately, that is the change. When they experience someone from another culture or hear their story, when their story becomes real, when his story and the Gospel story is connected with your own, that's when it becomes real.

Experiences correct mistaken facts by making new facts "real," imbuing everyday life with religious meaning and giving grads new ways to understand the world.

That firsthand accounts are transformative cannot be understated. JFM programs offer both direct and indirect firsthand experiences. Direct experience is meeting face-to-face with people undergoing some sort of hardship, typically encountered through immersion experiences or guest speakers. Indirect experience is the communication of these individuals' experiences, mainly through books and films. JustFaith and JusticeWalking offer both immersion experiences and speakers, Engaging Spirituality and GoodNewsPeople arrange only immersion experiences, and JustMatters modules have neither, depending on indirect experience to reshape the understandings of the participants. That both indirect and direct experience always focus on a particular person or situation, not a general plight, is important to note. For example, one might read about Eddie, a young man trying to start a new life after being in a gang. JustFaith rarely features more abstract stories about gang life in general or statistics without an accompanying story.

All JFM programs bring participants to those on the margins through indirect experience. Engaging Spirituality provides participants with "bearings letters," each written by a person or married couple very active in some sort of social outreach. The letters are a testimony of virtuous living and contain the difficulties of working in their ministry, the spiritual practices that sustain them in their work, and a challenge for the listeners for their own faith journey. They begin with a short biography and a photo, which is placed in an empty chair, as though the person were present with the group. Each letter closely follows the person in question, never generalizing a particular person's experience to her or his field of ministry broadly. At specific points in the reading of the letter, participants are invited to share words or phrases that resonate with them. The letters are quite personal, and facilitators ask participants not to discuss the contents outside of the group. Hearing the joys, triumphs, and struggles of the writers helps bring their experiences closer to one's own.

Every program features videos. The participants in GoodNewsPeople see a video of a man who works in a restaurant that mentors and employs young adults from at-risk communities. The Prison Reform module features a documentary that shows the psychological wear on several young adults who were sentenced to life in prison as teens. JustFaith shows participants a fictional video about a man who gradually revivified a small region of the Alps by planting trees. The content and style of the videos vary from program to program, but they share the focus on particular individuals.

The programs offer various reading materials. JFM created all the materials for GoodNewsPeople, but most of the other programs use third-party books and videos. With the exception of scripture and official church documents, the readings, like the videos, tend to follow specific events and individuals. There are books that feature short biographies of women and men who brought their faith into the world, from St. Francis of Assisi to Dorothy Day. Miguel Cruz enjoys Gregory Boyle's *Tattoos on the Heart*[7]: "I was in stitches because it was so well written! And the guy is funny! But at the same time, it just illustrated cases of where you feel for these people that have had a rough life, and have been born into situations that they didn't have any control over. They're just living their lives. It made you cry and it made you laugh." *Tattoos* is filled with stories of the joys and sorrows of a Jesuit priest who forms an organization that gives job skills to those looking to work after turning away from life in a gang. In a fast-paced, episodic fashion, Boyle jumps from one youth's story to the next, all cohered by the underlying story of his own faith journey through this ministry. Boyle's personal transformation shapes grads' understandings of their own direct experience.

Most programs offer direct experience through guest speakers, immersion experiences, or both. Guest speakers are not usually experts in their field; rather, they are people who have personal experience with the topic at hand. For example, when discussing racism, a group opted not for the sociology professor with books published on the topic and preferred instead an African American priest who had personally experienced discrimination. The immersion experiences in JustFaith are spread throughout the twenty-seven weeks, and grads claim that these are some of the most meaningful experiences in the program. The local groups arrange the immersions themselves, and the curriculum emphasizes that immersions are not service projects. Instead, they are times to sit with, talk to, and listen to people whose lives are different from their own in various ways. Megan Sims tells a story of when she was asked to sit-in on a JWalking group due to the absence of the female co-facilitator. What she witnessed among the teens that night had a profound impact on her:

> And I showed up and I remember the evening prayer and ritual, and I remember sitting—I remember where I was sitting if that tells you like how much of an impact it was—and I remember this one girl, this young girl crying and she was weeping because her heart really was just torn open by this experience of people who are homeless. And her ability to care and be really overwhelmed by compassion had so surfaced that it was just falling out of her eyes because it had nowhere else to go . . . What I witnessed was deep and true and real and it was not just being illuminated in her it was coming out of all of these young people who were talking about really how their lives were measurably different and the quality of their lives had just changed and their eyes were open to seeing things that they just had never seen before and they could never be the same.

The teen was weeping, according to this account, because she suddenly understood homelessness as the suffering of living human beings, pain that she came to feel as well. Grads have obvious affective responses to their experiences.

In order to change grads' behaviors, these experiences need to translate into moral lessons. Being saddened by a homeless person who sleeps on the cold, wet ground is one thing. Believing that not ensuring shelter for everyone is morally wrong is another thing. Still, making the leap from an affective experience to the moral injunction is an easy one. Experiences, unlike facts, also provide an evaluative frame to understand this knowledge. Staff person Cathy Meyers talks about her experience on a bike trip through Uganda:

> You are up close and personal with people and there were times when it just broke my heart, I would just have to cry. What you see, what you experience, what you smell. The people, whether they're challenging you or sharing a story with you, it is where I need to choose to put myself on a regular basis. It was kind of like the reverse evangelization, the reverse R&R. I have such a cushy life, I need to constantly be exposed and I don't mean exposed in the sense of "Oh, go drive through a poor neighborhood." I am talking about exposed like "I'm going to sit and talk with you and I'm going to know your name and I am going to know your story and I am going to tell you my name and I am going to tell you my story."

People receive knowledge in one of three genres: information, news, and stories. Information is defined here as a genre that presents facts without an apparent moral or affective frame for the speaker or listener.[8] News as a genre presents facts and the moral and affective frames of those involved without offering the receiver a particular frame of understanding, usually by presenting multiple frames for an issue or event.[9] As Meyers's last sentence indicates, story is the main genre of communicating knowledge in JFM programs as people most often share their experiences as stories.

Story as a Genre of Knowledge

Sharing stories is central to the JustFaith process. Members get to know one another by telling their story and listening to others' stories the night of the opening retreat, forming a community. They hear stories from those on the margins in order to transform the way they think about social issues. Stories transmit knowledge to the hearer in a way that is different from other genres of knowledge. Stories are told in a way that filters facts through the perspective of the speaker, connecting the facts to a particular moral and affective frame. The listener may accept, reject, or modify the moral and affective frame the storyteller offers, yet the frame of interpretation remains embedded in the story itself.[10] Because of the intimate connection between frame and event in the story genre, listeners will probably accept, reject, or modify the story according to their treatment of the frame (e.g., if they reject the frame, they will probably also reject the facts within the story).

The story that introduced this chapter illustrates that stories integrate an experience with an interpretive frame for the listener to understand it. In that story, the frame tells the listeners that the marginalized are active participants in the Gospel. Stories are an especially effective genre of knowledge given the personalist mores of American society. Before exploring the broader cultural trends that facilitate the story genre and the repercussions for JFM and American Catholics more broadly, examining the ways JFM uses stories to convey knowledge to its participants is useful.

Stories in JFM Programs

Stories are a critical component of the small-group dynamic in JFM programs. Storytellers create a "mentality" for themselves and others to understand the stories, omitting or embellishing parts to bring the listeners in and to create meaning around an event.[11] Stories help group members learn about one another by allowing people to discuss their failures and successes within a particular subjective frame. Because they believe fellow members will not contest their frame, group members divulge intimate parts of their past, bringing intimacy to strangers relatively quickly, as Janet Bolls explains: "I think we became a community because we did things like prayer, because we shared personal, meaningful things in our lives. We did things that we felt were important together. So, it wasn't just talking about issues, but our own stories." When asked if these stories are as important as the other elements of the program, Bolls continues: "Oh, *absolutely*. Otherwise, it's just a study club, [but] it's much more than that." More than the information one would get from a "study club," JFM programs offer affective experiences that educate as well as draw the group together. National small-group members who claim that their faith changed significantly since they joined the small group are far more likely to share stories within those groups.[12] Storytelling facilitates religious transformation as well as strengthens affective bonds, both of which reinforce one another. Affective bonds can pull people to a spiritual consensus they may not have arrived at without these ties. Furthermore, coming to shared religious beliefs can increase intimacy. In this way, friendship and religious transformation are mutually reinforcing and storytelling encourages both of these.

Stories in JFM programs are not simply a collection of well-crafted words and an entertaining plot. Cathy Meyers explains that in JustFaith stories are event-based and that they are sometimes rooted in uncomfortable but educative moments: "It is easier for me to throw money in the basket. It is hard for me to just stop and talk to you. The beggar on the street, the homeless person, drop some money and then feel good about yourself. But did you ever stop and say, 'Hey, can I help you? Do you need food? Could I help you get to a shelter? What is your name?' Share your name, share your story. This is what JustFaith is all about—sharing stories." Participants use stories as a launching point into a new friendship, perspective, and knowledge, all of which can be both unsettling and instructive.

Storytelling is a familiar form of instruction in American churches, as leaders recount and elaborate scripture and hagiography of the saints. These stories pull the listeners into the journey of the church in a vivid and relevant way, widening their moral imagination and inspiring them to act.[13] As Catholics hear stories of St. Francis—once a rich dandy—kissing a leper and St. Peter's climactic denial of Christ, they connect themselves to a larger community. They examine their own lives through the lives of the saints, judging how well their own lives approximate holy living. The bearings letters from Engaging Spirituality, as well as other testimony-style writings and videos in the programs, bring participants a contemporary vision of saintly living, as a regular facilitator says of JWalking: "One of the pieces of the process is that you learn about people who are good witnesses, people to follow, people who've made the path." The autobiographical style of the readings has a profound impact on the formation of the listeners, engaging them on a personal level and encouraging them to imitate the speaker.[14]

Lessons Worth Sharing: Parameters for Storytelling

Participants in some of the programs—GoodNewsPeople and Engaging Spirituality—write their own testimonies for the group. The bearings letters and GoodNews stories provide tacit parameters for the stories:

there can be struggle but not despair; there can be amazing accomplishments, but give the glory to God, not to oneself; and the more difficult the challenge one offers another, the more nebulous, rather than concrete, it should be. These parameters ensure that the participants learn lessons not only about each other but also specific values that JFM hopes they will learn about holy living in daily life. They also work as norms of group sharing, shaping the ways people tell their stories.[15]

Naming struggles without despairing ensures that Christians do not lose hope. A theological concern would be that Christians must always hope as this, along with faith and love, is a primary virtue. A practical concern would be that if someone loses hope, they would cease to seek change, having given up on the possibility of justice or peace; this illustrates the close connection of hope to compassion.[16] Megan Sims embodies this unwavering hope, despite the work remaining in the world:

> But there is the sense [that] there is never enough. There is when it comes to the limit for my heart to love people. There is always more, there is always more; it doesn't tap out—the desire to connect with people. There is always more—the desire to live these principles of JusticeWalking—there is always more. And that can seem like getting to the summit of Everest or it can seem like always having purpose and always having drive and always being able to do a little bit more. Not this sense of living in a dissatisfied state, but living in a hopeful state that until there is no one on the earth who knows hunger, until all suffering is eradicated then there is more for us to do.

Many might be overwhelmed at the prospect of having work until "all suffering is eradicated," yet JFM programs help participants to see this work as giving them a sense of purpose. Struggle is welcome, but it must invigorate and not diminish hope, encouraging the participants to go into the world and serve others.

In giving glory to God rather than themselves for their accomplishments, grads ensure humility while they inspire one another by discussing their good works. This is actually a very easy parameter for the grads. Considering the important positions of some grads or the many hours they volunteer weekly (some are full-time volunteers), they were surprisingly modest about their accomplishments and contributions, often casually revealing the extent of their involvement over the course of the interview. The groups often discuss the different ministries members work in, and some, like Engaging Spirituality, require modest commitments of outreach that provide experiences to contemplate over the sessions. To become boastful about accomplishments is self-defeating from a Christian moral perspective. From a group dynamics perspective, it is also very problematic if competition or hubris divides members. In the sessions, many people discuss their volunteer commitments only after the prompting of another member, for example, after being asked if something resonates with one's juvenile detention ministry. This parameter allows people to inspire and enliven without appearing "holier than thou."

By ensuring that harder challenges are less concrete than simpler ones, grads find many opportunities for action that are still practical given life in contemporary American society. This was explored in the previous chapter through the dilemma of efficacy. What is relevant for knowledge, experience, and compassion is that individuals in JFM programs are rarely given specific directives. Grads receive many difficult moral injunctions, from living in solidarity with the poor to loving their enemies. However, these nonnegotiables are extraordinarily vague. When Laura Dowell says that "God is love" should inform the life of the Christian, the lack of specificity in this tenet is obvious, but this ambiguity allows grads to adapt the idea to their own circumstances as she elaborates: "Stepping in to care for those in war and violence, the hungry, the homeless, the trafficked, that that all flows out of love because that is love, that is doing what God asked us to, what Jesus speaks to the people to do. So vague, big, overarching? Absolutely, but I really think the whole concept of the Gospel is about love and I think that's what Jesus talks about constantly." Dowell fills in her own sincere and other-regarding tasks to live out the notion that God is love and does not dilute it to another vague idea, such as being kind. Grads are comfortable with ambiguity as the challenge is immense and their individual circumstances are all very different. The indefinite quality allows them to discern ways to manifest these abstract injunctions into particular, concrete practices. Compare this to a list JustFaith gives participants to assess their use of resources: "I use cereal bags as freezer bags . . . I cancel junk mail solicitations . . . I plan meals for a week and make limited trips to the grocery store." When JFM is more concrete and specific, the challenges are less significant. These parameters for group sharing reflect the importance JFM gives to discernment and dialogue.

Influence of the Enlightenment: Dialogue and Discernment

Jürgen Habermas wrote that civil society cannot continue to progress without a vibrant and participatory public sphere.[17] Previously, there were public houses where people could come together to discuss and argue the issues of the day. People of all stations would offer their perspective on a current event and this fostered civic-mindedness and brought to light possible solutions. These public spaces no longer exist, and the media now shapes the sentiments of the day. Mass media outlets now *influence* public opinion, he argues, rather than people discussing events and *creating* a collective public opinion.[18] Civil society must create public forums with free exchanges of ideas in order to live in a more enlightened society.

Scholars debate the effects of the media on public opinion. Some studies show the media has a negligible impact on public opinion.[19] Others believe that the media influences the topics people think about, with little impact on the content of the beliefs themselves.[20] And still others contend that in setting the issues people consider, the media shapes public opinion a great deal.[21] A few grads spontaneously mention their concerns that the news media is inaccurate and the messages in popular entertainment are harmful. These suspicions cause them to prefer a Habermasian approach within their discipleship group through dialogue and discernment. These help the grads understand their social landscape, especially their roles as people of faith. Dialogue and discernment are also important from an organizational perspective. As grads share their thoughts and hear from others whom they care for and respect, they will more easily abandon ideas and interpretations of reality that are aberrant to the group, making their new attitudes consistent with the group's plausibility structure. These respected others provide participants a reference group and the members whose beliefs and lifestyle most closely approximate the ideals of JFM will have the largest impact on fellow group members.[22] When members identify the discipleship community as a select group of others who are morally and relationally significant, dialogue and discernment lead to a stronger ideological consensus among the members of the group.

JustFaith groups utilize dialogue, which allows for both unity and divergence in belief. Although there are important values and knowledge that JFM wants grads to learn, this does not mean that dialogue is insincere and alternative opinions are silenced.[23] Rather, groups welcome divergent views, with Pete London defining *community* as "an environment or a number of people that get together and have some common basis for belief or discussion, but still it's safe enough for disagreements and not feel like it's really going to change what people are going to think of you deeply." Groups attempt to make space for both commonality and diversity. Often, however, groups become more similar than when they began,[24] with individuals gradually harboring more compassion for the poor and vulnerable, as staff member Cathy Meyers elaborates: "[Our programs] are constantly pulling people into dialogue. Have the conversation. We are not trying to drive people to any political party. We are saying, though, we need to be able to talk to one another. Talk to one another on the basis of commonality; [that] commonality is your faith. So, on the basis of that faith . . . we are called to address [issues] in a compassionate and loving way." Caring dialogue grounded in faith will lead to compassion, which, according to JFM, means making poverty, peace, and justice issues higher priorities.

Dialogue in JustFaith must be elaborated both in process and content. First, a group can totally fall apart if any members fail to follow the guidelines for the dialogue process: "I think she wants to hear herself talk. But she doesn't listen. She doesn't listen." Caroline Dunn is remembering a group that slowly dwindled in members until only a handful were left, dissolving on the seventeenth session. She believes that a member's lack of ability to dialogue slowly drove members away. Second, the content is regulated by the group members. The fact that everyone is welcome to engage in dialogue does not mean that all perspectives are equally valid; tacit group norms state otherwise. JFM programs are for Christians—the vast majority of whom are Catholic—and the members are more traditional in their morality than one might imagine given the strong progressivism of many. Megan Sims believes that circumstances help us discern a moral course, yet she does not subscribe to moral relativism: "I want to be able to appreciate everyone's perspective, but I believe that a perspective that oppresses rather than liberates is contrary to Isaiah, which is contrary to Luke, which is contrary to Jesus." The groups welcome all people even while they do not believe all ideas are equally moral.

Grads are also very optimistic about the power of dialogue, revealing their belief that people are reasonable. Chris Miller, like many of the grads, comes from an occupation with social power and is very comfortable dialoguing with politicians and corporate giants: "We are going to invite that [mining] company vice-president to come with us and serve on the panel. We can discuss the pros and cons. Whether he would do it, we don't know but, so that would be a chance to listen to both sides of the issue, so to speak."[25] If the shared management–employee discussions Catholics initiated in the past are any indication of the efficacy of this strategy, meeting and discussion are unlikely to achieve the results grads desire.[26] Yet it is a tactic that he and others employ in hope.

Discernment is another important mode of transmitting knowledge and has both individualist and communal elements. Beginning with the individualist element, to discern is to discover the "true good in every circumstance and to choose the right means of achieving it."[27] Discernment in this definition has both a cognitive element to it and an expectation of action, as Dr. Emily Reese explains: "There's a lot of discernment built into every [JustFaith] experience. And true discernment leads toward some action, and it doesn't separate the contemplation and the action, the Martha/Mary kind of metaphors that somebody likes to use like that. It doesn't split them so much or isolate them so much." Discernment allows individuals to reflect on new experiences and act on their world.

In addition to this individualist element, there is likewise a communal element to discerning God's will. Having others whom one respects to evaluate his or her discernment can be invaluable. A person may be rash, fail to see another legitimate perspective, and so forth. Therese Brewer discusses the importance of the community in aiding individual discernment: "Community is so important. You need people that you can trust and that you respect enough on their opinion on what you are doing, or what you intend on doing. I think that's how I would define how to live an ethical life." Living an ethical life in this schema is much more difficult without the insights of others. Many discipleship communities are critical for members' action. A grad remembers when she was arrested for blocking the entrance to a country club that she and others believed was not paying a fair wage to its workers. She says that she was not sure she had the courage to go through with the action until a fellow grad said he would go with her for emotional support. In JustFaith, discernment is both an individual and a group process that teaches members ways to think about and act in their world.

Tying this to what was said earlier, experience and testimony bring stories to the group. Dialogue and discernment help them to collectively interpret these through a lens that JFM believes will make them more compassionate people, highlighting the intersubjectivity of knowledge.[28] As said at the outset, people typically present and receive knowledge as information, news, or story. The story genre provides listeners with a subjective frame to interpret the objective elements of the experience. When the story unfolds and its interpretive frame is accepted by the group, the moral and affective knowledge becomes intersubjective, with the group members collectively endorsing and reinforcing a particular understanding of an event. As the stories become more numerous, a whole narrative pattern, rather than an instance, emerges. Because the narrative is salient, relevant, and comprehensive, these stories can alter a person's worldview. The continuous telling of stories, giving grads a way to interpret theirs and others' experiences, is a major factor in grads' transformations.

As demonstrated earlier, the story is a very effective genre of knowledge in JFM. The story resonates with important American sensibilities, making it an especially effective tool in transmitting knowledge. The story owes much of its saliency to the personalist culture found within JFM, discipleship organizations and American life more generally.

Personalism as a Path to Compassion

Grads are especially critical of the individualism they see in American culture.[29] When the grads criticize "individualism," they are not describing a healthy honoring of the individual self. Rather, they mean that most people care only for themselves and those whom they choose (note the voluntarism) to care for. Grads worry about the withering of older forms of community, especially in cities and suburban areas.[30] People have lost the ability to speak in what sociologist Robert Bellah and his colleagues call their "second language."[31] In their renowned work *Habits of the Heart*, the Bellah team claims that Americans' first language is individualism: choice, identity, freedom, and self-interest.[32] These are the concepts Americans readily use to explain who they are and why they do what they do. A foreign-born staff member concurs with this: "*This* culture, that's the thing with this culture, it *very* strongly endorses individual preference. Choice is everything. Consumer choice is everything. You have the power with your individual consumer choices. If you don't like it, don't do it." Bellah and his colleagues assert that Americans are, in fact, familiar with concepts like community, obligation, service, and interdependence, but these are a part of Americans' second language. These are the concepts that percolate beneath the consciousness of most Americans, and many only draw on this communitarian language when their first language of individualism reaches its limits.[33] For example, Americans voice support or objections to political issues in terms of being personally affected in public and only speak beyond their self-interest when in private, apparently believing that self-interest is a more efficacious public tool.[34]

Other theorists have challenged this depiction of American mores and assert that Americans are not struggling with these individual and communal pulls as much as *Habits of the Heart* claims them to be. Instead, Americans are better understood as *personalists*. As sociologist Robert Wuthnow writes in *Acts of Compassion*, Americans are self-motivated individualists who do not usually care about nebulous others but will care deeply about particular individuals. Wuthnow found that 45 percent of all adults volunteer, averaging five hours per week per volunteer for their communities.[35] Yet, at the same time, he recognizes that even these volunteers live in a way that privileges individualism over community: those who volunteer hold just as many individualist beliefs as those who do not volunteer.[36] Americans, Wuthnow argues, have created their own way to be both individualists and altruistic by focusing their compassion on particular individuals and subjectivizing their volunteering.[37] According to this, a person might not care about the social isolation of the elderly, but he or she will make it a point to visit Ruth, an older next-door neighbor, at least weekly. Personalism is the way Americans, shaped by a rugged individualism, express compassion.

Within a personalist outlook, people will be more sensitive to and generous toward issues that affect those they know. Caroline Dunn explains that the wealthy, because they have fewer friends in low-income communities, are less likely to help the poor: "Here in JustFaith, they say that the poor give more relatively speaking, than the wealthy. Well, if your neighbor's kids are hungry, you're gonna help them. But if your neighbor's fifteen miles away you don't know about it, [you don't]." A personalist view, rather than undermining individualism, actually capitalizes on it. JFM programs bring the intimacy of traditional bonds shared with family and friends to those in vulnerable situations, with Megan Sims explaining, "When we don't care it doesn't matter if [other people don't] have clean water, because I do. And it doesn't matter who is hungry, because I'm not. All of the sudden when we start to know somebody we can't help but care." Personalist outlooks, even while rooted in individualist tendencies, direct people's concerns to others.

Two Expressions of Personalism

The irony in this is that while grads claim to reject individualism, their personalist logic is highly individualist. In many ways, the discipleship style privileges individual experience. These personalist expressions allow JFM programs to reject individualism as selfishness at the same time that they capitalize on certain individualist elements in contemporary American society. First, the programs and grads express personalism through the great weight they place on individual stories. Grads claim that learning about the suffering of individuals raises their awareness and gives them an urgency to act.[38] Stories, then, not only connect the members to one another and allow them to define events or the sacred through a particular frame; they also connect the members to others outside the group. Grads have always known that people are homeless or hungry. The important leap that personalism makes is to actually bring a person experiencing homelessness or food scarcity into the lives of participants: "I didn't know people who didn't eat every day, and I didn't know people who chose between paying their light and gas bill or paying their water bill. And I didn't know people who recycled cans as a way of making money. I didn't know people who were hugely traumatized by worse and have found themselves on the streets." Notice this grad does not say she was unaware that some people had difficulty paying their bills or recycled as a source of income. She simply had not met a specific individual who lived like this. Meeting those on the margins makes the abstract suffering in the world a reality and magnifies grads' urgency to become involved.[39]

Another personalist expression within the discipleship style is an emphasis on the transformation of individual actors.[40] These new stories are the impetus for the individual listener to change, as this Louisville grad emphasizes within her own faith journey, "I've never cared more about water than I did at the moment I got home from Nigeria because I spent time in this village where people are walking twenty-four miles a day to get water, twelve miles one way and twelve miles back. And all of the sudden I thought about washing my car, and I've never washed my car since then because why would I ever waste an ounce of water on a car . . . how many people all of the sudden became aware because they heard somebody's story?" Knowing the story of another's suffering, either through hearing an account or personally witnessing it, demands a change in one's life. Encounters with poor individuals also caused Gina McCormick to see those living in these situations as unique human beings:

> I was always of the opinion that the homeless can't be choosers. If you are homeless you are going to have to be, you really are supposed to be happy or grateful for a handout and blah, blah, blah. Well, going to those places [that provide services] I realized that, really, being choosey is part of being human—and they are humans and so they are choosey . . . At the other places [I volunteer], especially the one at Santa Monica, because you set out clothes, as well, and [they are] very fussy about the clothes . . . And then it surprised me and I thought that was great at the same time, because they have not lost their humanness. I think that's what it made me realize, is that really they are just like everyone else, they are not anything special. They are not anything to be pitied or anything, but just treated like a human being. And I think that's what has helped me— having the [JustFaith] class and seeing this—is that really, truly, these are all human beings.

A personalist understanding shapes the way grads view homelessness. Instead of seeing social problems and categories, they see suffering individuals. As these expressions of personalism demonstrate, American individualism shapes the ways grads understand their world. Individualism causes them to respond to these problems by ameliorating a person's suffering or by changing their own lifestyle rather than engaging in justice work.[41]

Moving from Caring for the Stranger to Caring for Family

As the preceding illustrates, personalism does not negate the individualist trends in American society. Rather, it uses the individualist elements already present in the participants to draw them closer to the suffering of those around them. These new experiences cause grads to expand their field of care to include people and issues different from those whom they typically encounter in their everyday lives.[42] Mike Campbell says of the youth program, "So the question we ask in JWalking is 'Do you care? [emphatic pause] Do you *really* care? [emphatic pause] How *much* do you care?' Do you care enough to change the way you live your life, for the sake of the world, future generations, all those kind[s] of things? Because if we don't change, how's it ever going to change?" Because people so often conceive of care in private terms, a personalist outlook allows people to understand their public ideas in intimate ways. Specifically, the care grads espouse makes reference to ideas about family in ways that are either expansive or analogous. An expansive notion of family means knowing that the concerns and well-being of others are as important as one's own. In this primarily cognitive frame, grads draw on notions of equal dignity and shared human family and apply their ideas in the abstract (e.g., the elderly). An analogous notion of family connects key people in one's life with others. This frame is emotive and draws the grad to a specific person's suffering (e.g., my friend, Hector, at the convalescent home). Families, having strong in-group bonds and considered a private institution, risk excluding others in need.[43] Expansive and analogical notions of family, however, draw grads more deeply into the suffering of others and motivate them to act.[44]

Expansive notions of family take familial care and extend it outside its traditional boundaries. Care for friends, family, and one's immediate world is important and valuable. For grads, these communities point them outward rather than eclipsing them from issues that do not immediately affect them. Under this new notion of care, there must be new avenues for showing care; people cannot show care for deforestation the same way they care for a sick child. Care changes from being only a private sentiment to include public action, expressed as justice activism. Bay Area retiree Joyce Roberts illustrates the ways her notion of care changed from being limited to her family to a more expansive understanding: "I was always an antiwar activist, antinuclear activist, my whole adult life, the last twenty or thirty years, but I didn't really see that so much as saving the world or saving individuals, as more like saving my family [laughing]. And I didn't realize that. But then as I got to go through JustFaith I was more concerned with everybody's welfare, at least trying to find some way to help a little bit more, with people who are struggling as opposed to more worried about what's going to happen to myself and my family." Caring for "everybody's welfare" causes this financially comfortable woman to become involved in concerns that would not be an issue for her if she cared only about her immediate social circle. This expanded care opens her up to activism for living wages, homelessness, third-world poverty, torture, and so forth.

Laura Dowell uses family analogically. Like the grad earlier, she shows that previous concerns for family and other loved ones are not ignored for more other-regarding pursuits. Instead, the love of one's family can *magnify* the suffering of a person living in poverty. Her church published a booklet featuring previous years' graduates and their experiences with JustFaith. She included two photos with her testimony: one with two young girls who were victims of human trafficking and another of her own two teenage boys. Next to the photos Dowell wrote, "Why should these children in the world [the girls], be treated with any less justice than these [her own]?" As she recounts this, the injustice brings her to tears as she adds, "[JustFaith] launched me much further out in caring. I look at my own kids and think, 'My God, what if nobody loved them? What if everybody wanted to hold on to their money and wouldn't save my kids?'" This analogical familial care magnifies the urgency of poverty and creates an interfamily sense of kinship and solidarity. JFM endorses this notion as well, including Dowell's testimony in their 2011 fund-raising letter.

Grads' major impetus for their civic involvement is compassion. Personalism allows compassion to be a private, intimate feeling as well as a public motivation. Grads appropriate a degree of familial feelings to social ills and feel responses of urgency similar to what they would feel for their biological family. Expansive notions of family make the victim cognitively abstract, mobilized grads around an issue and more readily invited responses of justice. Analogous ideas about social problems singled out a particular victim, mobilized grads around a particular person, and more readily invited responses of charity.[45] By increasing the compassion of religious and middle-class Americans, JFM hopes to ameliorate many peace and justice issues. JFM, as a ripple group, expects that this transformation of care will spill over into wider circles, affecting the lives of individual grads as well as their parish and world.

Knowledge and Personalism: The Church's Challenge in the Discipleship Style

The historical styles of public Catholicism each posed unique challenges for the church. The republican style, as it privatized Catholicism, did not leave a space for the church to evangelize the wider society. The immigrant style, with its total withdrawal from American society, left the church without a way to influence the wider society. The evangelical style rejected many of the dominant social institutions, also limiting the church's influence in the wider society. The discipleship style, situated in an organizationally weaker church and amid a society with strong individualist mores, leaves public action to individual discernment. Their moral, professional, and cultural tools include secular skills, personal experiences, and Catholic elements, and the Catholic elements they prioritize may not match those of their priest or bishop. This leaves the magisterium less able to control the energies of the laity. Far from awaiting orders, Catholics are discerning for themselves how to be Catholic in the world. However, although the magisterium may have lost *control* over the laity, it still has *influence* over the laity. This is a sociological lesson for the church if it wishes to be a cultural force in contemporary America.

Of all the national churches in the Western world, American Catholics are the most Catholic by numerous measures. Yet they challenge many traditional Catholic values. One of the most obvious, for both conservative and liberal Catholics, is their need to be persuaded by church teaching. From 1987 to 2011, increasing numbers of Catholics nationwide believed that *only* one's personal conscience—neither solely the bishops nor a dialogue between the clergy and laity—should determine one's beliefs on divorce and remarriage, abortion, nonmarital sex, and homosexuality.[46] Knowledge has always constructed reality, but Catholics of the past privileged the clergy's knowledge over their own. American Catholics, in short, no longer accept teaching simply because their priests or bishops proclaim it.

Part of the reason that the bishops' pastorals of the 1980s were so effective is that they consulted expert laypeople and released drafts to the public, who could then contact their bishops with feedback, effectively dialoguing with American Catholics. Before the release of *The Challenge of Peace*, 34 percent of Catholics, the same percentage as Protestants, believed the government was spending too much on defense. A year after its release, the number of Protestants objecting to the current level of military spending remained the same at 34 percent, while 54 percent of Catholics disagreed with the current spending policies.[47] Whereas Mass attendance, strength of identification with the church, and feelings toward abortion each had no effects on the reception of the pastoral letter, three factors did correlate: Democrats, self-described liberals, and those who voted for Jimmy Carter or John Anderson in the 1980 election were all much more likely to be persuaded by the bishops' pastoral.[48] The bishops had to dialogue with Catholics on the morality of nuclear arms. Those who were open to what the bishops had to say—in this case, progressive Catholics—changed their opinion on military spending. Catholics who were favorable to the Reagan administration generally ignored the pastoral letter, illustrating that religion has become more individually important than collectively important for many.[49] The larger point is that many Catholics received these teachings. Similarly, many rejected *Humanae Vitae*, which disregarded the advice of the consultative body. If the magisterium wants to influence the American laity, they must be persuasive and dialogical.[50]

JFM recognizes the role of reason and dialogue in transforming or deepening people's beliefs. However, everyday life does not often afford people the opportunity to discuss their beliefs on tax spending or abortion in a reasonable and noncombative manner. They are trying to make deadlines at work, help kids with homework, follow up with a sick friend, have a night with a friend in town, and follow their consciences the best they can given their circumstances. In providing two-and-a-half hours each week of thoughtful discussion, participants are allowed to disagree, question, and encourage each other. As a result, participants are usually more in agreement with church teaching than at the outset.

However, reason and dialogue are only part of the story. JFM recognizes the role of knowledge as experience and this intentional time with low-income individuals changes participants' outlook faster than any encyclical. Witness trumps catechesis. Through immersions and hearing personal accounts through books and films, participants are provided a new lens for viewing their world. By embedding this knowledge in stories, JustFaith helps grads understand that Catholic social teaching is a morally urgent and fundamental part of the Christian life, compelling them to transform their world.

Conclusion

Compassion is a central Christian virtue for grads. They claim that true compassion leads to caring actions at both the personal and social levels. Although knowledge as facts corroborates grads' beliefs, experience is the form of knowledge that actually transforms them. This experience is given to participants in the form of stories. Stories are an especially effective genre of knowledge for programs that are both affective and cognitive like JustFaith because stories do not simply convey facts; they also provide an interpretive frame with which to understand those facts. There are parameters for storytelling that help ensure that members accept the facts as well as the moral value of those facts. These parameters also help group members tell their own stories in a way that is conducive to the mission of the group as a whole. These parameters shape their beliefs and the way they act in the world. Dialogue and discernment further change the way participants understand a social issue as they do not interpret any story on their own but through weighing the opinions and beliefs within their discipleship community.

This all underscores the importance of personalism in JFM, discipleship groups, and American society more broadly. Compassion in JFM—as well as in the United States generally—is a concern for concrete individuals who are suffering, rather than more abstract issues.

This personalism affects the way grads view and address social problems, with this micro-level lens lending itself to charity more readily
than justice. The way contemporary Catholics treat knowledge, discernment, and authority has repercussions for American Catholicism. The
magisterium must dialogue with today's Catholics and take compassion
seriously if it seeks to influence the lives of the faithful.

Compassion is a central value of grads and JFM as it animates much
of what they do. Although grads are not as involved in activities that
could influence politics and structures as much as they indicate they
would like to be, their willingness to care deeply about the suffering of
others still brings them to the needs of others on a regular basis. What
this means for American Catholics and other issues more broadly is discussed next in the conclusion to this book.

Conclusion

JustFaith Ministries and the American Catholic Landscape

Although JustFaith Ministries (JFM) itself is relatively small, it undergirds theories and provides analytical frames with which to understand contemporary American life and Catholic civic engagement, in particular. This book follows the general scholarly pattern of finishing with a "conclusion." Here I briefly revisit the four characteristics of a personalist style of Catholic civic engagement—individual engagement, individual-level solutions, individual locus of moral authority, and integrating faith and society—as well as their ramifications for Catholic efforts toward social justice and for the perceived authority of the Catholic Church hierarchy. Still, the best conclusions also point readers onward. Rather than a summative ending, readers find a beginning. To this end, this conclusion also raises questions for further study. However, herein are also observations that invite pause, evoke disquiet, or are without easy resolution. So goes human life.

As we have seen, one way personalism manifests in the discipleship style is in mobilizing individual Catholics rather than collectives. Historically, American Catholics were institution builders, founding schools, hospitals, professional organizations, orphanages, relief societies, and more. If Catholics wanted to become more publicly involved, there were often a few Catholic organizations from which to choose. Now, Catholic engagement typically happens at the level of the individual, volunteering with a social project that could be Catholic or not. This is both an asset and a liability. The upside is that these professionalized Catholics can get involved in the ministries that best suit their talents and desires. However, this individual engagement has some drawbacks. First, working as individuals weakens the potential for justice activism, which is more effective when people work in collaboration. JFM, unlike some discipleship groups, seeks to foment justice in addition to charity, and working alone significantly impairs justice efforts. The second drawback is that working alone is an inefficient use of resources. The traditional bloc form of activism, even when charity-related, allowed for the formation of new organizations that could be run and funded at the local level. These contemporary Catholics have more money and education than their predecessors and could potentially create vibrant organizations, but they cannot do so if they continue to engage society independently. This raises a question of strategy: Can the discipleship style be attractive if it harnesses individual actors initially but then organizes them along traditional Catholic lines? Perhaps. For example, organizations could recruit active volunteers to create core leadership teams that mobilized their parishes to collectively engage the world. Discipleship-style Catholics could transform parishes, leading efforts to create organizations that channeled parish efforts to social problems in a systematic and dedicated way. This sustained and formal commitment would yield more efficacy in both charitable and justice-oriented endeavors. But would contemporary Catholics assent to bloc mobilization? They may if it still included a sense of relationship as a central piece.

This desire for relationship is connected to a second way in which personalism orients the discipleship style: it points Catholics to individual-level solutions. As we have seen, JFM grads more often engage in works of charity than of justice because of the one-on-one relationships charity provides. Yet these relationships and a reliance on individual-level solutions frustrate discipleship groups' commitments to justice, with Catholics engaging in work that ultimately fails to address the structural change that both JFM and the grads seek to effect. Because they all agree that justice work is a needed form of social activism, the way to increase justice work among grads may simply be to bring that same personalist feel to justice work.

One way to do this is to create a volunteer position at an extant social service agency that explicitly attends to justice. It might look like this: grads volunteer at a homeless shelter, initially building relationships with the residents and engaging in more typical forms of volunteering. Once they become a part of this community, they could change their role to be more activist and become advocates for the agency. Instead of preparing food or doing laundry, they might have one-on-one conversations with the residents about their concerns and compile these to bring to their legislators. Grads could become liaisons for the homeless shelter and their parish, mobilizing both parishioners and shelter residents in letter-writing campaigns. Evidence shows that people are less likely to be registered to vote the lower their income.[1] Having registration drives at the shelter would help residents participate in the policies that determine their access to goods and services that ultimately shape their life outcomes. All these strategies address justice as well as involve the building of community and relationships for grads, creating an avenue for a personalist form of justice.

A related question this study raises is whether American Catholic morality is doomed to stay personal. Even after grads brought faith to their daily lives, going beyond sex and stealing to issues of poverty and social welfare, they still overwhelmingly choose individualist ways to respond. For example, when looking at the problems with the market, they focus on consumption much more than production, and answers to problems in production are typically answered by supporting fair-trade goods. Most of their solutions are at the level of individual lifestyle, just like theft and adultery. If Catholicism wants to have a larger impact on American life, it must expand *notions* of Catholic morality—which it has done within official documents—as well as *responses* from the laity. Using the example of the homeless shelter, this sort of collaboration should also involve intentional efforts to illuminate for both parishioners and residents the religious meaning in their activism. Christian groups have been very active in American social justice issues, such as the civil rights movement,[2] the Central American peace movement,[3] and the nuclear freeze movement.[4] Discovering the ways new sorts of moral imaginations and religious responses arise in a personalist context would be fruitful scholarship.

The third characteristic of discipleship-style organizations is that they mobilize contemporary Catholics who have a strong sense of their personal moral authority. Calling to mind a quote from John Steinbeck's 1961 novel *The Winter of Our Discontent*, when it comes to moral choices among today's Catholics, "[n]o one wants advice—only corroboration." And it is not simply that discipleship groups mobilize Catholics who now have more ownership over their moral choices; the personalist emphasis within discipleship groups intensifies individual moral authority, inadvertently undermining the moral monopoly the church hierarchy once enjoyed. From vocation to discernment to experience to obligations of conscience, truths for discipleship Catholics are discovered, not passively received from an external authority, and this shapes their commitments, imagination, and ways they accept and understand church teaching. It is important to note that, as we have seen, although grads are generally progressive, dissent among US Catholics also occurs among conservatives, indicating that discipleship groups with more traditionalist orientations would probably likewise harbor a personalist morality. Individual moral authority is something American Catholics at every point on the political continuum have internalized, especially among discipleship Catholics.

This increased emphasis on personal moral authority brings both challenges and opportunities for the church. Something that the magisterium may consider a liability is the independence the laity assume in discerning their personal roles in public life. Members of discipleship organizations will be drawn to particular aspects of church teaching whether or not their local bishop deems these a priority. This individual moral discernment results in a church with less focus and cohesion than the previous styles offered. Catholics get involved in issues and projects that they themselves find personally meaningful. The magisterium is no longer *the* voice; it is *a* voice among many sources of moral influence. Discipleship Catholics will not be persuaded by the magisterium qua magisterium.

But this more morally sophisticated and discerning laity is also an asset. Catholicism has a developed intellectual tradition that should compel those in authority to rise to these challenges. Rather than understanding the move from "*the* voice" to "*a* voice" as an obstacle, it should be reframed as an opportunity. In needing to make sound arguments that appeal to reason, the church may enter into wider debates and concerns, becoming a relevant voice not just for Catholics but also for society more broadly.

Furthermore, this more competent and personalist laity should be viewed as a boon by the hierarchy. Rather than long for the "easier" days of an obedient and less educated flock, church officials should plumb the depths of tradition, reason, scripture, and experience in a thoughtful, robust, and nuanced way, relying more on a position's cogency than on their ecclesial office when dialoguing with the laity. Magisterial leaders will no doubt find it takes more time and patience to dialogue than to promulgate. But in doing the long work of dialogue, they will have earned an arguably stronger, more respected, and more authentic fidelity than they currently enjoy. In fact, given the findings discussed in this volume, a wise pastoral move may be for a bishop to be less single-minded with his own civic priorities—be those immigration, abortion, poverty, capital punishment, same-sex marriage, peace, or others—and simply to encourage every parish and individual Catholic to promote the church's mission in the world as they are called. Likewise, parish priests might inspire more Catholics if they, too, are less directive and more generally supportive. This trust from their bishops and priests will no doubt help the laity to feel a connection to their parish, diocese, and global church more readily. And in trusting, they may also expand their engagement to the issues that most concern their leaders. Finally, bishops and clergy who reach out in more pastoral ways—capitalizing on Catholics' desires for relationship and the personal—can expect to be met warmly.

The final characteristic of personalism in the discipleship style is a stronger integration of religious beliefs with the rest of a person's life. Many signs indicate that the church is in trouble as an institution: falling Mass attendance, the priest shortage, rising rates of disagreement with official teachings, high rates of attrition, and numerous other measures. Except for the religious social activism of the 1980s, the contemporary American Church has not made efforts to help Catholics connect their faith to public life. Catholic institutions, such as hospitals and schools, are no longer distinctly "Catholic" and are run similarly to their secular counterparts. Discipleship groups combat some of these tendencies of declining Catholic identity and the bifurcation of faith and everyday life, giving Catholics a way to enter public life *as Catholics*.

The discipleship style simultaneously revivifies Catholics' faith and sense of mission, as these mutually reinforce one another. From Opus Dei to Catholic Christian Outreach to JFM, discipleship Catholics generally have a strengthened faith and more readily connect religion to their public life. Part of this robustness comes from discipleship communities' embracing of two "rules."[5] The first rule is that strict churches are strong. Churches—or other ideologically bound groups—that have strong in- and out-group boundaries and demand much from their members are better at fostering religious identity and helping members connect their faith to other aspects of their life. The second rule initially seems to contradict the first: churches wishing to remain vibrant and relevant must engage the major changes in their culture, such as industrialization, the transition from rural to urban life, and so forth. Discipleship groups take seriously the waning religious identity of American Catholics, the decrease in traditional forms of religious expression and the possibility of spiritual lethargy or heterodoxy in the unsettled times of Catholicism today. These discipleship communities provide participants with a space to draw distinct boundaries between themselves and the world but in a way that still compels them to engage the world. By studying Catholic teaching, integrating the lives of Jesus and the saints with their own, utilizing familiar components of the liturgy, attending Mass together, and encouraging friendships, discipleship communities create a renewed sense of pride in and identity with one's Catholic tradition, distinct from and critical of the world "out there." Despite their critique of society, there is also a sense of mission that pushes members of these communities into the world, a world they repair, are grateful for, participate in, find joy in, and pray for and with. Discipleship communities creatively bring together a high-tension outlook with the concern to be embedded in and relevant to the world.

Even with a preference for individual-level solutions, JFM programs can play a critical role in bringing outreach and even justice to parishes. The common outreach strategy among parishes is to establish a social justice or outreach committee that handles the mission of serving the poor. This is effective in some regards and self-defeating in others. When there is a social justice or outreach committee, a designated group of individuals are trained and experienced in handling the needs that arise. The presence of this committee can cause fellow parishioners to believe that the poor are taken care of and that the uninvolved somehow participate in this ministry by dint of it being in their parish. This participation-by-proxy can allow the vast majority of the parish to neglect or distance themselves from poverty and related issues, ultimately participating in few charitable works themselves. When Catholics perceive justice and outreach as peripheral, their charity atrophies. The strategy of JFM is to change the definition of what it means to be a Christian, bringing the traditional works of mercy, charity, justice, and

almsgiving to a twenty-first-century context. This would not abolish social justice committees, but it would restructure how parishes handle
social ministry. Parish social ministry would be a component of faith
formation, Lenten practices, and so forth, getting the whole parish involved while connecting justice to Catholic piety. Just as a living and
merciful faith is the foundation of discipleship Catholics' lives, so, too,
can this social relevance permeate the faith life of the parish. Again, faith
and mission strengthen one another.

Personalist Catholics: To Be Continued . . .

Shifting Catholic demographics requires considering these findings
in light of the future of American Catholicism. Engagement in the
discipleship style requires a fair amount of skill, public savvy, and
professionalism. Relatedly, the introduction noted the dominance of
white grads in this study. However, within a generation or two, the
Catholic Church in the United States will be predominantly Latinx.[6]
Will Latinx Catholics, as they stay for more generations in the United
States and continue to vote and attend college in increasing numbers,
also find the characteristics of the discipleship style attractive? Or will
the discipleship style wane as the percentage of white Catholics diminishes? Christian Smith and his team found that the third-generation
young adult Latinx Catholics looked similar to their white counterparts in some, but not all, ways.[7] We must recognize that the significant
absence of Catholics of color among these participants—also found in
another discipleship group, the Jesuit Volunteer Corps—could affect
this style's staying power as Catholicism becomes more ethnically
diverse.[8] However, much in this style resonates with Latinx theology,
such as an emphasis on community, storytelling, and experience.[9]
With the multiple factors at play and the notable absence of Catholics
of color in this study, determining whether this style will characterize Catholic civic engagement in a more ethnically diverse church is
difficult.

Another question that is beyond the scope of this research is, Is this
really a discipleship style? That is, is this unique to Catholicism? Do other
religious denominations have organizations that demonstrate these similar traits, like ripple groups, individual mobilization, and a theology of

pragmatic reverence? A brief story might illustrate the broader relevance of this analysis. I was presenting some of these findings at a meeting of the Association for the Sociology of Religion. Among those presenting in the session was a group of four young women. They discussed their experiences of earning their master's degree in sociology at their Protestant college while simultaneously enrolled in a program that required them to live together and spend time doing community engagement with marginalized groups. I noticed that they kept exchanging glances with one another during my presentation. When the time for questions came, one of these women said, "Just to explain our glances, everything you said described our year perfectly!" Her housemates nodded in agreement.

Although there were differences between Catholic and Protestant grads, that the similarities were far more apparent is worth noting. Also, the social changes that precipitated the discipleship style affected many non-Catholic Americans as well. Some Protestant denominations boast memberships with greater income and education than most Americans, just like these Catholics. Additionally, increased geographic mobility characterizes Americans generally. Finally, the increased emphasis on personal moral authority rather than institutional authority characterizes all Americans, even those of conservative denominations.[10] Perhaps this "discipleship style" is merely a Catholic expression of a larger "personalist style" that characterizes contemporary American civic engagement more broadly. Discovering whether this style exists within other denominations or even in secular volunteer groups is a question ripe for scholarly inquiry.

The smallest unit of analysis is JustFaith's impact on the individual. As JFM's strategy is that of the ripple group, it pours its organizational energies into the participants. Still, many grads struggle with dilemmas and are unsure how to best engage the world. Given the tensions and challenges, two final remarks are in order. The first is that, despite the dilemma of efficacy, JustFaith provides its participants with ways to be faithful and effective within their middle- to upper-class social location. The second concerns the subjective transformation of the grads, a transformation that brings them hope as they engage the world.

In *To Change the World*, sociologist James Davidson Hunter offers his readers a "theology of faithful presence." To summarize, just as God is faithfully present to people, so should Christians be faithfully present to each other, to their tasks, and within their spheres of influence.[11] This faithful presence "gives priority to what is right in front of us."[12] It is communities of work, family, church, and others that offer invitations to grow in goodness, love, and faith, as well as opportunities to minister and be ministered to. Hunter also discusses the practical reality of a theology of faithful presence. In the Great Commission, Jesus tells his followers to go out into all the world. Hunter claims that Christians should interpret this call geographically as well as, importantly, socially, meaning that the faithful should be found in all social arenas and socioeconomic classes.[13] This notion of faithful presence resonates with much of what grads say as they grapple with ways to live faithfully as Christians in the modern world.

Some grads are more comfortable with privilege than others. Given their enthusiasm and high survey-response rate, grads took this study quite seriously. So it was unsurprising when a follow-up came in after the Louisville interviews. Caroline Dunn returned a lengthy letter along with her survey. An excerpt reveals her struggles:

> I wish I could tell you that [my husband] and I worked with Mother Theresa's sisters in Calcutta or in a leper colony in India, but our steps were definitely "baby steps," including donating to a priest who works in a leper colony in India. Still, we are painfully aware of the difference between sending a check and holding the hand of a sick leper. But we have tried to support the missionaries by hosting them often in our home. We have tried to make small but positive changes: We have been much more conscious of our effect on the planet's limited resources. We have volunteered at clothing drives, food drives, shoe drives and Habitat for Humanity. I have taken our grandchildren to deliver food packages in poor neighborhoods and as a family we have eliminated gift exchanges at Christmas and donated the money to various charities.[14]

Her letter is filled with self-doubt. However, it also shows that while she may fail to hold the hand of a leper in India, she looks around at her world in Louisville and affects it in positive ways. She is an excellent example of a middle-class person trying to live her faith and morality in a complex world filled with challenges and ambiguity. Still, her unsettledness reveals not only her dissatisfaction but also her goodness, efforts, and sense that more is yet possible.

Another grad draws more confidently upon a theology of faithful presence. When asked about how wealthy Christians should manage economic disparity, James O'Reilly begins to answer the question but then changes it in an important way: "But I think the question is, How much effort am I giving to this relationship with God and what does God continue to reveal to me about what I'm to do?" Rather than scrutinizing one's bank account, Christians should be examining their relationship with God and discerning how God is calling them to be servants of others in the world. And this is not a "rationalization," as many grads worry when they say things such as these. O'Reilly worked full-time at a homeless shelter and lives a simple, joy-filled lifestyle. Grads live their religious values with intentionality, and many are confident— even while they recognize the difficulties—that the faithful can challenge themselves and serve God in a plethora of circumstances.

Second, JustFaith helps grads to frame their volunteering in such a way that they grow in hope, love, and joy. Sociologist Robert Wuthnow contends that volunteering is of limited efficacy in materially solving society's problems, yet it has profound effects on the volunteer and wider society. In *Acts of Compassion*, he writes that, despite the inability of volunteer work to cure social ills, it still "inspires goodness in the human condition, in the goodness of those who are truly needy and deserve our help. To participate in voluntary organizations means we are making a change for the better, siding with the good, doing something, rather than idly sitting by while the specter of chaos and corruption advances."[15] Most grads say that, in one way or another, their engagement or activism changes them in a profound way, leaving them filled with a sense of goodness and hope, with Megan Sims saying, "When I see [my homeless friend], I don't pretend to know everything about him, but I know that I've eaten a meal with him, I know where he goes during the day, and I'm pretty positive I know where he sleeps in the night. And I'm a better, fuller human being because of it, because I get to carry him with me. And it doesn't—it doesn't change much, *but it changes me* [my emphasis]." Her numerous volunteer commitments might feed a hungry person or get a jacket to someone who would have otherwise been cold. Yet she humbly acknowledges that the biggest change she sees is the change within herself. Sims continues, beginning by paraphrasing author Marianne Williamson: "We were born to manifest the glory of God, which is not in some of us, it is in all of us. If we're going to live into that then it starts by recognizing that everybody is born to manifest the glory of God, recognizing that is imperative." Getting to know her homeless friend and the countless others she encounters makes her more optimistic and gives her faith in humanity, seeing all people as participants in the glory of God. These JustFaith grads view society and those in it as a gift that they, in true freedom, care for.[16] JFM strives to change the world and still the problems—from hunger to war—remain. Determining whether JustFaith affects these issues is difficult. What JustFaith clearly succeeds in doing is forming individuals, encouraging them to grow in faith, hope, and love for God and humanity. If discipleship groups accomplish only this, they have given much to our world.

ACKNOWLEDGMENTS

This book would not be what it is without the steadfast support of many people. For their feedback, support, and all-around spunk, I thank key people who mentored me and helped shape this project. Lisa Fullam started teaching at the Jesuit School of Theology of Santa Clara University, the same semester I started learning there; thank you for your enthusiasm and for asking the questions that helped me to think in new ways, here and elsewhere. I first met Tricia Bruce, University of Notre Dame, through her joyful willingness to provide feedback to this manuscript; who knew that this project would be just the beginnings of our collaboration? To many more! Finally, Jerome Baggett, Jesuit School of Theology of Santa Clara University, my advisor, committee chair, and friend. Jerome, I offer you my abbreviated sappiness as you already know how deeply I appreciate the way you have taken on each of these roles; you continue to bring me happiness and insight while reminding me of what's most important in life. You're an amazing human being. Thanks.

Immense thanks to my editor at New York University Press, Jennifer Hammer, and the great team of folks who work with her. Others also in the process of writing their first book know too well the importance of quick communication, warm professionalism, and concrete direction. Jennifer, you are a wonderful editor in these ways, and I thank you for your dedication to this project and the craft more broadly. Thanks also to the three reviewers of this manuscript. One of these remained anonymous, and two, Michele Dillon and Jim Cavendish, disclosed their identities and let me probe them even further. The feedback from all three helped me see new things, greatly improving this book.

A host of others improved this book or facilitated the research in some way. A longtime friend who is an Oblate of Saint Joseph read a chapter of the manuscript and offered feedback on theological themes contained herein. In addition to my own transcribing of the interviews, many others assisted: Christy Fuller, Mariana Castañeda, Violeta Castañeda, and Shannon Day. Amy LaGoy offered many helpful tips for data collection and analysis. Eileen Limburg helped connect me to many churches that participated in this research. Many thanks to those congregations, the names of which, as promised, I will not disclose.

Because of the confidentiality I promised, I cannot list the many people associated with JustFaith Ministries (JFM) who so graciously shared their time and, often, intimate parts of their faith journey to make this book possible. Know that I am incredibly appreciative of your participation in this project. Those who were instrumental in connecting me with key individuals associated with the program include Meg Bowerman, Tony Fadale, Carol Harr, Amy LaGoy, Patricia Parfett, and Pat Plant. Given the spiritually sensitive nature of these programs and my research interests, I am especially grateful to the four JFM groups that allowed me to participate with them. Also, any organization that opens itself up to research and scrutiny takes a risk. I thank the founder of JustFaith Ministries, Jack Jezreel, and the board and staff for allowing me to pursue this project. I owe special thanks to staff member Mary Wright for her perpetual willingness, efficiency, and cheer when I needed data on the organization.

Thank you to my colleagues. Those at the Association for the Sociology of Religion, the Society for the Scientific Study of Religion, and the Religious Research Association have provided great company and conversation, especially my fellow sociologists of Catholicism: Gary Adler, Jerome Baggett, Tricia Bruce, Jim Cavendish, Michele Dillon, Stephen Fichter, Tom Gaunt, Mary Gautier, Brett Hoover, Linda Kawentel, April Manalang, Tony Pogorelc, Tia Pratt, Lucas Sharma, Brian Starks, and Pat Wittberg. A big thanks to my home institution, the Franciscan School of Theology, for its enthusiasm for my first publication and the many opportunities it has facilitated for me since my arrival. Special thanks to Jeff Burns, who has brightened countless mornings with his friendship, playful teasing, and genuine goodness. Keep it up!

I want to thank my family and my husband's parents for the ways they have aided me in this project. I thank my mother- and father-in-law, Cheryl and Pete Palermo, for hosting "camp" at their farm, giving their grandchildren two hundred acres to play on and a few days for me to delve deeply into writing or research. I am grateful in so many ways for my mother and my sister, Shannon and Megan Day, for these purposes for opening their homes and visiting with us, also giving me a chance to catch up on whatever was falling behind. I thank my father, David O'Day, who passed away when I was an undergrad. Although he would have preferred a book on Irish Catholic union organizers, his love of the church and tireless work for justice no doubt planted the seeds for this project and those to come.

Countless acknowledgments note the immense contributions of the author's indefatigable spouse who reads drafts, talks through ideas, or transcribes. This *cannot* be said of Joseph Palermo, my wonderful husband of sixteen years! What can be said is that he knows his strengths, and he was always there to play a board game Friday and Saturday nights after the kids were tucked in or offer a brilliant solution in ten seconds or less whenever I was experiencing technical problems. Thank you for *not* reading my drafts, and thank you, instead, for spending your time being my friend and an amazing father. Veronica, fourteen years old, and David, ten years old, took after Dad in knowing their strengths. After the first week of writing, Veronica looked at me with the compassion characteristic of the saint for whom she was named and said, "Mom, can I make you some turmeric tea?" David knew exactly when I needed an interruption for a great big hug. Care and affection came abundantly from all three of them throughout this process. I thank you all for making our home a place of generosity, fun, beauty, and love.

APPENDIX A

Detailed Methods

The methodological choices discussed in the Introduction are elaborated here. The geographic diversity of the interviewees (San Francisco, Los Angeles, and Louisville) was meant to allow me to observe the differences, if any, between red- or blue-state participants. Only one person whom I asked to interview declined (a Louisville resident who was not in town during my visit). The transcripts were coded using ATLAS.ti.

The four-page survey contained demographic questions as well as those asking about beliefs and practices. So they would be easily comparable to coreligionists nationally, some of the survey questions come from larger studies. Because I drew some questions for the Catholic survey from the William V. D'Antonio team's national Catholic study and from several national studies for the Protestant survey, this resulted in slightly different surveys for Catholics and Protestants. Because of the small number of Protestants in my sample, I gave surveys to an additional thirteen Protestants, whom I did not interview, which totaled twenty surveys from Protestant graduates. I also surveyed a small group of thirty-six people—twelve Protestants and twenty-four Catholics— within their first three weeks of beginning JustFaith. This was to see the propensities of those who would enroll in a JustFaith Ministries (JFM) program as well as to gather a baseline to estimate the effects, if any, of JustFaith on the participants. Unless indicated otherwise, the survey findings draw on both those interviewed and the supplementary Protestants ($n = 66$) but exclude the thirty-six just beginning the program as the latter are used only to study the effects of the programs on individual graduates—explored extensively in the third chapter.

I also conducted participant observation in four JFM programs: JustFaith, Engaging Spirituality, the JustMatters module on prison reform, and GoodNewsPeople. In these sessions, I fully participated in readings and discussion as any other member would. Each member of the groups I was in understood my project and consented to my being there.[1] At many JFM events, I openly took notes, and I revealed my research interests to anyone who asked.

APPENDIX B

Overview of JustFaith Ministries Programs

JustFaith

JustFaith is the original program that began with a dozen or so Catholics in Louisville's Church of the Epiphany. It started out as a thirty-five-week program that aimed to transform lives and the world through an experience of Catholic social teaching in a small-group setting. Once there was a real intention to spread this program, sessions became far more scripted, from the prayers to the symbols on the table. As the years have gone by, the program has changed. The first notable change was the addition of the ecumenical version, which does not include Catholic social teaching or prayers and symbols that are specific to Catholicism. The program length also decreased, dropping from thirty-five weeks to thirty weeks. In 2013, the Catholic version of the program further reduced the number of sessions, from thirty sessions to twenty-four or twenty-seven sessions,[1] while the ecumenical version remained unchanged. The decrease in sessions accompanied a reduction in the amount of time the groups met, from two-and-a-half hours to two hours. JustFaith Ministries (JFM) made these adjustments primarily in response to the fact that participants felt the length of the program was prohibitive, discouraging many who would have otherwise registered. The popularity of JustFaith peaked between 2006 and 2009, with roughly 280 to 300 groups yearly, and has been slowly declining, stabilizing at about 50 groups per year in 2018. For most of 2016, JFM decided to only run the ecumenical version but, after much feedback, brought back the Catholic version in the fall of 2016.

The format of the program involves a considerable amount of reading, fifty to seventy-five pages per week, and weekly meetings in which typically between eight and fourteen participants gather to pray, watch videos, discuss the readings, and share reflections on their struggles and growth through the program. There are also three three-hour immersion experiences at local nonprofits. Here participants do not serve a meal to the homeless but, instead, sit and share a meal with them, emphasizing relationship with the marginalized. There is a daylong Journey to Justice Day retreat that involves learning more about organizations in the area receiving local grants from the Catholic Campaign for Human Development. These featured organizations are deliberate in their justice approach to social problems, rather than taking a purely charitable approach. There are also two day-and-a-half retreats, one at the start of the program that facilitates the forming of community within the group and a second at the end to commission the graduates.

JusticeWalking

JusticeWalking (JWalking) began in 2004 as a response to the many graduates hoping for a similar program for their teen children. Mike Campbell was running youth retreats at Crossroads Ministry, an inner-city retreat house in Louisville. Youth, some of whom had never encountered situations of poverty, would go there to learn about what Jesus and the church taught about poverty and come face-to-face with things they had only seen before on the evening news. The methods he used here became the foundations for JWalking. JWalking is for seven to twelve high schoolers, preferably juniors and seniors, and consists of twelve two-hour sessions that, according to the group's needs, can run weekly for three months or every other week for six months. In 2009, JFM extended JWalking to college students. After one year of running it in a manner identical to the high school program, Campbell condensed it to seven sessions. The change respected the fact that college students brought more life experience to the program than high school students did and could process the material more quickly. The alteration was also pragmatic in that college students can only structure their schedules on a semester-by-semester basis, making a six-month program quite difficult.

JWalking has a structure very similar to JustFaith with some notable adjustments. The opening and closing retreats for JWalkers are over-
night. In JWalking, the visits to local nonprofits comprise half of their

meetings. They also have a daylong justice retreat, called a Justice Pilgrimage. Two notable additions are a journal that participants use regularly and five "spiritual practices," such as fasting from their cell phone and praying more or for one week carrying around all the garbage they generate. There is also a notable difference between the targets of the program. Although JFM claims that JustFaith is a program for anyone who wants to learn more about Catholic social teaching with no previous knowledge or experience required, they go to great lengths to explain that JWalking is not for everyone. In fact, this program will only be a good fit for a handful of youth. Campbell uses the metaphor of a wedge to explain different types of youth and their corresponding ministries:

> We often use this wedge model with the young people. One end of the wedge is really wide and that's where you have your parties, and you have disco nights, you have pizza parties. You . . . maybe throw Jesus in there a couple of times . . . And as you get farther down they may have service. Far fewer people are going to come but it's still going to be really easy to do. It's one day, let's do Habitat . . . And you go farther down: let's actually begin bonding . . . and maybe make a mission trip or whatever. Then you get to that very narrow end of the wedge where even fewer people come. That's for the inner circle of the really motivated kids . . . they're really motivated to ask harder questions and want to make definite plans and commitments. *That's* who JWalking is for . . . rather than try to get *everybody* to a *popular* program, let's do something prophetic.

At the JusticeWalking webinar on March 22, 2013, the instructor underscored this point: "Here's another countercultural message: JWalking is *not* for everyone." She qualified that it "isn't because the Gospel invitation isn't for everyone—in fact, Jesus calls all of us to follow Him—but [JWalking is] not for everyone because not everyone is ready or willing to respond to such a radical invitation." Rather than interpreting JWalking's small market as elitism, JFM believes that only a small few are ready to become, as Campbell sees the JWalkers, prophets. The webinar also specified that the program could not be a requirement or confirmation[2] class, emphasizing the no-strings-attached voluntarism that needs to accompany a more intense and countercultural program looking to foster transformation in the youth. As of 2015, JWalking is no longer offered.

JustSkills

JFM introduced a third program called JustFaith II. This was a "how-to" for the formation that the first JustFaith program offered. It offered skills in getting involved in direct service, doing legal advocacy, organizing committees, and so forth. It did not, however, receive great feedback from its participants. Because of the name, too many people expected it to be an extension of the first program. They renamed it JustSkills, but it remained unpopular. JFM discontinued the program in 2010, but many of the skills are now offered as a JustMatters module, elaborated below.

JustMatters

JustMatters started in 2007 as a way to allow program graduates or those totally new to JFM to dive more deeply into a contemporary issue in a faith-based way. This program began quite popular, with seventy-one groups the first year and more than doubling that two years later. Registrations are lower as of this writing, with eighty-five groups in 2017. The breadth of topics these modules cover has grown over time. Their first module was *God's Creation Cries for Justice; Climate Change: Impact and Response*. The next year they added *Prison Reform: The Church of the Second Chance*. In 2009 they offered four new modules, the first being *Living Solidarity: Government, the Budget, and the Common Good*. The second was *New Wineskins: Forming Mission Based Communities*, for JustFaith groups who wish to stay together and discern next steps following JustFaith. The third module was *Engaging Our Conflicts: An Exploration of Nonviolent Peacemaking*. The fourth was *Crossing Borders: Migration, Theology, and the Human Journey*. There were two new modules in 2010: *Faith Encounters the Ecological Crisis* and *In the Footsteps of the Crucified: Torture is Never Justified*. With 2011 came *Sanctity of All Life* and *In the Spirit of St. Francis and the Sultan: Muslims and Christians Working Together for the Common Good*. The latter of these is JFM's first and, so far, only attempt at an interreligious offering, bringing together Christians and Muslims. From year to year, JFM has changed, added or updated the modules as needed, sometimes changing the name of the module to better reflect the new content. These groups were eight to fifteen people in size and run anywhere from six to twelve sessions, depending on the module, and each session lasts two-and-a-half hours. By 2018 they had standardized the modules so that they are each eight weeks in length.

The format is quite similar to JustFaith, with prayer, respectful listening, study, and sharing. Because of the brevity of the modules, they do not include immersion experiences. Still, the curriculum usually encourages the groups to arrange something themselves. By dint of the focus on a particular topic, they draw a wide range of people, from those already active in the issue to JustFaith grads and others seeking to learn more. Several interviewees said that their JustFaith group continued to meet after the thirty weeks through their collective participation in a module. As of this writing there are four JustMatters modules.

Engaging Spirituality

The story about the birth of Engaging Spirituality is different from the others in that it was brought into being by a generous donor. Luke Bender found a great deal of insight and growth through contemplative prayer. Because he was wealthy, Bender was able to go on numerous retreats and study under the modern masters of Catholic techniques in centering prayer. He realized many others could not afford these expensive retreats that he enjoyed frequently. Because Bender considered contemplative prayer a means that others, like himself, might find necessary to living a prayerful life, he wanted to make them more financially available. He approached two retreat centers and a famous practitioner and teacher of contemplative prayer, and each said that designing something for independent use was outside of the scope of their mission. As a fourth option, Bender approached JFM, having gone through the JustFaith course previously and appreciating the national availability of its programs. The staff considered whether centering prayer was a part of their mission. After much thought, they came to see it as an important complement to JustFaith. JFM describes JustFaith as "leading us out and into a world filled with problems and possibilities" and Engaging Spirituality as "draw[ing] this world down into ourselves, to hold it together in prayer and practice living deeply."[3] Because Campbell, creator of JusticeWalking, was the point person for this program, he wrote up a proposal of the way he envisioned the program and the donor did the same. They exchanged proposals and met the following day, both pleased with the similarities between the proposals and Bender excited about the small overhead and creativity of JFM. The program had a pilot year in 2008, with Campbell laughing that fifty-six groups "in my mind is not a pilot. That's a small launch." Engaging Spirituality has continued to be a popular program, for both JustFaith grads and those new to JFM.

This twenty-one-week program is actually quite different from Just-Faith, with a real emphasis on interior prayer and an invitation to make a modest commitment of two hours of service each month. There are the same recommended group sizes, immersion experiences, guidelines for dialogue, and the content of the program centers on the poor and marginalized. In contrast with JustFaith, the program has less reading and the added expectations of journaling and daily centering prayer, meant to foster greater introspection and quiet than JustFaith lends itself to. Every session begins with centering prayer, starting the participants with just two minutes and, by the end of the twenty-one weeks, allowing participants twenty minutes of contemplative prayer. Another unique part of the weekly sessions is the reading of bearings letters. To illustrate the diversity of these, one contributor is the director of a Christian peace association; another advocates against torture; there is a couple living a life of service, material simplicity, and grandparenting; and still another is a priest who works for racial justice. These letters come in three sections: the writer's "struggle," the day-to-day difficulties that illustrate that holiness is not easy or even something readily embraced; a "practice," what the writer does to keep focused on God, fueling a desire to serve despite the apparent difficulties or impossibilities; and a "challenge," parting words for the listeners to encourage them to a richer, holier, and more rewarding life. Following each of these three parts, participants are invited to share a word or phrase that they found compelling, difficult, or that simply resonated with them in some way. Participants are likewise asked to write their own bearings letter to share with the group.

Belonging

Belonging is a program that was born out of Engaging Spirituality and designed especially for Protestants. Although Protestants have successfully run Engaging Spirituality with denominationally specific adjustments, JFM wanted a resource that would bring them centering prayer in more familiar terms. It is very similar to Engaging Spirituality in style and content, with the notable exception that it is much shorter at seven two-hour sessions. This program was small when it piloted in 2012 and was discontinued in 2013.

GoodNewsPeople

GoodNewsPeople was perhaps the most exciting program for the Louisville staff at its launch. As they began to see the registrations for JustFaith decline, they wondered how they could reach more Catholics and teach them how they could be good news for the poor. They realized that the vast majority of those who signed up for JustFaith were usually among the most active and faithful of their parish; who else would want to meet for two-and-a-half hours weekly, engage in fair amounts of spiritual reading, sacrifice Saturdays to spend time with the poor, and so forth except those who already took their faith rather seriously. These were highly committed Catholics, and although JustFaith was increasing their spirituality, awareness, and activism, it would never reach less active Catholics. JFM refers to these less active Catholics as "middle-pew" Catholics. They are not the front-pew Catholics already involved in the St. Vincent de Paul or parish council or the first to come help when there is a need. Nor are they the back-pew Catholics who leave immediately after communion. The middle-pew Catholics attend Mass faithfully, perhaps bring a bag of groceries when there is a food drive, but are not as engaged in their faith as they could be or, as JFM might argue, as much as their church or world needs them to be.

JFM created a program specifically for these Catholics, one that is shorter and presents the church's teaching as "good news." Another thing that shaped the program was the desire to touch more people; if the program would not go as deep, then it would go wide. It is less demanding, with fourteen ninety-minute sessions. Yet it reaches more people, asking parishes to commit to ten groups of ten participants. The hope is that whole parishes will transform through the collective transformation of a large group of individuals, as well as encourage the participants to ask more probing questions about faith and society, pointing them to other JFM curriculum. In its pilot year of 2012, it had twenty-four groups, and in 2013, their first year of launch, they had ninety groups, for a staggering total of nine thousand Catholics in the program. Their most notable pocket of support was the Diocese of Stockton, where, in 2013, Bishop Stephen Blaire strongly encouraged all the parishes to run the program. However, they have not had a diocese support the program to such an extent since.

Group sessions are shorter than in JustFaith (I was a participant-observer during the pilot year and heard that several groups at the parish elected to meet for two or three hours so they could accommodate more discussion). Each session has a focus, such as "Created in God's Image," and this lesson connects to a virtue, like generosity, through lessons taken from *The Catechism of the Catholic Church*. Participants engage scripture through the traditional Benedictine practice of *Lectio Divina*, that is, reading Bible verses several times with contemplative pauses between. Because of the group setting, JFM adapted the practice to include discussion. Next, there is a GoodNews Story, featuring, like the bearings letters of Engaging Spirituality, an inspirational figure of the contemporary world. These stories come in three sections: the storyteller's "call," when the author began his or her spiritual journey; "belonging," the milestones and community in this faith journey; and "mission," how the author brings this faith into the world. Sometimes participants watch a DVD of a GoodNews story, with theologians and prominent Catholic leaders discussing the theological underpinnings of the featured person's activism, and other times, they read their own stories that they prepared in advance. The discussion of scripture, the story, and the *Catechism* is the focus of the ninety minutes, which opens and closes with prayer. The binder offers essays, journal prompts, and quotes from saints and others of deep faith to inspire and enliven participants throughout the week.

NOTES

INTRODUCTION

1 Other than Jack and Maggie Jezreel and the Church of the Epiphany, the names of all people and churches have been changed.

2 David J. O'Brien, *Public Catholicism*, 2nd ed. (New York: Orbis Books, 1996).

3 Robert Wuthnow, *Loose Connections: Joining Together in Americas Fragmented Communities* (Cambridge, MA: Harvard University Press, 2002), 50.

4 William V. D'Antonio, Michele Dillon, and Mary L. Gautier, *American Catholics in Transition* (Lanham, MD: Rowman & Littlefield Publishers, 2013), 78.

5 Michele Dillon, *Postsecular Catholicism: Relevance and Renewal* (New York: Oxford University Press, 2018), 19, 158.

6 I did not give one staff member a survey as the primary purpose of her interview was to collect historical data on the founding and development of JFM.

7 Compare these to JFM-provided statistics for 2017–2018 participants: seventy-one percent were fifty-five or older, and 41 percent were sixty-five or older. Seventy-seven percent were female, and 23 percent were male. Seventy-four percent were Catholic, 21 percent were members of different Protestant traditions, 4 percent opted not to disclose affiliation, and 1 percent were unaffiliated (although, as discussed earlier, JFM participants have historically been overwhelmingly Catholic).

8 Some of this is because these are older Catholics who went to college at a time when it was more common for Catholics to attend a religious school. D'Antonio, Dillon, and Gautier, *American Catholics in Transition*, 177.

CHAPTER 1. JUSTFAITH MINISTRIES AND THE DISCIPLESHIP STYLE

1 For an example, see Sharon Erickson Nepstad, *Religion and War Resistance in the Plowshares Movement*, Cambridge Studies in Contentious Politics (New York: Cambridge University Press, 2008).

2 Christian Smith, *Resisting Reagan: The U.S. Central America Peace Movement* (Chicago: University of Chicago Press, 1996).

3 United States Catholic Bishops, *The Challenge of Peace: God's Promise and Our Response*, 1983, in *Catholic Social Thought: The Documentary Heritage*, ed. David J. O'Brien and Thomas A. Shannon (Maryknoll, NY: Orbis, 1992).

4 United States Catholic Bishops, *Economic Justice for All*, 1986, in O'Brien and Shannon, eds., *Catholic Social Thought*.

5 Doug McAdam, *Political Process and the Development of Black Insurgency, 1930–1970* (Chicago: University of Chicago Press, 1999), 40–43.

6 To clarify, JustFaith is a parish program that began in 1989 and still runs today, albeit with many changes over the years. JFM is the organization that eventually forms in 2004 that runs JustFaith and a variety of other programs.

7 William V. D'Antonio, Michelle Dillon, and Mary L. Gautier, *American Catholics in Transition* (Lanham, MD: Rowman & LittleField Publishers, 2013), 172.

8 Peter Steinfels, *A People Adrift: The Crisis of the Roman Catholic Church in America* (New York: Simon and Schuster, 2004).

9 Thomas Merton, *Conjectures of a Guilty Bystander* (Garden City, NY: Image Books, 1968), 155.

10 Unless otherwise stated, all quotes come from personal interviews.

11 Pope Paul IV, Sacrosanctum Concilium, no. 64, December 4, 1963, accessed July 7, 2019, http://www.vatican.va.

12 David Yamane and Sarah MacMillen, with Kelly Culver, *Real Stories of Christian Initiation: Lessons for and from the RCIA* (Collegeville, MN: Liturgical Press, 2006), xii.

13 National Conference of Catholic Bishops, *Rite of Christian Initiation of Adults*, 1988, no. 75, cited in Yamane and MacMillen, *Real Stories of Christian Initiation*, xiv.

14 All the Christians who attend denominationally unaffiliated churches number more than the second-largest denomination, behind only Catholics. These account for more congregations than any denomination. Mark Chaves, *American Religion: Contemporary Trends* (Princeton, NJ: Princeton University Press, 2011), 58.

15 Taken from "JustFaith Group Guidelines." Week 1: Attachment B.

16 Jay P. Dolan, *The American Catholic Experience: A History from Colonial Times to the Present* (Notre Dame, IN: University of Notre Dame Press, 1992), 116.

17 Dolan, *The American Catholic Experience*, 167.

18 Dolan, *The American Catholic Experience*, 166.

19 David J. O'Brien, *Public Catholicism*, 2nd ed. (New York: Orbis Books, 1996), 23.

20 Dolan, *The American Catholic Experience*, 166.

21 Dolan, *The American Catholic Experience*, 117.

22 Jay Dolan, *In Search of American Catholicism: A History of Religion and Culture in Tension* (New York: Oxford University Press, 2002), 45.

23 O'Brien, *Public Catholicism*, 26.

24 Charles R. Morris, *American Catholic: The Saints and Sinners Who Built America's Most Powerful Church* (New York: Vintage, 1997).

25 O'Brien, *Public Catholicism*, 43.

26 Mary J. Oates, *The Catholic Philanthropic Tradition in America* (Indianapolis: Indiana University Press, 1995), 7, 39.

27 Hannah Barker and Simon Burrows, eds., *Press, Politics and the Public Sphere in Europe and North America 1760–1820* (New York: Cambridge University Press, 2002), 141.

28 Dolan, *The American Catholic Experience*, 102.

29 Dolan, *The American Catholic Experience*, 263.

30 O'Brien, *Public Catholicism*, 45.

31 O'Brien, *Public Catholicism*, 47.

32 Dolan, *The American Catholic Experience*, 263.

33 The 1875 Blaine Amendment intended to remove public funding from church-sponsored schools and was often promoted as a solution to the backwardness of Catholic schools, as anti-Catholic sentiment was growing more common and severe. Although defeated, thirty-four states passed legislation similar to the Blaine Amendment over the next several decades.

34 O'Brien, *Public Catholicism*, 107.

35 Edwin S. Gaustad and Mark A. Noll, *A Documentary History of Religion in America: Since 1877*, 3rd ed. (Grand Rapids, MI: Eerdmans, 2003), 16.

36 O'Brien, *Public Catholicism*, 49.

37 Dolan, *In Search of American Catholicism*, 147.

38 Dolan, *In Search of American Catholicism*, 73.

39 Readership dropped precipitously to fifty thousand during World War II, mostly because of the strict pacifist stance of the Catholic Worker while the church had declared the war just. Likewise, the thirty-two houses of hospitality in 1942 had shriveled to only ten in 1945. Dolan, *The American Catholic Experience*, 412.

40 O'Brien, *Public Catholicism*, 191.

41 Robert Wuthnow, *Loose Connections: Joining Together in Americas Fragmented Communities* (Cambridge, MA: Harvard University Press, 2002), 50.

42 Robert Putnam, *Bowling Alone: The Collapse and Revival of American Community* (New York: Simon & Schuster, 2000), 128.

43 William V. D'Antonio, Michele Dillon, and Mary L. Gautier, *American Catholics in Transition* (Lanham, MD: Rowman & Littlefield Publishers, 2013), 78.

44 Catholics are in the bottom ranks of the social hierarchy in 1945 and rise to the middle ranks by 1987. Wade Clark Roof and William McKinney, *American Mainline Religion: Its Changing Shape and Future* (New Brunswick, NJ: Rutgers University Press, 1987), 110.

45 Professionalism and ample financial resources also contributed to the quick organization of Voice of the Faithful. Tricia Colleen Bruce, *Faithful Revolution: How Voice of the Faithful is Changing the Church* (New York: Oxford, 2011), 90–91.

46 James Martin, "Opus Dei in the United States," *America*, February 25, 1995, accessed November 7, 2014, http://americamagazine.org/.

CHAPTER 2. THE CULTURE OF CATHOLIC CIVIC ENGAGEMENT

1 Michele Dillon, *Catholic Identity: Balancing Reason, Faith, and Power* (Cambridge, MA: Cambridge University Press, 1999), 12. Michael W. Cuneo, *The Smoke of Satan: Conservative and Traditionalist Dissent in Contemporary American Catholicism* (New York: Oxford University Press, 1997).

2 S. L. Hansen, "Vatican Affirms Excommunication of Call to Action Members in Lincoln," *Catholic News Service*, December 8, 2006, accessed November 27, 2013, www.catholicnews.com/.

3 Anthony Giddens, *The Constitution of Society* (Berkeley: University of California Press, 1984), 25–26, 173–174.

4 Compare the way seeking to maintain a Catholic identity shapes Voice of the Faithful in Tricia Colleen Bruce, "On Being Catholic," in *Faithful Revolution: How Voice of the Faithful is Changing the Church* (New York: Oxford University Press, 2011), 95–108.

5 Bruce, *Faithful Revolution*, 30.

6 Voice of the Faithful, "Our Beginnings," 2018, accessed August 15, 2018, www.votf .org/.

7 Call to Action, "FAQ," 2018, accessed August 15, 2018, http://cta-usa.org/faq/.

8 Rev. Joseph F. Donnelly, "'But They Are not Dogmas!,'" *Catholic Mind* (1956): 265–267.

9 Ralph Gorman, "Can a Catholic Be a Liberal?," *Catholic Mind* (1959): 341–343.

10 Senator Barry Goldwater, "The Conscience of a Conservative," *Catholic Digest* (August, 1960): 46–49.

11 Cuneo, *The Smoke of Satan*, 52.

12 Charles E. Curran, *Catholic Social Teaching 1891–Present: A Historical, Theological, and Ethical Analysis* (Washington, DC: Georgetown University Press, 2002), 113.

13 The other labels he uses are "separatists" and "Marianists." For more on conservatives, see chapters 2 and 3 in Cuneo, *The Smoke of Satan*.

14 Cuneo, *The Smoke of Satan*, 30, 51–54.

15 "Sounding the Alarm about JustFaith Ministries," *Fidelity and Action*, August 7, 2012, accessed July 8, 2014, http://fidelityandaction.wordpress.com/.

16 William A. Borst, "Blowin' in the Wind: Just/Faith [*sic*] and the Socialist Indoctrination of the Church," *Mindszenty Report* 53, no. 11 (November 2011): 1–3, accessed July 8, 2014, www.mindszenty.org/.

17 See Tricia Colleen Bruce's work on Voice of the Faithful to see that Catholic organizations risk criticism not only for their ideas but also can have their Catholic identity challenged. Bruce, *Faithful Revolution*, 96.

18 The seven themes of Catholic social teaching are (1) the life and dignity of the human person; (2) call to family, community, and participation; (3) rights and responsibilities; (4) option for the poor and vulnerable; (5) the dignity of work and the rights of workers; (6) solidarity; and (7) care for God's creation.

19 Stephanie Block, "Part 3 in a Series on JustFaith: The Seven Themes of Catholic Social Justice," *Spero News*, May 24, 2012, accessed July 9, 2014, www.speroforum .com/.

20 Pontifical Council for Justice and Peace, *Compendium of the Social Doctrine of the Church*, no. 66, April 2, 2004, accessed July 11, 2014, www.vatican.va/.

21 *Compendium of the Social Doctrine of the Church*, no. 580

22 Stephanie Block, "Part 3 in a Series on JustFaith." Block cites Pontifical Council for Justice and Peace, *Compendium of the Social Doctrine of the Church*, Libreria Editrice Vaticana, nos. 66–67, 2004, referencing John Paul II, Encyclical Letter, *Centesimus annus*, 5.

23 Stephanie Block, "Culturing Peace: Part 15 in a Series on JustFaith," *Spero News*, May 24, 2012, accessed July 9, 2014, www.speroforum.com/.

24 Block cites Catechism of the Catholic Church (CCC) 677.

25 Dillon, *Catholic Identity*, 254.

26 CCC 2816.

27 CCC 2818.

28 The CCHD is the social justice arm of the American bishops. They award grant money each year to organizations that promote the social teaching of the church.

29 John P. Hogan, *Credible Signs of Christ Alive: Case Studies from the Catholic Campaign for Human Development* (Lanham, MD: Rowman & Littlefield Publishers, 2003).

30 Stephanie Block, "Credible Signs: Part 13 in a Series on JustFaith," *Spero News*, May 7, 2012, accessed July 8, 2014, www.speroforum.com.

31 See the discussion in chapter 4.

32 CRS is the international charitable arm for American Catholics; Maryknoll is a missionary congregation of priests, brothers, sisters, and laity; and Catholic Charities is the church's primary agency for handling relief work in the United States.

33 United States Conference of Catholic Bishops, "Partner Organizations," 2014, accessed July 11, 2014, www.usccb.org/.

34 In contrast, the Christian Right names feminists, secularists, and gays as social threats. Tanya Erzen, *Straight to Jesus: Sexual and Christian Conversions in the Ex-Gay Movement* (Berkeley: University of California Press, 2006), 195. See also movement/countermovement tactics in Tina Fetner, *How the Religious Right Shaped Lesbian and Gay Activism*, Social Movements, Protest and Contention, vol. 31 (Minneapolis: University of Minnesota Press, 2008).

35 William V. D'Antonio, James D. Davidson, Dean R. Hoge, and Katherine Meyer, *American Catholics: Gender, Generation, and Commitment* (Walnut Creek, CA: AltaMira Press, 2001), 91–92.

36 "Ruined for life" was the motto of the Jesuit Volunteer Corps and refers to the dramatic change the JVs experience in their year of living in solidarity with the poor. See Simon J. Hendry, "'Ruined for Life': The Spirituality of the Jesuit Volunteer Corps" (PhD diss., Graduate Theological Union, 2002), 464.

37 Sant'Egidio, "Friendship with the Poor," June 27, 2000, accessed August 17, 2018, www.santegidiousa.org/.

38 John R. Donahue, "The Bible and Catholic Social Teaching: Will This Engagement Lead to Marriage?" in *Modern Catholic Social Teaching: Commentaries and Interpretations*, ed. Kenneth R. Himes, and Lisa Sowle Cahill, Charles E. Curran,

David Hollenbach, and Thomas Shannon as associate editors (Washington, DC: Georgetown University Press, 2005), 13–15.

39 Faith-based community organizing also works to ensure that participants ground their efforts in religious beliefs. Joseph M. Palacios, *The Catholic Social Imagination: Activism and the Just Society in Mexico and the United States* (Chicago, University of Chicago Press: 2007), 99.

40 Catholic Christian Outreach, "Our Focus" (n.d.), accessed November 12, 2014, http://cco.ca/.

41 Catholic Christian Outreach, *The Ultimate Relationship*, October 14, 2014, p. 10 of online booklet, accessed November 13, 2014, http://issuu.com/.

42 See, for example, "Message: Work, Family Life, and Other Ordinary Activities are Opportunities for Spiritual Union with Jesus Christ," *Opus Dei*, March 2, 2006, accessed November 12, 2014, www.opusdei.org/.

43 Opus Dei has two levels of membership: Prelature and Cooperators. The Prelature, a more demanding involvement, is reserved for Catholics and Cooperators can come from any faith, and they currently list Cooperators who are Orthodox Christian, Anglican, Lutheran, Jewish, Muslim, Buddhist, and those of no religion. "Questions: Frequently Asked Questions About Opus Dei," *Opus Dei*, n.d., accessed November 13, 2014, www.opusdei.org/.

44 Doug McAdam, *Political Process and the Development of Black Insurgency, 1930–1970* (Chicago: University of Chicago Press, 1999), 48–51.

45 Sidney Verba, Kay Schlozman, and Henry Brady, *Voice and Equality: Civic Voluntarism in American Politics* (Cambridge, MA: Harvard University Press, 1995), 319, 188.

46 Annette Lareau, *Unequal Childhoods: Class, Race, and Family Life* (Berkeley: University of California Press, 2003), 141.

47 Laura Deavers, "JustFaith in Jail," *U.S. Catholic*, June 2010, accessed May 27, 2014, www.uscatholic.org/.

48 This was also found among Jesuit Volunteers. Hendry, "'Ruined for Life,'" 214.

CHAPTER 3. FROM PRIVATE BELIEF TO PUBLIC CALL

1 Taken from the JFM mission statement.

2 See the discussion of "awkward movements" in Francesca Polletta, "Awkward Movements," *Mobilization* 11, no. 4 (December 2006): 475–478.

3 This chart differs from David Aberle's classification of social movements in that it is not a classification of social movements but efforts at change more broadly (e.g., support groups). It is similar in that it examines the locus of change (individual or society), and this schema differs from Aberle's in that this typology looks at where the organization expends efforts (individual or society), and Aberle differentiates between the degree of change movements seek (total or partial). David F. Aberle, *The Peyote Religion Among the Navaho* (Oklahoma: University of Oklahoma Press, 1991), 316.

4 Elizabeth Cherry, "Veganism as a Cultural Movement: A Relational Approach," *Social Movement Studies* 5, no. 2 (September 2006): 156.

5 Peter Berger, *The Sacred Canopy: Elements of a Sociological Theory of Religion* (Garden City, NY: Doubleday, 1967), 45.

6 Robert N. Bellah, Richard Madsen, William M. Sullivan, Ann Swidler, and Steven M. Tipton, *Habits of the Heart: Individualism and Commitment in American Life* (Berkeley: University of California Press, 1985), 286.

7 Bellah et al., *Habits of the Heart*, 286.

8 Cf. "man" as a functional concept in Alasdair MacIntyre, *After Virtue*, 2nd ed. (Notre Dame, IN: University of Notre Dame Press, 1984), 58–59.

9 Bellah et al., *Habits of the Heart*, 286.

10 Bellah et al., *Habits of the Heart*, 153–154.

11 Jerald C. Brauer, "Conversion: From Puritanism to Revivalism," *Journal of Religion* 58, (1978): 227.

12 Richard Travisano, "Alternation and Conversion as Qualitatively Different Transformations," in *Social Psychology through Symbolic Interaction*, ed. Gregory Prince Stone and Harvey A. Farberman (Waltham, MA: Ginn-Blaisdell, 1970), 594.

13 Max Heirich, "Change of Heart: A Test of Some Widely Held Theories about Religious Conversion," *American Sociological Review* 83 (1977): 674.

14 People have "narratives" about their transformation through community organizing. Stephen Hart, *Cultural Dilemmas of Progressive Politics: Styles of Engagement among Grassroots Activists* (Chicago: University of Chicago Press, 2001), 87.

15 This use of "motif" is not to be confused with that of Lofland and Skonovd. Conversion "motifs" there refer to both the account of the conversion as it is remembered and the objective events that led to the conversion; these together make up Lofland and Skonovd's motif. The use here is simply the more prominent aspects of a person's conversion story. John Lofland and Norman Skonovd, "Conversion Motifs," *Journal for the Scientific Study of Religion* 20, no. 4 (December 1981): 373–385.

16 Sociologists debate the extent to which religious beliefs permeate one's life with Courtney Bender showing that religious belief emerges in nonreligious settings in *Heaven's Kitchen: Living Religion at God's Love We Deliver* (Chicago: University of Chicago Press, 2003), 8. Whether these grads already bring their religion to daily life is unclear, yet religion-centering transformation gives them tools to *deliberately* bring their religious values to other spheres, increasing the likelihood of doing so.

17 David A. Snow and Richard Machalek, "The Sociology of Conversion," *Annual Review of Sociology* 10 (1984): 170.

18 One of the grads, a college student, does not believe in God, and a motif like "religion-centering transformation" may not be appropriate for her. However, she definitely believed her moral values—which she could articulate clearly—should shape all of her life. There is still a "centering" for her even without the theological aspect.

19 There is some evidence that this integration of religion and public life will be culturally easier for Catholics than Protestants. Stephen Hart found that very few of the Catholics he interviewed "compartmentalized" their faith—keeping it from other aspects of their life—while this was more common among his Protestant interviewees. Stephen Hart, *What Does the Lord Require? How American Christians Think about Economic Justice* (New Brunswick, NJ: Rutgers University Press, 1996), 76–77.

20 This integrity is tremendously important to the grads. This has implications for their sense of self, emphasizing the "I" over the "me." George Herbert Mead, *Mind, Self, and Society from the Standpoint of a Social Behaviorist* (Chicago: University of Chicago Press, 1934). In contrast to Goffman's understanding of the self as "me" and "impression management," grads focus on the I, making sure for themselves that the various aspects of their lives are centered on Christ. Erving Goffman, *The Presentation of Self in Everyday Life* (Garden City, NY: Doubleday, 1959).

21 More political party switching may have been found if more of the sample were in a conservative area. It is important to note that there were a handful of people who remained Republicans and had glowing reviews for JustFaith. This demonstrates the JFM stance that concern for the poor and other Gospel values are the concern of all Christians, regardless of their political stripes.

22 Robert Putnam, *Bowling Alone: The Collapse and Revival of American Community* (New York: Simon & Schuster, 2000), 35.

23 Gay Christian men who seek to become straight have intense experiences of crises. Tanya Erzen, *Straight to Jesus: Sexual and Christian Conversions in the Ex-Gay Movement* (Berkeley: University of California Press, 2006), 87. See also a sense of dying in Puritan conversion stories. Brauer, "Conversion," 231.

24 "Final Report: National Geographic-Roper Public Affairs 2006 Geographic Literacy Study," National Geographic/Roper Public Affairs, May 2006, accessed July 7, 2019, https://media.nationalgeographic.org .

25 Other research shows that understanding the connection between faith and politics is difficult for many Americans. Mark Mulder and Gerardo Marti, "Rustbelt Religion: Faith and Politics in Central Wisconsin" (presentation at the 2018 Association for the Sociology of Religion, Philadelphia, PA).

26 Conservatives' faith is generally more central to their lives than it is for liberals. Robert, Wuthnow, *Acts of Compassion: Caring for Others and Helping Ourselves* (Princeton, NJ: Princeton University Press, 1991), 133. Part of JustFaith's success among those already sympathetic to progressive causes is to help them realize the religious meaning in their extant beliefs.

27 Mark Chaves, *American Religion: Contemporary Trends* (Princeton, NJ: Princeton University Press, 2011), 20–21.

28 Arthur L. Greil, "Previous Dispositions and Conversion to Perspectives of Social and Religious Movements," *Sociological Analysis* 38, no. 2 (1977): 116.

29 Henri Gooren, "Towards a New Model of Conversion Careers: The Impact of Personality and Situational Factors," *Exchange* 34 (2005) 149–166.

30 Aristotle, *Nicomachean Ethics*, trans. Martin Ostwald (New York: Macmillan Publishing, 1962), 34.

31 Ziad W. Munson, *The Making of Pro-Life Activists: How Social Movement Mobilization Works* (Chicago: University of Chicago Press, 2009).

32 This second form of intensification initially seems similar to the form of political transformation that entailed increased knowledge of political issues. They are different in that the second form of political transformation refers mainly to the expansion of political beliefs and knowledge. This form of intensification is more practiced-based, an expansion of one's ministries, going from, for example, volunteering at a homeless shelter to adding tutoring and environmental advocacy to one's service commitments.

33 See the excellent discussion of this in "The Human Person" in Richard Gula's *Reason Informed by Faith* (New York: Paulist Press, 1989).

34 See the examination of multitarget social movements in Grace Yukich, *One Family Under God: Immigration Politics and Progressive Religion in America* (New York: Oxford University Press, 2013).

35 Robert Wuthnow, *Sharing the Journey: Support Groups and America's New Quest for Community* (Princeton, NJ: Princeton University Press, 1994), 326.

36 Wuthnow, *Sharing the Journey*, 327.

37 Wuthnow, *Sharing the Journey*, 329.

38 Stephen Hart, *Cultural Dilemmas of Progressive Politics: Styles of Engagement Among Grassroots Activists* (Chicago: University of Chicago Press, 2001), 62.

39 Munson, *The Making of Pro-Life Activists*, 168.

40 There were several that were excluded from analysis. Six had been through the twenty-one-week Engaging Spirituality course (the two who had taken JustMatters modules were included), one returned their survey after the time limit of three weeks had passed and one Catholic was given the Protestant survey (she was taking the course through a local United Methodist church).

41 "General" is the small group type in Bernard Lee's typology that JustFaith would fall under. His other types are Latino, Charismatic, Call to Action, and Eucharist Centered Communities. Bernard J. Lee, with William V. D'Antonio, Virgilio P. Elizondo, Patricia O'Connell Killen, and Jeanette Rodriguez, *The Catholic Experience of Small Christian Communities* (New York: Paulist Press, 2000), 70.

42 Some findings are only reported for Catholics or Protestants as there were different surveys for each group, which did not include all the questions. When there are not denominationally specific questions that warrant one group's exclusion (e.g., frequency of Confession), this was due to data gathered from D'Antonio, Dillon, and Gautier's national study that only surveyed Catholics. Other relevant questions were culled from other national surveys to create a survey for Protestants that could compare them to national data. When data for only one group are presented, it is because there are no data for that question for the other group, not because there was no difference between the groups.

43 William V. D'Antonio, Michelle Dillon, and Mary L. Gautier, *American Catholics in Transition* (Lanham, MD: Rowman & Littlefield Publishers, 2013), 170.

44 Baylor University, *The Baylor Religion Survey, Wave II* (Waco, TX: Baylor Institute for Studies of Religion, 2007).

45 General Social Survey, 2012, Cross Section and Panel Combined, www.thearda .com.

46 Wuthnow, *Sharing the Journey*, 252–253.

47 D'Antonio, Dillon, and Gautier, *American Catholics in Transition*, 174.

48 D'Antonio, Dillon, and Gautier, *American Catholics in Transition*, 167.

49 D'Antonio, Dillon, and Gautier, *American Catholics in Transition*, 171.

50 D'Antonio, Dillon, and Gautier, *American Catholics in Transition*, 176.

51 D'Antonio and his team assigned low-level commitment if the person met two of the three following criteria: attending Mass seldom or never, saying that the church is not very important at all, and choosing a 5, 6, or 7 to describe her likelihood of leaving the church. A medium level was assigned to all who did not fit either the high- or low-commitment criteria. D'Antonio, Dillon, and Gautier, *American Catholics in Transition*, 57.

52 Jerome Baggett, *Habitat for Humanity: Building Private Homes, Building Public Religion* (Philadelphia: Temple University Press, 2000), 196. This missionary outlet JustFaith provides might also increase loyalty to the institution. Catholics for whom mission is an important aspect of their faith would be upset by the relatively few engagement opportunities in their parishes compared to parishes historically. They might exercise options of "exit" or "voice." For these outreach-minded Catholics, JustFaith gives them a meaningful space to be Catholic, allowing them to exercise "loyalty." Albert O. Hirschman, *Exit, Voice, and Loyalty: Responses to Decline in Firms, Organizations, and States* (Cambridge, MA: Harvard University Press, 1970).

53 General Social Survey, 2012, Cross-Section and Panel Combined.

54 General Social Survey, 2012, Cross-Section and Panel Combined.

55 Baylor University, *The Baylor Religion Survey, Wave II*.

56 The percentages of particular practices are, with those in small groups listed first, daily prayer (78 percent vs. 46 percent), reconciliation within the last two years (71 percent vs. 32 percent), retreat attendance (55 percent vs. 12 percent), weekly Mass attendance (93 percent vs. 32 percent), or a Catholic social justice meeting (39 percent vs. 8 percent). Lee, *The Catholic Experience of Small Christian Communities*, 60.

57 D'Antonio, Dillon, and Gautier, *American Catholics in Transition*, 172.

58 Christian Smith and Michael Emerson, with Patricia Snell, *Passing the Plate: Why American Christians Don't Give Away More Money* (New York: Oxford University Press, 2008), 50.

59 Smith and Emerson, *Passing the Plate*, 30.

60 Nina Eliasoph, *Avoiding Politics: How Americans Produce Apathy in Everyday Life* (New York: Cambridge University Press, 1998), 69.

61 Although there does not appear to be an attitude change that precedes volunteer involvement, JustFaith channels these new energies to local nonprofits, putting participants' inner convictions into action and facilitating transformation. Jone L. Pearce, *Volunteers: The Organizational Behavior of Unpaid Workers* (New York: Routledge, 1993), 89.

62 Jone L. Pearce, *Volunteers*, 71.

63 This figure was calculated using the answers to two survey questions. The first question asked respondents, "In the last 12 months, how often have you participated in the activities of one of the following associations or groups? A community-service or civic association?" The second question asked the same for "a political party or organization." General Social Survey, 2008, Cross-Section and Panel Combined, Questions 881 and 882. Admittedly, these questions are not exactly the same as the survey questions grads answered, which asked them how frequently they volunteer in charitable activities and political activities. Yet, they would be expected to generate similar answers from respondents and offer, if not a perfect comparison, a general difference between grads and Americans more broadly.

64 Thom File, "The Diversifying Electorate—Voting Rates by Race and Hispanic Origin in 2012 (and Other Recent Elections)," *United States Census Bureau*, May 2013, accessed November 18, 2014, www.census.gov/.

65 General Social Survey, 2010, Cross-Section and Panel Combined.

66 Baylor University, *The Baylor Religion Survey, Wave II*.

67 In the civil rights movement, the black churches played a crucial role. This was not because churches simply recruited members; church membership itself was redefined to necessarily include activism. In the same way, grads redefine what it means to be a Christian to necessarily include active concern for others. Doug McAdam, *Political Process and the Development of Black Insurgency, 1930–1970* (Chicago: University of Chicago Press, 1999), 128.

68 The percentages are helping others, 83 percent; the environment, 51 percent; and political issues, 24 percent. Lee, *The Catholic Experience of Small Christian Communities*, 54.

69 Lee, *The Catholic Experience of Small Christian Communities*, 94.

70 See, for example, his talk titled "St. Francis, Pope Francis, and a Vision for the 21st Century Parish" given at the Catholic Charities Conference, September 14, 2013, San Francisco, CA.

71 This is a reference to Matthew 18:20 that many use to illustrate God's presence in small gatherings.

72 Mark M. Gray, Mary L. Gautier, and Melissa A. Cidade, *The Changing Face of U.S. Catholic Parishes* (Washington, DC: National Association for Lay Ministry, 2011), 17.

73 "Justice action" events are events that attempt to make a structural impact on an issue (such as writing politicians for transitional housing funds). "Prayer for Justice/Peace" events are prayer or liturgical events that have a justice or peace

issue as its central intention. "Education (social issue)" events refers to teaching events that are not explicitly theological and touch on public themes, such as abortion or human trafficking. "Charity action" events are events that attempt to make a micro-level impact on an issue (such as a coat drive). "Prayer" includes a rosary group or centering prayer. "Bible study/Theology" refers to regularly meeting bible groups or a guest speaking on a spiritually relevant topic. "Retreat" includes any extended period (four hours or more) of communal prayer or study. "Justice" and "Charity" fund-raisers are efforts (such as a bake sale, not simply second collections) to raise money for systemic change or immediate aid, respectively. "Protest/Demonstration" refers to a collective effort to wield political power. "Social" events would include a movie night or a gathering at a restaurant. I excluded ministries that did not fall into one of these eleven categories, such as small therapeutic groups (e.g., an overeaters support group) or educational programming that did not address a social issue (e.g., preparing one's tax forms).

74 In one study, 61 percent of people in a church-sponsored small group became more active in their church or synagogue and half increase their contributions at their place of worship. For those in small groups not sponsored by their religious congregation, the corresponding figures are 12 and 13 percent, respectively. Wuthnow, *Sharing the Journey*, 321.

75 This time that offers people both a time to visit and a time to offer outreach was also found in Rebecca Anne Allahyari's *Visions of Charity: Volunteer Works and Moral Community* (Berkeley: University of California Press, 2000), 125.

76 Nina Eliasoph, *Making Volunteers* (Princeton, NJ: Princeton University Press, 2011), 106–107.

77 Robert Wuthnow, *Loose Connections: Joining Together in Americas Fragmented Communities* (Cambridge, MA: Harvard University Press, 2002), 349.

78 Wuthnow, *Loose Connections*, 366. Lee, *The Catholic Experience of Small Christian Communities*, 95.

CHAPTER 4. CHRIST-CENTERED DISCIPLESHIP

1 Exodus 23:9. Translation not specified in worship aid.

2 Leviticus 19:34. Translation not specified in worship aid.

3 Isaiah 61:1. Translation not specified in worship aid.

4 Hebrews 13:1–2. Translation not specified in worship aid.

5 In actuality, even Catholic institutions are quite secular. A 1974 poll showed that Catholic social service directors in Minnesota were upset about the growing secularization of their organizations. Also, the importance of Catholic financial support in the budgets of even in diocesan charities is diminishing, with 63 percent of their money coming from the government and a mere 11 percent from private donations in 1991. Mary J. Oates, *The Catholic Philanthropic Tradition in America* (Indianapolis: Indiana University Press, 1995).

6 Clifford Geertz, "Thick Description: Toward an Interpretive Theory of Culture," in *The Interpretation of Cultures* (New York: Basic Books, 1973), 5.

7 Christian Smith, "Correcting a Curious Neglect, or Bringing Religion Back In," in *Disruptive Religion: The Force of Faith in Social Movement Activism*, ed. Christian Smith (New York: Routledge, 1996), 1–25.

8 Charles R. Morris, *American Catholic: The Saints and Sinners Who Built America's Most Powerful Church* (New York: Vintage, 1997), 323.

9 Gaudium et Spes 4.

10 Lumen Gentium 31.

11 GS 43.

12 William V. D'Antonio, Michelle Dillon, and Mary L. Gautier, *American Catholics in Transition*, (Lanham, MD: Rowman & Littlefield Publishers, 2013), 57.

13 D'Antonio, Dillon, and Gautier, *American Catholics in Transition*, 168.

14 D'Antonio, Dillon, and Gautier, *American Catholics in Transition*, 168.

15 D'Antonio, Dillon, and Gautier, *American Catholics in Transition*, 167.

16 D'Antonio, Dillon, and Gautier, *American Catholics in Transition*, 168.

17 Avery Dulles, *Models of the Church*, expanded ed. (New York: Doubleday, 1987).

18 Mysteries in a Catholic theological sense refer to something that is beyond the full understanding of the human mind, "hidden in God, which can never be known unless they are revealed by God" (Catechism of the Catholic Church [CCC] 237).

19 Dulles, *Models of the Church*, 28.

20 Dulles, *Models of the Church*, 89.

21 See, for example, Pope Francis's homily at the Chrism Mass of March 28, 2013, accessed April 30, 2014, http://w2.vatican.va/.

22 Carol Klatz reported in the Catholic Herald on March 28, 2013, that Cardinal Jorge Mario Bergoglio used the phrase "theological narcissism" to describe the state of the church as he convened with fellow cardinals in the days leading to the conclave. Accessed April 30, 2014, www.catholicherald.co.uk/.

23 John Paul II, *Redemptor Hominis*, no. 21, Vatican website, March 4, 1979, accessed May 1, 2014, www.vatican.va/.

24 JFM's ecclesiology shifted during the study. A discipleship model dominated the organizational literature and Jezreel's public addresses, but with the papacy of Francis—and the servant model he emphasizes—the servant model came more to the fore.

25 Richard L. Wood, *Faith in Action: Religion, Race, and Democratic Organizing in America* (Chicago: University of Chicago Press, 2002), 239.

26 Stephen Hart, *What Does the Lord Require? How American Christians Think about Economic Justice* (New Brunswick, NJ: Rutgers University Press, 1996), 52.

27 Grace Yukich, *One Family under God: Immigration Politics and Progressive Religion in America* (New York: Oxford University Press, 2013), 50.

28 The most commonly cited negative trait in Baggett's study of American Catholics is judgementalism, which shares many characteristics with exclusion. Jerome Baggett, *Sense of the Faithful: How American Catholics Live Their Faith* (New York: Oxford University Press, 2009), 81. Compare this to a nonjudgmentalism that is permissive in Alan Wolfe, *One Nation, After All: What Middle-Class Americans*

Really Think about God, Country, Family, Racism, Welfare, Immigration, Homo-sexuality, World, the Right, the Left and Each Other (New York: Viking Penguin, 1988), 298.

29 Wood, *Faith in Action*, 212.

30 Hart, *What Does the Lord Require?*, 53–60.

31 Referred to as "SASI," this program gathers Catholics from across the nation—there were more than two hundred in attendance in 2012—for workshops on ways to spread the church's social mission in their local communities.

32 Wood, *Faith in Action*, 212.

33 Baylor University, *The Baylor Religion Survey, Wave II* (Waco, TX: Baylor Institute for Studies of Religion, 2007).

34 Pew Forum on Religion and Public Life, U.S. Religious Landscape Survey, 2007, www.thearda.com.

35 General Social Survey, 2010, Cross-Section and Panel Combined.

36 General Social Survey, 2010, Cross-Section and Panel Combined.

37 Baylor University, *The Baylor Religion Survey, Wave II*.

38 The Angelus is a traditional Catholic prayer said at 6 a.m., noon, and 6 p.m. The pope hosts an audience for the Angelus Sundays at noon when he is in Rome.

39 Compare St. Jude devotees' use of prayer in Robert A. Orsi, *Thank You, St. Jude: Women's Devotion to the Patron Saint of Hopeless Causes* (New Haven, CT: Yale University Press, 1996), 189, 193–197.

40 CCC 2446.

41 Francis, *Evangelii gaudium*, Vatican website, November 24, 2013, accessed May 6, 2013, http://w2.vatican.va/, 57.

42 Ann Swidler, *Talk of Love: How Culture Matters* (Chicago: University of Chicago Press, 2003).

43 Iris Marion Young, "Five Faces of Oppression," in *Justice and the Politics of Difference* (Princeton, NJ: Princeton University Press, 2011), 39–65.

44 See Genesis 1:26–27.

45 CCC 1938.

46 GS 27.

47 Charles R. Morris, *American Catholic: The Saints and Sinners Who Built America's Most Powerful Church* (New York: Vintage, 1997), 332.

48 GS 16.

49 Thomas Aquinas, *Summa Theologiae*, I–II, q. 19, a 5, ed. Benzinger Brothers and trans. Fathers of the English Dominican Province, 1947, accessed June 27, 2014, http://dhspriory.org/.

50 This response might be read with concern for Orthodox Catholics supportive of teachings that emphasize properly formed conscience but more often see Catholics using teachings on conscience to blithely disregard inconvenient teachings. Grads take moral realities very seriously and claim to regularly weigh and reexamine issues in light of particular circumstances and magisterial teaching.

51 John Paul II, *Sollicitudo rei socialis*, December 30, 1987, in *Catholic Social Thought: The Documentary Heritage*, ed. David J. O'Brien and Thomas A. Shannon (Maryknoll, NY: Orbis, 1992), no. 38. For a brief overview on how the understanding solidarity has changed and developed over the last century, see Joseph M. Palacios, *The Catholic Social Imagination: Activism and the Just Society in Mexico and the United States* (Chicago: University of Chicago Press, 2007), 38–57, especially 50.

52 Jerome Baggett, "Citizenship and its Class-Based Distortions" in *Habitat for Humanity: Building Private Homes, Building Public Religion* (Philadelphia: Temple University Press, 2000).

53 Rebecca Anne Allahyari, *Visions of Charity: Volunteer Works and Moral Community* (Berkeley: University of California Press, 2000), 138.

54 Pius XI, *Quadragesimo anno* (After Forty Years), May 15, 1931, in *Catholic Social Thought: The Documentary Heritage*, ed. David J. O'Brien and Thomas A. Shannon (Maryknoll, NY: Orbis, 1992), no. 79.

55 John XXIII, *Pacem in terris* (Peace on Earth), April, 11 1963, in *Catholic Social Thought: The Documentary Heritage*, ed. David J. O'Brien and Thomas A. Shannon (Maryknoll, NY: Orbis, 1992), no. 141.

56 Heidi J. Swarts, *Organizing Urban America: Secular and Faith-based Progressive Movements* (Minneapolis: University of Minnesota Press, 2008).

57 Liberation theology began in the early 1960s in Latin America and is a theology that makes the perspective of the poor central. The approach draws heavily on experience and scripture with the goal of praxis, defined by well-known liberation theologian Gustavo Gutiérrez as a "transforming activity marked and illuminated by Christian love." Thomas L. Schubeck, *Liberation Ethics: Sources, Models, and Norms* (Minneapolis, MN: Augsburg Fortress, 1993), 57. Liberation theology, briefly, offers social, moral, and religious critiques of a given political situation, attempting to find a solution that removes oppression and comes closer to actualizing the Reign of God. For a thorough treatment of liberation theology, see Schubeck, *Liberation Ethics* (1993).

58 Charles E. Curran, *Catholic Social Teaching 1891-Present: A Historical, Theological, and Ethical Analysis* (Washington, DC: Georgetown University Press, 2002), 183–188.

59 John Paul II, *Centesimus annus* (On the Hundredth Anniversary of *Rerum Novarum*), May 1, 1991, in *Catholic Social Thought: The Documentary Heritage*, ed. David J. O'Brien and Thomas A. Shannon (Maryknoll, NY: Orbis, 1992), no. 11.

60 United States Catholic Bishops, *Economic Justice for All* (1986), in *Catholic Social Thought: The Documentary Heritage*, ed. David J. O'Brien and Thomas A. Shannon (Maryknoll, NY: Orbis, 1992), no. 52.

61 Alessandro Bianchi, "Pope Says Communists Are Closet Christians," *Reuters*, June 29, 2014, accessed July 1, 2014, www.reuters.com/.

62 C. Melissa Snarr, *All You that Labor: Religion and Ethics in the Living Wage Movement* (New York: New York University Press, 2011), 55.

63 Faith-based organizing has shown that religion can transcend political differences. Wood, *Faith in Action*, 180.

64 James Davison Hunter, *To Change the World: The Irony, Tragedy, and Possibility of Christianity in the Late Modern World* (New York: Oxford, 2010), 138–139.

65 In Matthew 25:40, Jesus tells those who have cared for the hungry, thirsty, naked, homeless, sick, and imprisoned that in attending to the "least of these who are members of my family, you did it to me" (New Revised Standard Version Catholic Edition).

66 Allahyari, *Visions of Charity*, 36.

67 Richard Gula, *Reason Informed by Faith* (New York: Paulist Press, 1989), 116–121.

68 GS 25.

69 John Paul II, *Sollicitudo Rei Socialis*, no. 36.

70 John Paul II, *Sollicitudo Rei Socialis*, no. 39.

71 Compare the appropriation of Our Lady of Guadalupe in Palacios, *The Catholic Social Imagination*, 107–109.

72 Stephanie Block, "Culturing Peace: Part 15 in a Series on JustFaith," *Spero News*, May 24, 2012, accessed July 13, 2014, www.speroforum.com/.

73 Pope Francis, General Audience, St. Peter's Square, April 16, 2014, accessed July 13, 2014, http://w2.vatican.va/.

74 He said of the Shroud of Turin, "This disfigured Face resembles all those faces of men and women marred by a life that does not respect their dignity, by war and the violence that afflict the weakest." "Pope: I Join All of You Gathered around the Holy Shroud," *News.Va Official Vatican Network*, March 30, 2013, accessed November 7, 2013, www.news.va/.

75 Fifty-six percent of grads versus 73 percent of Catholics generally. D'Antonio, Dillon, and Gautier, *American Catholics in Transition*, 167.

76 CCC 459 and 460.

77 Palacios, *The Catholic Social Imagination*, 37–38.

78 Michele Dillon, *Postsecular Catholicism: Relevance and Renewal* (New York: Oxford University Press, 2018).

79 Mary Ellen Konieczny, Charles C. Camosy, and Tricia Colleen Bruce. *Polarization in the US Catholic Church: Naming the Wounds, Beginning to Heal* (Collegeville, MN: Liturgical Press, 2016). Maureen K. Day, "Why Are We at Each Others' Throats? Healing Polarization in Our Church," National Catholic Reporter, November 30, 2018, accessed August 6, 2019, https://www.ncronline.org/.

80 Michele Dillon, *Catholic Identity: Balancing Reason, Faith, and Power* (Cambridge, MA: Cambridge University Press, 1999), 206–216.

CHAPTER 5. TRANSFORMING COMMUNITY

1 Ephesians 4:1–7, 11–13 (New Revised Standard Version Catholic Edition).

2 Courtney Bender, *Heaven's Kitchen: Living Religion at God's Love We Deliver* (Chicago: University of Chicago Press, 2003).

3 Ziad W. Munson, *The Making of Pro-Life Activists: How Social Movement Mobili-zation Works* (Chicago: University of Chicago Press, 2009), 166.

4 Munson, *The Making of Pro-Life Activists*, 189.

5 Munson, *The Making of Pro-Life Activists*, 168.

6 Munson, *The Making of Pro-Life Activists*, 169. Illustrating Munson's point, some sociologists of religion look for religious practice "with others outside their own home" nearly exclusively within the congregation. Mark Chaves, *American Religion: Contemporary Trends* (Princeton, NJ: Princeton University Press, 2011), 55.

7 Alasdair MacIntyre, *After Virtue*, 2nd ed. (Notre Dame, IN: University of Notre Dame Press, 1984), 187.

8 Stephen Hart, "Faith and Politics: Integration or Compartmentalization?" in *What Does the Lord Require? How American Christians Think about Economic Justice* (New Brunswick, NJ: Rutgers University Press, 1996), 65–81.

9 Cf. James 2:26.

10 Compare Aristotle's role of friendship in the cultivation of virtue in Alasdair MacIntyre, *After Virtue*, 155.

11 Most parishes do not challenge their members on contentious moral issues, such as war, the death penalty, or abortion, as they prefer to preserve the cohesion of the parish. Jerome Baggett, *Sense of the Faithful: How American Catholics Live Their Faith* (New York: Oxford University Press, 2009), 120.

12 There was a stark shift in the interview data on the election of Pope Francis, due, no doubt, to his open preaching and practicing of many of the JustFaith values surrounding peace, justice, and poverty. When I first started interviewing grads, many were ambivalent toward the institutional church, claiming a strong affinity to their parish. There was definitely a "Francis effect" among interviewees. When asked about the institutional church post-Francis, many spoke enthusiastically of him and few mentioned serious criticisms of the church.

13 This desire for an affinity with one's parish is giving rise to an increasing number of "personal parishes," which are canonically distinct from the more common territorial parish. Tricia Bruce, *Parish and Place: Making Room for Diversity in the American Catholic Church* (New York: Oxford University Press, 2017).

14 Scholars have noted that unique religious goods can be an incentive to remain within a denomination. See, for example, Matthew Loveland, "Religious Switching: Preference Development, Maintenance, and Change," *Journal for the Scientific Study of Religion* 42 (2003): 154.

15 Bernard J. Lee found that for a small minority of Catholics, their small group became their only communal expression of faith and they dropped out of parish life. More often, however, his interviewees said the opposite: if it were not for their small group, they would have dropped out of parish life. Rather than being an alternative, for the vast majority, participation in a small group more firmly an-chored them to their parish and, by extension, the global church. Likewise, some grads say that JustFaith is the only thing that keeps them from leaving the church

and many claim that participation in JustFaith strengthened their faith. Bernard J. Lee, with William V. D'Antonio, Virgilio P. Elizondo, Patricia O'Connell Killen, and Jeanette Rodriguez, *The Catholic Experience of Small Christian Communities* (New York: Paulist Press, 2000), 128–133.

16 These grads illustrate that JustFaith might offer parishes a chance to do away with some of the "perils" and flex the "promises" of the role of the church in civil society. Baggett, *Sense of the Faithful*, 175–202.

17 Robert Wuthnow, *Sharing the Journey: Support Groups and America's New Quest for Community* (Princeton, NJ: Princeton University Press, 1994), 4.

18 Christian Smith, *American Evangelicalism: Embattled and Thriving* (Chicago: University of Chicago Press, 1998), 116–117.

19 William V. D'Antonio, Michelle Dillon, and Mary L. Gautier, *American Catholics in Transition* (Lanham, MD: Rowman & Littlefield Publishers, 2013), 169.

20 R. Stephen Warner, "Religion, Boundaries, and Bridges," *Sociology of Religion* 58, no. 3 (1997): 224.

21 David I. Kertzer, *Ritual, Politics, and Power* (New Haven, CT: Yale University Press, 1988), 67–69.

22 Kertzer, *Ritual, Politics, and Power*, 69–72.

23 Lee, *The Catholic Experience*, 71.

24 Lee, *The Catholic Experience*, 44.

25 Some groups do, in fact, dissipate to nothing, never meeting again or perhaps dissolving after meeting only a few times after finishing. However, there are also stories of profound group commitment following the program, with some groups investing significant personal resources to buy blocks of housing and begin non-profits and others selling their homes to move in together in intentional community.

26 Robert Wuthnow, *Sharing the Journey*, 84.

27 Roger A. Straus, "Religious Conversion as a Personal and Collective Accomplishment," *Sociological Analysis* 40 (1979): 162.

28 Brock Kilbourne and James T. Richardson, "Paradigm Conflict, Types of Conversion, and Conversion Theories," *Sociological Analysis* 50, no. 1 (1989): 15. See also Jasper's work illustrating the ways collective emotions mutually reinforce one another. Reciprocal emotions—care of one another—strengthens shared emotions—concern for a group, person, or issue—and vice versa. As a person becomes fond of another, she cares about what the other person cares about. Likewise, we like people more as we discover shared interest. James M. Jasper, *The Art of Moral Protest: Culture, Biography, and Creativity in Social Movements* (Chicago: University of Chicago Press, 1999), 187. Also, Smith, *American Evangelicalism*, 104–107.

29 Some social groups can cohere without agreement, but in others, disagreement is a serious threat to solidarity. JustFaith groups encourage agreement amongst the members, yet when members disagree, the intimacy keeps maintains the group bonds. For more on these social groupings and the effect of disagreement, see

Nina Eliasoph, *Avoiding Politics: How Americans Produce Apathy in Everyday Life* (New York: Cambridge University Press, 1998), 45–47.

30 Arthur L. Greil, "Previous Dispositions and Conversion to Perspectives of Social and Religious Movements," *Sociological Analysis* 38, no. 2 (1977): 120–121. Peter Berger and Thomas Luckmann, *The Social Construction of Reality: A Treatise in the Sociology of Knowledge* (Garden City, NY: Doubleday, 1966), 151.

31 Wuthnow, *Sharing the Journey*, 319.

32 Wuthnow, *Sharing the Journey*, 320, 325–326. Regular participation in a small group is related linearly to more positive attitudes, as well. Sixty-five percent of those who participate regularly in a small group say that volunteering time is "absolutely essential" or "very important" to them, compared to 51 percent who attend occasionally and 29 percent who do not attend a small group. Small-group participation also increases church involvement (254).

33 Wuthnow, *Sharing the Journey*, 322.

34 Family-to-Family is a ministry that invites a family or small group of people to offer social and some material support to a family that is just coming out of poverty in the hope that the extra support will keep them out.

35 Wuthnow, *Sharing the Journey*, 324.

36 A pilgrimage that ends at the Cathedral of St. James in northwestern Spain.

37 For an example of community reinforcing group values, see Irwin R. Baker and Raymond F. Currie's "Do Converts Always Make the Most Committed Christians?," *Journal for the Scientific Study of Religion* 24 (1985): 312. Also, for veganism and punk culture, see Elizabeth Cherry's "Veganism as a Cultural Movement: A Relational Approach," *Social Movement Studies* 5, no. 2 (September 2006): 155–170.

38 Peter G. Stromberg, "Ideological Language in the Transformation of Identity," *American Anthropologist*, New Series, 92, no. 1 (1990): 43.

39 Drawing on Rosabeth Moss Kanter's work on community and commitment, Jone Pearce found that among volunteers, personal relationships are the most important factor in anchoring individuals to their volunteer commitments. This might indicate that, even though these grads do not often share volunteer commitments, their JustFaith relationships—centered on values including outreach—push them into activism and sustain their commitments. Jone L. Pearce, *Volunteers: The Organizational Behavior of Unpaid Workers* (New York: Routledge, 1993), 102.

40 Christian Smith, *Resisting Reagan: The U.S. Central America Peace Movement* (Chicago: University of Chicago Press, 1996), 78.

41 Smith, *Resisting Reagan*, 342.

42 The Kentucky and California grads look very similar to one another when "strongly agree" and "agree" are combined. This would signal that while both sets of grads have close friends that are more like them rather than unlike them, it is truer for Bay Area grads.

43 Many men understand their employment as an expression of love and care for their family. Nicholas Townsend, "The Four Facets of Fatherhood," in *Family in*

Transition, 15th ed., ed. Arlene S. Skolnick and Jerome H. Skolnick (Boston: Allyn and Bacon, 2009), 290–291.

44 Twenty-one percent of women are in a service-oriented job compared to 9 percent of men. Arlie Russell Hochschild, *The Managed Heart: Commercialization of Human Feeling* (Berkeley: University of California Press, 1983), 171. In 1991, women accounted for far fewer degrees in engineering (15 percent) and physical science (32 percent) and achieved parity in business (47 percent). There is even some difference in high school curriculum, with boys taking more math and science courses and girls taking more courses in commercial arts and foreign language. Joseph G. Altonji and Rebecca M. Blank, "Race and Gender in the Labor Market," in *Handbook of Labor Economics, Volume 3*, ed. Orley C. Ashenfelter and David Card (Amsterdam: Elsevier B.V., 1999), 3205.

45 Altruism is making a sacrifice for another with no gain, only loss, for oneself. Prosocial actions, in contrast, may not maximize the self-interest of the actor but are personal sacrifices that benefit oneself as well as the group. Many people volunteer with prosocial motives, recognizing how they benefit from their activism and often volunteers move from altruistic to prosocial attitudes as they remain at an organization. The speaker revalorizes altruism here as a fundamental Christian enterprise, with sacrifice taking on its more traditional Christian spirit. Pearce, *Volunteers*, 77.

46 Jasper, *The Art of Moral Protest*, 83.

47 Compare this to Victor Turner's use of "communitas" as a place to nourish individuals who then go out to act in (or on, depending on their context) "structure" that is the larger organizational mechanisms of society. This dialectical relationship is essential, he argues, for a healthy society. Victor Turner, *The Ritual Process: Structure and Anti-Structure* (Ithaca, NY: Cornell University Press, 1969), 129.

48 Cf. chapter 4, "Christ Above Culture" in H. Richard Niebuhr's *Christ and Culture* (New York: Harper and Row, 1951).

49 Compare works that have found group bonds are strengthened when members are imagined to be superior to the wider world. James M. Jasper, *The Art of Moral Protest*, 80.

50 This is a risk for any community that has a mission to serve those outside the group. Rosabeth Moss Kanter, *Commitment and Community: Communes and Utopias in Sociological Perspective*. (Cambridge, MA: Harvard University Press, 1972), 192.

51 Jerome Baggett, *Habitat for Humanity: Building Private Homes, Building Public Religion* (Philadelphia: Temple University Press, 2000), 128.

52 Nina Eliasoph, *Making Volunteers* (Princeton, NJ: Princeton University Press, 2011), 48.

53 The slow, cumulative building of relationship is an important part of civic engagement and increases its efficacy. Eliasoph, *Making Volunteers*, 119, 125–126.

54 Cf. Catechism of the Catholic Church 1822–1829, especially 1829, "[C]harity demands beneficence and fraternal correction; it is benevolence; it fosters reciprocity and receives disinterested and generous, it is friendship and communion."

55 Habitat for Humanity volunteers also minimize differences between themselves and the clients, discovering "these folks are just like we are." Baggett, *Habitat for Humanity*, 133.

56 The interrelationship of charity, justice, the common good, friendship, forgiveness, and other values central to Christianity are discussed in MacIntyre, *After Virtue*, 174.

57 Harry T. Ries, Michael R. Maniaci, Peter A. Caprariello, Paul W. Eastwick, and Eli J. Finkel, "Familiarity Does Indeed Promote Attraction in Live Interaction," *Journal of Personality and Social Psychology* 101, no. 3 (2011): 561, 564.

CHAPTER 6. THE STATE, THE MARKET, AND POVERTY

1 Compare institutional differentiation—rather than secularization writ large—in Rodney Stark and Roger Finke, *Acts of Faith: Explaining the Human Side of Religion* (Berkeley, University of California Press, 2000), 59–61. This is a secular, rather than postsecular, understanding of society as described in Michele Dillon's *Postsecular Catholicism: Relevance and Renewal* (New York: Oxford University Press, 2018).

2 Joseph B. Tamney, Ronald Burton, and Stephen Johnson, "Christianity, Social Class, and the Catholic Bishops' Economic Policy," *Sociological Analysis* 49 Supplement: Presidential Issue (December 1988): 82S. This is even more true for Catholics specifically; Jerome Baggett, *Sense of the Faithful: How American Catholics Live Their Faith* (New York: Oxford University Press, 2009), 186. See also the salience for religiosity as a predictor of stance on homosexuality and abortion, with little to no correlation on the respondents' beliefs on the government's role in reducing inequality, spending on foreign aid, immigration, the death penalty and other issues in Robert D. Putnam and David E. Campbell's *American Grace: How Religion Divides and Unites Us* (New York: Simon & Schuster, 2012), 386.

3 Including Latinos increases the number of Democrats. William V. D'Antonio, Michelle Dillon, and Mary L. Gautier, *American Catholics in Transition* (Lanham, MD: Rowman & Littlefield Publishers, 2013), 126.

4 For the ideological division among Catholics on women, see Maureen K. Day, "From Consensus to Division: Tracing the Ideological Divide Among American Catholic Women, 1950–1980," *Journal of Media and Religion* 16, no. 4 (2017): 129–140. For division on work and family, see Mary Ellen Konieczny, *The Spirit's Tether: Family, Work, and Religion among American Catholics* (New York: Oxford University Press, 2013).

5 Putnam and Campbell, *American Grace*, 400.

6 Edwin S. Gaustad and Mark A. Noll, *A Documentary History of Religion in America: Since 1877*, 3rd ed. (Grand Rapids, MI: Eerdmans, 2003), 688. This does not necessarily mean that Republicans are more religious than their Democratic counterparts. It is important to remember that church attendance is a more traditional way of practicing faith and that those who conceive of their faith in more

conservative terms are more likely to conceive of their politics in conservative terms.

7 D'Antonio, Dillon, and Gautier, *American Catholics in Transition*, 130.

8 Black Protestants are another clear exception. They are one of the most churchgoing groups in the country and one of the least likely to be Republican. Putnam and Campbell, *American Grace*, 371.

9 Stockholm International Peace Research Institute, "World Military Spending Was $1.69 Trillion in 2016," (no date), accessed November 12, 2017, http://visuals.sipri.org/.

10 Catechism of the Catholic Church (CCC) #2309 reads, "The power of modem means of destruction weighs very heavily in evaluating this condition." See also, Pope Benedict XVI, then cardinal Josef Ratzinger, in an interview of Pope John Paul II's condemnation of the American attacks on Iraq said, "Given the new weapons that make possible destructions that go beyond the combatant groups, today we should be asking ourselves if it is still licit to admit the very existence of a 'just war.'" "Cardinal Ratzinger on the Abridged Version of Compendium," Zenit.org-Avvenire, May 2, 2003, accessed September 25, 2014, www.zenit.org/.

11 For example, a letter from the USCCB to President George W. Bush stating, "We conclude, based on the facts that are known to us, that a preemptive, unilateral use of force is difficult to justify at this time." President of USCCB Bishop Wilton D. Gregory, "Letter to President Bush on Iraq," USCCB, September 13, 2002, accessed September 25, 2014, www.usccb.org/.

12 E. J. Dionne Jr., "There Is No Catholic Vote—And it's Important," in *American Catholics and Civic Engagement: A Distinctive Voice*, ed. Margaret O'Brien Steinfels (Lanham, MD: Rowman and Littlefield Publishers, 2004), 253.

13 Charles R. Morris, *American Catholic: The Saints and Sinners Who Built America's Most Powerful Church* (New York: Vintage, 1997), 303.

14 D'Antonio, Dillon, and Gautier, *American Catholics in Transition*, 135.

15 Catholics favor a more lenient immigration policy (69 percent of Republican Catholics vs. 78 percent of Democratic Catholics), more health care for poor children (68 percent Republican vs. 89 percent Democrat), and less spending on nuclear weapons (75 percent Republican, 85 percent Democrat). D'Antonio, Dillon, and Gautier, *American Catholics in Transition*, 135.

16 For an excellent historical overview of American church–state relationships, see Philip Hamburger, *Separation of Church and State* (Cambridge, MA: Harvard University Press, 2004).

17 Baylor University, *The Baylor Religion Survey, Wave II* (Waco, TX: Baylor Institute for Studies of Religion, 2007).

18 Forty-one percent of Americans believe that it is important or very important to serve in the military to be a good person. Additionally, 68 percent of Americans believe the government spends too much on education, and only 29 percent say the same of the nation's military. Baylor University, *The Baylor Religion Survey, Wave II*.

19 For examples of the church supporting pacifism and absolute conscientious objection, see GS 78. Also, USCCB, *Declaration on Conscientious Objection and Selective Conscientious Objection*, October 21, 1971, accessed November 26, 2014, www .catholicpeacefellowship.org/.

20 Cf. Pope Francis's notion of "integral ecology" in *Laudato Si'*, May 24, 2015, accessed September 21, 2018, http://w2.vatican.va/.

21 Putnam and Campbell, *American Grace*, 392.

22 For a closer examination of the role of abortion in American Catholic politics, see Peter Steinfels, *A People Adrift: The Crisis of the Roman Catholic Church in America* (New York: Simon and Schuster, 2004), 82–98.

23 David C. Leege and Paul D. Mueller, "How Catholic Is the Catholic Vote?" in *American Catholics and Civic Engagement: A Distinctive Voice*, ed. Margaret O'Brien Steinfels (Lanham, MD: Rowman and Littlefield Publishers, 2004), 239.

24 D'Antonio, Dillon, and Gautier, *American Catholics in Transition*, 169.

25 D'Antonio, Dillon, and Gautier, *American Catholics in Transition*, 167.

26 Simon J. Hendry, "Ruined for Life: The Spirituality of the Jesuit Volunteer Corps" (PhD diss., Graduate Theological Union, 2002), 464. Michele Dillon, *Catholic Identity: Balancing Reason, Faith, and Power* (Cambridge, MA: Cambridge University Press, 1999), 199.

27 Christel Manning, *God Gave Us the Right: Conservative Catholic, Evangelical Protestant, and Orthodox Jewish Women Grapple with Feminism* (New Brunswick, NJ: Rutgers University Press, 1999), compare 198–199 with 26 and 231.

28 See Marvin L. Krier Mich's *The Challenge and Spirituality of Catholic Social Teaching*, rev. ed. (Maryknoll, NY: Orbis Books, 2011), ix. Mich acknowledges Jack Jezreel, thanking him "for the invitation to work on this text and for his suggestion to revise and update the first edition . . . both the JustFaith staff and participants in the JustFaith program surfaced a number of suggestions for improving the text." For the participants in the JustFaith group that I participated in, some had the original, and others used the revised edition. The only substantive difference they found was the more frequent discussion of abortion in the revised edition.

29 Kristen Luker examines the ways women's cultural understandings shape the abortion debate in *Abortion and the Politics of Motherhood* (Berkeley: University of California Press, 1984), 158–191. For a closer look at how the pro-choice movement is framed as a social issue in Germany compared to the individualist strategy in the United States, see Myra Marx Ferree's "Resonance and Radicalism: Feminist Framing in the Abortion Debates in the United States and Germany," *American Journal of Sociology* 109, no. 2 (September 2003): 304–344.

30 An excerpt reads, "There are two ways, one of life and one of death, and there is a great difference between the two ways. The way of life is this. First of all, you must love the God who made you; secondly, your neighbor as yourself. All things you wouldn't have befall yourself, neither do to another . . . But the way of death is this: . . . not pitying the poor man, not toiling for the one who is oppressed with toil, not recognizing Him who made them, murderers of children, corrupters of

the creatures of God, turning away from the one who is in want, oppressing those who are afflicted, advocates of the wealthy, unjust judges of the poor, altogether sinful." "The Good News of the Judgment," in *Present Truth Magazine*, trans. J. B. Lightfoot (1891), ed. Baruch (1993), accessed October 21, 2014, www.presenttruth mag.com/.

31 Pope John Paul II's *Evangelium Vitae*, Vatican website, May 25, 1995, accessed October 21, 2014, www.vatican.va/.

32 Cardinal Joseph Bernardin was president of the National Conference of Catholic Bishops and worked to bring Catholic concern for poverty, immigration, war, abortion, euthanasia, capital punishment, and so forth under the theological umbrella of a "consistent ethic of life."

33 Pope Francis's *Evangelii gaudium*, Vatican website, November 24, 2013, accessed October 28, 2014, http://w2.vatican.va/, n. 54.

34 For more on the difficulty of leaving one's economic class of origin, see David Card, "The Causal Effect of Education on Earnings," in *Handbook of Labor Economics, Volume 3*, ed. Orley C. Ashenfelter and David Card (Amsterdam: Elsevier Science B.V, 1999), 1801–1863. Also see Michael Hout, "Status, Autonomy, and Training in Occupational Mobility," *American Journal of Sociology* 89 (1984): 1379–1409. Furthermore, it has been calculated that it takes the average family at the poverty line five generations to reach double the poverty line; in Bhaskar Mazunder, "The Apple Falls Even Closer to the Tree than We Thought: New and Revised Estimates of the Intergenerational Inheritance of Earnings," in *Unequal Chances: Family Background and Economic Success*, ed. Samuel Bowles, Herbert Gintis, and Melissa Osborne Groves (New York: Russell Sage Foundation, 2006), 80–99.

35 Dennis Gilbert, *The American Class Structure in an Age of Growing Inequality* (Thousand Oaks, CA: Sage Publications, 2018), 91–93.

36 Not all sociologists believe that consumption patterns since the 1950s indicate a growing materialism or obsession with acquisition. Elizabeth Warren and Amelia Warren Tyagi, "Why Middle-Class Mothers and Fathers Are Going Broke," in *Family in Transition*, 15th ed., ed. Arlene S. Skolnick and Jerome H. Skolnick (Boston: Allyn and Bacon, 2009).

37 Christian Smith and Michael O. Emerson, with Patricia Snell, *Passing the Plate: Why American Christians Don't Give Away More Money* (New York: Oxford University Press, 2008), 63. People also care more about money than previous generations—73 percent listed "being well-off financially" as a top goal in 1985 compared to just 39 percent in 1970. Herbert J. Gans, *Middle American Individualism: The Future of Liberal Democracy* (New York: The Free Press, 1988), 99.

38 This was the college undergrad, and one would expect this low income to be temporary.

39 For a family of four in 1994, $50,000 is more than double the federal poverty line. "2014 Poverty Guidelines," *U.S. Department of Health and Human Services,* accessed November 16, 2014, http://aspe.hhs.gov/.

40 Baylor University, *The Baylor Religion Survey, Wave II.*

41 Meredith B. McGuire, "Testimony as a Commitment Mechanism in Catholic Pentecostal Prayer Groups," *Journal for the Scientific Study of Religion* 16 (1977): 166.

42 Compare the softer criticism of corporations from Habitat for Humanity staff: There is very little discussion of reform, and much of generosity. Jerome Baggett, *Habitat for Humanity: Building Private Homes, Building Public Religion* (Philadelphia: Temple University Press, 2000), 173.

43 This underscores discipleship style Catholics' need to be in the world, changing "structures of sin" to "structures of grace." Joseph M. Palacios, *The Catholic Social Imagination: Activism and the Just Society in Mexico and the United States* (Chicago, University of Chicago Press: 2007), 213.

44 Jim Wallis and Joyce Hollyday, *Cloud of Witnesses*, new rev. ed. (Maryknoll, NY: Orbis Books, 2005).

45 The "foot" of social justice, which removes root causes of injustice and improves structures, walks the "Path of Caritas" with the "foot" of charitable works, which meets basic needs and aids individuals. See "The Two Feet of Love in Action" in *JustFaith Participant Handbook*, Week 7: Attachment B.

46 CCC #1822, #1829.

47 Smith and Emerson, *Passing the Plate*, 53. "Outside organizations" do not include denominational or diocesan contributions, which average 8 percent of a congregation's expenditures.

48 Ram A. Cnaan, *The Invisible Caring Hand: America's Congregations and the Provision of Welfare* (New York: New York University Press, 2002), 9.

49 Nina Eliasoph, *The Politics of Volunteering* (Malden, MA: Polity Press, 2013), 43. Although these word associations come from college undergrads, there is no reason to think that the opinion of the wider culture is significantly different.

50 General Social Survey, 2008, Cross-Section and Panel Combined.

51 "Fundamentalist" Catholics are more likely to assent to the charitable elements in the American bishops' letter on the economy, and "non-Fundamentalist" Catholics are more in favor of reform. Tamney, Burton, and Johnson, "Christianity, Social Class, and the Catholic Bishops' Economic Policy," 86S, 93S.

52 Robert Wuthnow, *Acts of Compassion: Caring for Others and Helping Ourselves* (Princeton, NJ: Princeton University Press, 1991), 254–255.

53 These individualist tendencies are perhaps more dangerous for the poor; more often Americans want policies that remove obstacles for individuals but are hostile to removing obstacles that hinder a class of people. Gans, *Middle American Individualism*, 37.

54 Wuthnow, *Acts of Compassion*, 170–173.

55 Wuthnow, *Acts of Compassion*, 168–170.

56 Karl Marx, "The Eighteenth Brumaire of Louis Bonaparte," in *The Marx-Engels Reader*, 2nd ed., ed. Robert C. Tucker (New York: W. W. Norton & Company, 1978), 595.

57 Max Weber, "The Social Psychology of the World Religions," in *From Max Weber: Essays in Sociology*, ed. and trans. Hans H. Gerth and C. Wright Mills (Cambridge, MA: Oxford University Press, 1946), 280.

58 He calls power "a complex strategical situation in a particular society." Michel Foucault, *The History of Sexuality: An Introduction, Volume I*, trans. Robert Hurley (New York: Vintage Books, 1990), 92–94.

59 James Davison Hunter, *To Change the World: The Irony, Tragedy, and Possibility of Christianity in the Late Modern World* (New York: Oxford, 2010), 273.

60 There are similar findings in Nina Eliasoph, *Making Volunteers* (Princeton, NJ: Princeton University Press, 2011), 96.

61 Stephen Hart, *Cultural Dilemmas of Progressive Politics: Styles of Engagement Among Grassroots Activists* (Chicago: University of Chicago Press, 2001), 190.

62 This preference of charity over justice is common among American congregations. There are, however, a handful of steadfast congregations that pursue justice causes. Being more purposeful in explaining justice in their curricula could help JFM get the results it desires. Cnaan, *The Invisible Caring Hand*, 242–243.

63 General Social Survey 2008, Cross-Section and Panel Combined.

CHAPTER 7. COMPASSION

1 Jean-Françios Lyotard, *The Postmodern Condition: A Report on Knowledge* (Minneapolis: University of Minnesota Press, 1995), 53–60. Also see David Harvey, *The Condition of Postmodernity: An Enquiry into the Origins of Cultural Change* (Malden, MA: Blackwell Publishers, 1991), 328.

2 Compare his use of "narrative knowledge" in Lyotard, *The Postmodern Condition*, 18–23.

3 Peter L. Berger, *The Sacred Canopy: Elements of a Sociological Theory of Religion* (New York: Anchor Books, 1967), 11–15.

4 Christian Smith, *Moral, Believing Animals: Human Personhood and Culture* (New York: Oxford University Press, 2003), 56–57.

5 Robert Wuthnow, *Acts of Compassion: Caring for Others and Helping Ourselves* (Princeton, NJ: Princeton University Press, 1991), 285.

6 Compare Wolfe's idea of middle-class experience as contrasting to their ideological commitment, divorcing morality from politics. Grads bring experience and ideology and morality and politics, together. Alan Wolfe, *One Nation, After All: What Middle-Class Americans Really Think about God, Country, Family, Racism, Welfare, Immigration, Homosexuality, World, the Right, the Left and Each Other* (New York: Viking Penguin, 1988), 315.

7 Greg Boyle, *Tattoos on the Heart: The Power of Boundless Compassion* (New York: Free Press, 2011).

8 Compare MacIntyre's use of "fact," in which he criticizes the imagined separation of reality and evaluation of the reality. Alasdair MacIntyre, *After Virtue*, 2nd ed. (Notre Dame, IN: University of Notre Dame Press, 1984), 84.

9 Not all news is news in this sense. News media may offer "news" in the information, news, or story genre.

10 Our personal narratives shape our acceptance or rejection of knowledge. Smith, *Moral, Believing Animals*, 2003, 65, 87–88.

11 George Herbert Mead, *On Social Psychology*, ed. Anselm Strauss (Chicago: University of Chicago Press, 1964), 194.

12 Robert Wuthnow, *Sharing the Journey: Support Groups and America's New Quest for Community* (Princeton, NJ: Princeton University Press, 1994), 297.

13 Jerome Baggett, *Habitat for Humanity: Building Private Homes, Building Public Religion* (Philadelphia: Temple University Press, 2000), 16.

14 Lewis R. Rambo, *Understanding Religious Conversion* (New Haven, CT: Yale University Press, 1993), 159.

15 James M. Jasper, *The Art of Moral Protest: Culture, Biography, and Creativity in Social Movements* (Chicago: University of Chicago Press, 1999), 53.

16 Wuthnow, *Acts of Compassion*, 224–225.

17 Jürgen Habermas, *The Structural Transformation of the Public Sphere: An Inquiry into a Category of Bourgeois Society*, trans. Thomas Burger with the assistance of Frederick Lawrence (Cambridge, MA: MIT Press, 1991).

18 Habermas, *The Structural Transformation of the Public Sphere*, 249.

19 William J. McGuire, "Attitudes and Attitude Change," in *Handbook of Social Psychology*, 3rd ed., ed. Gardner Lindzey and Elliot Aronson (New York: Random House, 1985), 277–281.

20 Maxwell E. McCombs and Donald L. Shaw, "The Agenda Setting Function of Mass Media," *The Public Opinion Quarterly* 36, no. 2 (Summer, 1972): 184.

21 Robert M. Entman, "How the Media Affect What People Think: An Information Processing Approach," *Journal of Politics* 51, no. 2 (May, 1989): 361.

22 In a similar but more dramatic example, prisoners of war are more effectively brainwashed not when they are subjected to more extreme forms of torture but when they are with other prisoners who are more advanced in their stage of brainwashing. Arthur L. Greil, "Previous Dispositions and Conversion to Perspectives of Social and Religious Movements," *Sociological Analysis* 38, no. 2 (Summer, 1977):118.

23 Despite the fact that many grads say that their group offers a chance to disagree, there are also group norms that discourage disagreement. In one of the groups I observed there was a woman who one week said that it was important to care for the homeless but that one should never give them money directly. She proceeded to recount a story of her friend who works daily with the homeless and who claims that often she is very close to getting a person on the streets to come to a shelter. But then they get enough money to get drugs and then they want nothing to do with help. When she was absent for the session that discussed homelessness, someone brought up that position (notably not mentioning her specifically), and several people voiced their objections to that position, yet they said nothing

when she was present. This illustrates the tension in the competing values of open dialogue and sacred listening.

24 This is also corroborated in Habermas, who claims that it is the most informed who are most likely to enter into dialogue and that the most common outcome of this is to confirm their own beliefs or to persuade those lukewarm in their opinion to come to their side. Habermas, *The Structural Transformation of the Public Sphere*, 213. Also, in contrast to "volunteers," who tend to avoid discussing political issues, "activists" learn through such dialogue. Nina Eliasoph, *Avoiding Politics: How Americans Produce Apathy in Everyday Life* (New York: Cambridge University Press, 1998), 173.

25 Mountaintop removal in the coal-mining industry is a very serious issue for many of the Louisville grads.

26 David J. O'Brien, *Public Catholicism*, 2nd ed. (New York: Orbis Books, 1996), 156.

27 CCC 1806.

28 Berger and Luckmann, *The Social Construction of Reality*, 23.

29 However, this is by no means an exclusively American phenomenon. The falling away of the epic and other traditional plot-based stories in favor of the novel, with its concentration on the development of individuals and subjectivity, reflects this larger shift. Ian Watt, *The Rise of the Novel: Studies in Defoe, Richardson and Fielding* (Berkeley: University of California Press, 1957). It is even appearing in the traditionalist countryside of Andalusia, as the people there have come to look at the world with eyes of "modern subjectivity." Jane Fishburne Collier, *From Duty to Desire: Remaking Families in a Spanish Village* (Princeton, NJ: Princeton University Press, 1997).

30 Robert Putnam, *Bowling Alone: The Collapse and Revival of American Community* (New York: Simon & Schuster, 2000). Bender is more positive in his assessment of contemporary American society yet still asserts that we give more of our lives to rational market logic than the affection and obligation of community. Thomas Bender, *Community and Social Change in America* (Baltimore, MD: Johns Hopkins University Press, 1982), 146.

31 Robert N. Bellah, Richard Madsen, William M. Sullivan, Ann Swidler, and Steven M. Tipton, *Habits of the Heart: Individualism and Commitment in American Life* (Berkeley: University of California Press, 1985), 154.

32 Bellah et al., *Habits of the Heart*, 20, 32–35.

33 Bellah et al., *Habits of the Heart*, 156–157.

34 Eliasoph, *Avoiding Politics*, 3–8.

35 Wuthnow, *Acts of Compassion*, 6.

36 Wuthnow, *Acts of Compassion*, 22–23.

37 Wuthnow, *Acts of Compassion*, 71–73.

38 Experiences and stories also motivated many to become involved in the Central American Peace Movement. Christian Smith, *Resisting Reagan: The U.S. Central America Peace Movement* (Chicago: University of Chicago Press, 1996), 181.

39 At housing organization Habitat for Humanity, staff and volunteers also "put human faces on social problems." Baggett, *Habitat for Humanity*, 135.

40 Believing that civic engagement is also for the benefit of the person doing the engaging is a theme in Empowerment Talk, and it is in tension with the desire of nonprofits to make volunteering there seem manageable and non-threatening. Nina Eliasoph, *Making Volunteers* (Princeton, NJ: Princeton University Press, 2011), 48.

41 Nina Eliasoph has found that personalism is a tactic some use to make a more unwieldy problem, like the transformation of a structure, into something more manageable, such has handling the needs of a particular individual. Eliasoph, *Avoiding Politics*, 13. Courtney Bender, *Heaven's Kitchen: Living Religion at God's Love We Deliver* (Chicago: University of Chicago Press, 2003), 65.

42 James M. Jasper calls this sort of other-regarding activism "post-citizenship" and is found among those integrated into the systems of power in their society. As they do not need to secure goods or services for themselves, they look to ensure them for others. Jasper, *The Art of Moral Protest*, 7. This appears to be in contrast to what Doug McAdam found in his examination of the civil rights movement. McAdam found that resources from elites are unnecessary and can even damage social movements. Doug McAdam, *Political Process and the Development of Black Insurgency, 1930–1970* (Chicago: University of Chicago Press, 1999), 141, 167. However, solidarity and relationship can cause one to see oneself as a part of the offended class even when one is not personally threatened.

43 The American family was once an institution that tied members to the larger public world. Now it has largely become a retreat from the public world. Bellah et al. *Habits of the Heart*, 112.

44 Compare the way some volunteers use care and personalism to *limit* their sphere of care and activism in Eliasoph, *Avoiding Politics*, 25.

45 This does not happen to be true for the woman who uses family analogically for human trafficking. She was very passionate about the issue of human trafficking and discussed legislative options. However, generally an analogical approach is more focused on a specific victim and directing charity to him or her.

46 The percentage increase on these range from 7 to 18 percent, depending on the issue. William V. D'Antonio, Michelle Dillon, and Mary L. Gautier, *American Catholics in Transition* (Lanham, MD: Rowman & Littlefield Publishers, 2013), 78.

47 Andrew M. Greeley, *American Catholics since the Council: An Unauthorized Report* (Chicago: The Thomas More Press, 1985), 93–94.

48 Greeley, *American Catholics since the Council*, 96.

49 Phillip E. Hammond, *Religion and Personal Autonomy: The Third Disestablishment in America* (Columbia: University of South Carolina Press, 1992), 10.

50 Michele Dillon, *Catholic Identity: Balancing Reason, Faith, and Power* (Cambridge, MA: Cambridge University Press, 1999), 15.

CONCLUSION

1 Fifty-two percent of people whose income is lower than $10,000 are registered to vote. Compare this to 62 percent of those who make between $20,000 and $29,999 yearly, 73 percent who make between $50,000 and $74,999 yearly, and 80 percent who make $100,000 or more. For complete data, see table 7 of "Voting and Registration," United States Census Bureau, last modified October 2011, accessed October 30, 2014, www.census.gov/.

2 Doug McAdam, *Political Process and the Development of Black Insurgency, 1930–1970* (Chicago: University of Chicago Press, 1999).

3 Christian Smith, *Resisting Reagan: The U.S. Central America Peace Movement* (Chicago: University of Chicago Press, 1996).

4 Sharon Erickson Nepstad, *Religion and War Resistance in the Plowshares Movement*, Cambridge Studies in Contentious Politics (New York: Cambridge University Press, 2008).

5 Peter Steinfels, *A People Adrift: The Crisis of the Roman Catholic Church in America* (New York: Simon and Schuster, 2004), 354–356. Smith, *Resisting Reagan*.

6 Charles E. Zech, Mary L. Gautier, Mark M. Gray, Jonathon L. Wiggins, and Thomas P. Gaunt, S.J. *Catholic Parishes of the 21st Century* (New York: Oxford University Press, 2017), 11. William V. D'Antonio, Michele Dillon, and Mary L. Gautier, *American Catholics in Transition* (Lanham, MD: Rowman & Littlefield Publishers, 2013), 33.

7 Smith, Christian, Kyle Longest, Jonathan Hill, and Kari Christoffersen. *Young Catholic America: Emerging Adults In, Out of, and Gone from the Church* (New York: Oxford University Press, 2014), 69–76.

8 Simon Hendry, "'Ruined for Life': The Spirituality of the Jesuit Volunteer Corps" (PhD diss., Graduate Theological Union, 2002), 214.

9 Natalia Imperatori-Lee, *Cuéntame: Narrative in the Ecclesial Present* (Maryknoll, NY: Orbis, 2018).

10 See his discussion of the shift from collective-expressive agency to individual-expressive agency in Phillip E. Hammond, *Religion and Personal Autonomy: The Third Disestablishment in America* (Columbia: University of South Carolina Press, 1992).

11 James Davison Hunter, *To Change the World: The Irony, Tragedy, and Possibility of Christianity in the Late Modern World* (New York: Oxford, 2010), 244–248.

12 Hunter, *To Change the World*, 253.

13 Hunter, *To Change the World*, 256–257.

14 Personal letter dated August 6, 2012. Used with permission of sender.

15 Robert Wuthnow, *Acts of Compassion: Caring for Others and Helping Ourselves* (Princeton, NJ: Princeton University Press, 1991), 233–234.

16 Alan Wolfe, *Whose Keeper? Social Science and Moral Obligation* (Berkeley: University of California Press, 1989), 237–259.

APPENDIX A

1 JFM was clear that while I had their approval for this project, I also needed the approval of any group I participated in. Of the five groups I approached, one group's facilitators declined to have me participate.

APPENDIX B

1 The number is listed as twenty-four or twenty-seven because the core program is twenty-four sessions with an additional three sessions of discernment that groups can elect to do, as well.

2 Confirmation is the final sacrament of initiation into the Catholic Church. Those raised Roman Catholic typically receive this sacrament in eighth or tenth grade in the United States.

3 "JustFaith Ministries, Programs, Engaging Spirituality: Frequently Asked Questions," n.d., JustFaith Ministries, accessed November 12, 2013, http://justfaith.org/.

BIBLIOGRAPHY

Aberle, David F. *The Peyote Religion among the Navaho*. Norman: University of Oklahoma Press, 1991.

Allahyari, Rebecca Anne. *Visions of Charity: Volunteer Works and Moral Community*. Berkeley: University of California Press, 2000.

Altonji, Joseph G., and Rebecca M. Blank. "Race and Gender in the Labor Market." In *Handbook of Labor Economics, Volume 3*, edited by Orley C. Ashenfelter and David Card, 3143–3259. Amsterdam: Elsevier B.V., 1999.

Aquinas, Thomas. *Summa Theologiae*. Edited by Benzinger Brothers. Translated by Fathers of the English Dominican Province. 1947. Accessed June 27, 2014. http://dhspriory.org.

Aristotle. *Nicomachean Ethics*. Translated by Martin Ostwald. New York: Macmillan Publishing, 1962.

Baggett, Jerome. *Habitat for Humanity: Building Private Homes, Building Public Religion*. Philadelphia: Temple University Press, 2000.

———. *Sense of the Faithful: How American Catholics Live Their Faith*. New York: Oxford University Press, 2009.

Baker, Irwin R., and Raymond F. Currie. "Do Converts Always Make the Most Committed Christians?" *Journal for the Scientific Study of Religion* 24 (1985): 305–313.

Barker, Hannah, and Simon Burrows, eds. *Press, Politics and the Public Sphere in Europe and North America 1760–1820*. New York: Cambridge University Press, 2002.

Bellah, Robert N., Richard Madsen, William M. Sullivan, Ann Swidler, and Steven M. Tipton. *Habits of the Heart: Individualism and Commitment in American Life*. Berkeley: University of California Press, 1985.

Bender, Courtney. *Heaven's Kitchen: Living Religion at God's Love We Deliver*. Chicago: University of Chicago Press, 2003.

Bender, Thomas. *Community and Social Change in America*. Baltimore, MD: Johns Hopkins University Press, 1982.

Berger, Peter. *The Sacred Canopy: Elements of a Sociological Theory of Religion*. New York: Anchor Books, 1967.

———, and Thomas Luckmann. *The Social Construction of Reality: A Treatise in the Sociology of Knowledge*. Garden City, NY: Doubleday, 1966.

Brauer, Jerald C. "Conversion: From Puritanism to Revivalism." *Journal of Religion* 58 (1978): 227–248.

Bruce, Tricia Colleen. *Faithful Revolution: How Voice of the Faithful Is Changing the Church*. New York: Oxford University Press, 2011.

———. *Parish and Place: Making Room for Diversity in the American Catholic Church.* New York: Oxford University Press, 2017.

Card, David. "The Causal Effect of Education on Earnings." In *Handbook of Labor Economics, Volume 3*, edited by Orley C. Ashenfelter and David Card, 1801–1863. Amsterdam: Elsevier Science B.V., 1999.

Chaves, Mark. *American Religion: Contemporary Trends.* Princeton, NJ: Princeton University Press, 2011.

Cherry, Elizabeth. "Veganism as a Cultural Movement: A Relational Approach." *Social Movement Studies* 5, no. 2 (September 2006): 155–170.

Cnaan, Ram A. *The Invisible Caring Hand: America's Congregations and the Provision of Welfare.* New York: New York University Press, 2002.

Collier, Jane Fishburne. *From Duty to Desire: Remaking Families in a Spanish Village.* Princeton, NJ: Princeton University Press, 1997.

Cuneo, Michael W. *The Smoke of Satan: Conservative and Traditionalist Dissent in Contemporary American Catholicism.* New York: Oxford University Press, 1997.

Curran, Charles E. *Catholic Social Teaching 1891–Present: A Historical, Theological, and Ethical Analysis.* Washington, DC: Georgetown University Press, 2002.

D'Antonio, William V., James D. Davidson, Dean R. Hoge, and Katherine Meyer. *American Catholics: Gender, Generation, and Commitment.* Walnut Creek, CA: AltaMira Press, 2001.

———, Michelle Dillon, and Mary L. Gautier. *American Catholics in Transition.* Lanham, MD: Rowman & Littlefield Publishers, 2013.

Day, Maureen K. "From Consensus to Division: Tracing the Ideological Divide among American Catholic Women, 1950–1980." *Journal of Media and Religion* 16, no. 4 (2017): 129–140.

Dillon, Michele. *Catholic Identity: Balancing Reason, Faith, and Power.* Cambridge, MA: Cambridge University Press, 1999.

———. *Postsecular Catholicism: Relevance and Renewal.* New York: Oxford University Press, 2018.

Dionne, E. J., Jr. "There Is No Catholic Vote—And It's Important." In *American Catholics and Civic Engagement: A Distinctive Voice*, edited by Margaret O'Brien Steinfels, 251–260. Lanham, MD: Rowman & Littlefield Publishers, 2004.

Dolan, Jay P. *The American Catholic Experience: A History from Colonial Times to the Present.* Norte Dame, IN: University of Notre Dame Press, 1992.

———. *In Search of American Catholicism: A History of Religion and Culture in Tension.* New York: Oxford University Press, 2002.

Donahue, John R. "The Bible and Catholic Social Teaching: Will This Engagement Lead to Marriage?" In *Modern Catholic Social Teaching: Commentaries and Interpretations*, edited by Kenneth R. Himes, with Lisa Sowle Cahill, Charles E. Curran, David Hollenbach, and Thomas Shannon as associate editors, 9–40. Washington, DC: Georgetown University Press, 2005.Dulles, Avery, S.J. *Models of the Church.* Expanded edition. New York: Doubleday, 1987.

Eliasoph, Nina. *Avoiding Politics: How Americans Produce Apathy in Everyday Life*. New York: Cambridge University Press, 1998.

——. *Making Volunteers*. Princeton, NJ: Princeton University Press, 2011.

——. *The Politics of Volunteering*. Malden, MA: Polity Press, 2013.

Entman, Robert M. "How the Media Affect What People Think: An Information Processing Approach." *Journal of Politics* 51, no. 2 (May, 1989): 347–370.

Erzen, Tanya. *Straight to Jesus: Sexual and Christian Conversions in the Ex-Gay Movement*. Berkeley: University of California Press, 2006.

Ferree, Myra Marx. "Resonance and Radicalism: Feminist Framing in the Abortion Debates in the United States and Germany." *American Journal of Sociology* 109, no. 2 (September 2003): 304–344.

Fetner, Tina. *How the Religious Right Shaped Lesbian and Gay Activism*. Social Movements, Protest and Contention series. Minneapolis: University of Minnesota Press, 2008.

Foucault, Michel. *The History of Sexuality: An Introduction, Volume I*. Translated by Robert Hurley. New York: Vintage Books, 1990.

Francis. *Evangelii Guadium*. Vatican website. November 24, 2013. Accessed May 6, 2013. http://w2.vatican.va/.

——. *Laudato Si'*. Vatican website. May 24, 2015. Accessed September 21, 2018. http://w2.vatican.va.

Gans, Herbert J. *Middle American Individualism: The Future of Liberal Democracy*. New York: The Free Press, 1988.

Gaustad, Edwin S., and Mark A. Noll. *A Documentary History of Religion in America: Since 1877*. 3rd ed. Grand Rapids, MI: Eerdmans, 2003.

——, and Leigh E. Schmidt. *The Religious History of America: The Heart of the American Story from Colonial Times to Today*. San Francisco: HarperSanFrancisco, 2002.

Geertz, Clifford. "Thick Description: Toward an Interpretive Theory of Culture." In *The Interpretation of Cultures*, 3–32. New York: Basic Books, 1973.

Giddens, Anthony. *The Constitution of Society*. Berkeley: University of California Press, 1984.

Gilbert, Dennis. *The American Class Structure in an Age of Growing Inequality*. Thousand Oaks, CA: Sage Publications, 2018.

Goffman, Erving. *The Presentation of Self in Everyday Life*. Garden City, NY: Doubleday, 1959.Gooren, Henri. "Towards a New Model of Conversion Careers: The Impact of Personality and Situational Factors" *Exchange* 34 (2005): 149–166.

Gray, Mark M., Mary L. Gautier, and Melissa A. Cidade. *The Changing Face of U.S. Catholic Parishes*. Washington, DC: National Association for Lay Ministry, 2011.

Greeley, Andrew M. *American Catholics since the Council: An Unauthorized Report*. Chicago: The Thomas More Press, 1985.

Greil, Arthur L. "Previous Dispositions and Conversion to Perspectives of Social and Religious Movements." *Sociological Analysis* 38, no. 2 (1977): 115–125.

Gula, Richard. *Reason Informed by Faith*. New York: Paulist Press, 1989.

Habermas, Jürgen. *The Structural Transformation of the Public Sphere: An Inquiry into a Category of Bourgeois Society*. Translated by Thomas Burger with the assistance of Frederick Lawrence. Cambridge, MA: MIT Press, 1991.

Hamburger, Philip. *Separation of Church and State*. Cambridge, MA: Harvard University Press, 2004.

Hammond, Phillip E. *Religion and Personal Autonomy: The Third Disestablishment in America*. Columbia: University of South Carolina Press, 1992.

Hart, Stephen. *What Does the Lord Require? How American Christians Think about Economic Justice*. New Brunswick, NJ: Rutgers University Press, 1996.

———. *Cultural Dilemmas of Progressive Politics: Styles of Engagement among Grassroots Activists*. Chicago: University of Chicago Press, 2001.

Harvey, David. *The Condition of Postmodernity: An Enquiry into the Origins of Cultural Change*. Malden, MA: Blackwell Publishers, 1991.

Heirich, Max. "Change of Heart: A Test of Some Widely Held Theories about Religious Conversion." *American Sociological Review* 83 (1977): 653–680.

Hendry, Simon J. "'Ruined for Life': The Spirituality of the Jesuit Volunteer Corps." PhD diss., Graduate Theological Union, 2002.

Hirschman, Albert O. *Exit, Voice, and Loyalty: Responses to Decline in Firms, Organizations, and States*. Cambridge, MA: Harvard University Press, 1970.

Hochschild, Arlie Russell. *The Managed Heart: Commercialization of Human Feeling*. Berkeley: University of California Press, 1983.

Hogan, John P. *Credible Signs of Christ Alive: Case Studies from the Catholic Campaign for Human Development*. Lanham, MD: Rowman & Littlefield Publishers, 2003.

Hout, Michael. "Status, Autonomy, and Training in Occupational Mobility." *American Journal of Sociology* 89 (1984): 1379–1409.

Hunter, James Davison. *To Change the World: The Irony, Tragedy, and Possibility of Christianity in the Late Modern World*. New York: Oxford, 2010.

Imperatori-Lee, Natalia. *Cuéntame: Narrative in the Ecclesial Present*. Maryknoll, NY: Orbis, 2018.

Jasper, James M. *The Art of Moral Protest: Culture, Biography, and Creativity in Social Movements*. Chicago: University of Chicago Press, 1999.

John XXIII. *Pacem in Terris* (Peace on Earth). April, 11 1963. In *Catholic Social Thought: The Documentary Heritage*, edited by David J. O'Brien and Thomas A. Shannon, 129–162. Maryknoll, NY: Orbis, 1992.

John Paul II. *Centesimus Annus* (On the Hundredth Anniversary of *Rerum Novarum*). May 1, 1991. In *Catholic Social Thought: The Documentary Heritage*, edited by David J. O'Brien and Thomas A. Shannon, 437–488. Maryknoll, NY: Orbis, 1992.

———. *Redemptor Hominis*. Vatican website. March 4, 1979. Accessed May 1, 2014. www.vatican.va.

———. *Sollicitudo Rei Socialis* (On Social Concern). December 30, 1987. In *Catholic Social Thought: The Documentary Heritage*, edited by David J. O'Brien and Thomas A. Shannon, 393–496. Maryknoll, NY: Orbis, 1992.

———. *Evangelium Vitae.* Vatican website. May 25, 1995. Accessed October 21, 2014. www.vatican.va.

Kanter, Rosabeth Moss. *Commitment and Community: Communes and Utopias in Sociological Perspective.* Cambridge, MA: Harvard University Press, 1972.

Kertzer, David I. *Ritual, Politics, and Power.* New Haven, CT: Yale University Press, 1988.

Kilbourne, Brock, and James T. Richardson. "Paradigm Conflict, Types of Conversion, and Conversion Theories." *Sociological Analysis* 50, no. 1 (1989): 1–21.

Konieczny, Mary Ellen. *The Spirit's Tether: Family, Work, and Religion among American Catholics.* New York: Oxford University Press, 2013.

Konieczny, Mary Ellen, Charles C. Camosy, and Tricia Colleen Bruce. *Polarization in the US Catholic Church: Naming the Wounds, Beginning to Heal.* Collegeville, MN: Liturgical Press, 2016.

Lareau, Annette. *Unequal Childhoods: Class, Race, and Family Life.* Berkeley: University of California Press, 2003.

Lee, Bernard J., with William V. D'Antonio, Virgilio P. Elizondo, Patricia O'Connell Killen, and Jeanette Rodriguez. *The Catholic Experience of Small Christian Communities.* New York: Paulist Press, 2000.

Leege, David C., and Paul D. Mueller. "How Catholic Is the Catholic Vote?" In *American Catholics and Civic Engagement: A Distinctive Voice*, edited by Margaret O'Brien Steinfels, 213–243. Lanham, MD: Rowman & Littlefield Publishers, 2004.

Lofland, John, and Norman Skonovd. "Conversion Motifs." *Journal for the Scientific Study of Religion* 20, no. 4 (December 1981): 373–385.

Loveland, Matthew. "Religious Switching: Preference Development, Maintenance, and Change." *Journal for the Scientific Study of Religion* 42 (2003): 147–157.

Luker, Kristen. *Abortion and the Politics of Motherhood.* Berkeley: University of California Press, 1984.

Lyotard, Jean-François. *The Postmodern Condition: A Report on Knowledge.* Minneapolis: University of Minnesota Press, 1995.

MacIntyre, Alasdair. *After Virtue.* 2nd ed. Notre Dame, IN: University of Notre Dame Press, 1984.

Manning, Christel. *God Gave Us the Right: Conservative Catholic, Evangelical Protestant, and Orthodox Jewish Women Grapple with Feminism.* New Brunswick, NJ: Rutgers University Press, 1999.

Marx, Karl. "The Eighteenth Brumaire of Louis Bonaparte." In *The Marx-Engels Reader*, 2nd ed., edited by Robert C. Tucker, 594–617. New York: W. W. Norton & Company, 1978.

Mazunder, Bhaskar. "The Apple Falls Even Closer to the Tree than We Thought: New and Revised Estimates of the Intergenerational Inheritance of Earnings." In *Unequal Chances: Family Background and Economic Success*, edited by Samuel Bowles, Herbert Gintis, and Melissa Osborne Groves, 80–99. New York: Russell Sage Foundation, 2006.

McAdam, Doug. *Political Process and the Development of Black Insurgency, 1930–1970.* Chicago: University of Chicago Press, 1999.

McCombs, Maxwell E., and Donald L. Shaw. "The Agenda Setting Function of Mass Media." *The Public Opinion Quarterly* 36, no. 2 (Summer 1972): 176–187.

McGuire, Meredith B. "Testimony as a Commitment Mechanism in Catholic Pentecostal Prayer Groups." *Journal for the Scientific Study of Religion* 16 (1977): 165–168.

McGuire, William J. "Attitudes and Attitude Change." In *Handbook of Social Psychology*, 3rd ed., edited by Gardner Lindzey and Elliot Aronson, 233–346. New York: Random House, 1985.

Mead, George Herbert. *On Social Psychology.* Edited by Anselm Strauss. Chicago: University of Chicago Press, 1964.

Merton, Thomas. *Conjectures of a Guilty Bystander.* Garden City, NY: Image Books, 1968.

Mich, Marvin L. Krier. *The Challenge and Spirituality of Catholic Social Teaching.* Rev. ed. Maryknoll, NY: Orbis Books, 2011.

Morris, Charles R. *American Catholic: The Saints and Sinners Who Built America's Most Powerful Church.* New York: Vintage, 1997.

Munson, Ziad W. *The Making of Pro-Life Activists: How Social Movement Mobilization Works.* Chicago: University of Chicago Press, 2009.

Nepstad, Sharon Erickson. *Convictions of the Soul: Religion Culture and Agency in the Central American Solidarity Movement.* New York: Oxford University Press, 2004.

———. *Religion and War Resistance in the Plowshares Movement.* Cambridge Studies in Contentious Politics. New York: Cambridge University Press, 2008.

Niebuhr, H. Richard. *Christ and Culture.* New York: Harper and Row, 1951.

O'Brien, David J. *Public Catholicism.* 2nd ed. New York: Orbis Books, 1996.

Oates, Mary J. *The Catholic Philanthropic Tradition in America.* Indianapolis: Indiana University Press, 1995.

Orsi, Robert A. *Thank You, St. Jude: Women's Devotion to the Patron Saint of Hopeless Causes.* New Haven, CT: Yale University Press, 1996.

Palacios, Joseph M. *The Catholic Social Imagination: Activism and the Just Society in Mexico and the United States.* Chicago: University of Chicago Press, 2007.

Paul VI. *Gaudium et Spes* (Pastoral Constitution on the Church in the Modern World). December 7, 1965. In *Catholic Social Thought: The Documentary Heritage*, edited by David J. O'Brien and Thomas A. Shannon, 164–237. Maryknoll, NY: Orbis, 1992.

Pearce, Jone L. *Volunteers: The Organizational Behavior of Unpaid Workers.* New York: Routledge, 1993.

Pius XI. *Quadragesimo Anno* (After Forty Years). May 15, 1931. In *Catholic Social Thought: The Documentary Heritage*, edited by David J. O'Brien and Thomas A. Shannon, 40–79. Maryknoll, NY: Orbis, 1992.

Polletta, Francesca. "Awkward Movements." *Mobilization* 11, no. 4 (December 2006): 475–478.

Putnam, Robert. *Bowling Alone: The Collapse and Revival of American Community.* New York: Simon & Schuster, 2000.

Putnam, Robert D., and David E. Campbell. *American Grace: How Religion Divides and Unites Us*. New York: Simon & Schuster, 2012.

Rambo, Lewis R. *Understanding Religious Conversion*. New Haven, CT: Yale University Press, 1993.

Ries, Harry T., Michael R. Maniaci, Peter A. Caprariello, Paul W. Eastwick, and Eli J. Finkel. "Familiarity Does Indeed Promote Attraction in Live Interaction." *Journal of Personality and Social Psychology* 101, no. 3 (2011): 557–570.

Roof, Wade Clark, and William McKinney. *American Mainline Religion: Its Changing Shape and Future*. New Brunswick, NJ: Rutgers University Press, 1987.

Schubeck, Thomas L. *Liberation Ethics: Sources, Models, and Norms*. Minneapolis, MN: Augsburg Fortress, 1993.

Smith, Christian, ed. *American Evangelicalism: Embattled and Thriving*. Chicago: University of Chicago Press, 1998.

———. *Disruptive Religion: The Force of Faith in Social Movement Activism*. New York: Routledge, 1996.

———. *Moral, Believing Animals: Human Personhood and Culture*. New York: Oxford University Press, 2003.

———. *Resisting Reagan: The U.S. Central America Peace Movement*. Chicago: University of Chicago Press, 1996.

———, and Michael O. Emerson, with Patricia Snell. *Passing the Plate: Why American Christians Don't Give Away More Money*. New York: Oxford University Press, 2008.

———, Kyle Longest, Jonathan Hill, and Kari Christoffersen. *Young Catholic America: Emerging Adults In, Out of, and Gone from the Church*. New York: Oxford University Press, 2014.

Snarr, C. Melissa. *All You that Labor: Religion and Ethics in the Living Wage Movement*. New York: New York University Press, 2011.

Snow, David A., and Richard Machalek. "The Sociology of Conversion." *Annual Review of Sociology* 10 (1984): 167–190.

Stark, Rodney, and Roger Finke. *Acts of Faith: Explaining the Human Side of Religion*. Berkeley, University of California Press, 2000.

Steinfels, Peter. *A People Adrift: The Crisis of the Roman Catholic Church in America*. New York: Simon and Schuster, 2004.

Straus, Roger A. "Religious Conversion as a Personal and Collective Accomplishment" *Sociological Analysis* 40 (1979): 158–165.

Stromberg, Peter G. "Ideological Language in the Transformation of Identity" *American Anthropologist*, New Series, 92, no. 1 (1990): 42–56.

Swarts, Heidi J. *Organizing Urban America: Secular and Faith-Based Progressive Movements*. Minneapolis: University of Minnesota Press, 2008.

Swidler, Ann. *Talk of Love: How Culture Matters*. Chicago: University of Chicago Press, 2003.

Tamney, Joseph B., Ronald Burton, and Stephen Johnson. "Christianity, Social Class, and the Catholic Bishops' Economic Policy." *Sociological Analysis* 49 Supplement: Presidential Issue (December 1988): 78S–96S.

Townsend, Nicholas. "The Four Facets of Fatherhood." In *Family in Transition*, 15th ed., edited by Arlene S. Skolnick and Jerome H. Skolnick, 283–292. Boston: Allyn and Bacon, 2009.

Travisano, Richard. "Alternation and Conversion as Qualitatively Different Transformations." In *Social Psychology through Symbolic Interaction*, edited by Gregory Prince Stone and Harvey A. Farberman, 594–606. Waltham, MA: Ginn-Blaisdell, 1970.

Turner, Victor. *The Ritual Process: Structure and Anti-Structure*. Ithaca, NY: Cornell University Press, 1969.

United States Catholic Bishops. *The Challenge of Peace: God's Promise and Our Response* (1983). In *Catholic Social Thought: The Documentary Heritage*, edited by David J. O'Brien and Thomas A. Shannon, 572–680. Maryknoll, NY: Orbis, 1992.

United States Catholic Bishops. *Economic Justice for All* (1986). In *Catholic Social Thought: The Documentary Heritage*, edited by David J. O'Brien and Thomas A. Shannon, 572–680. Maryknoll, NY: Orbis, 1992.

Verba, Sidney, Kay Schlozman, and Henry Brady. *Voice and Equality: Civic Voluntarism in American Politics*. Cambridge, MA: Harvard University Press, 1995.

Wallis, Jim, and Joyce Hollyday. *Cloud of Witnesses*. New rev. ed. Maryknoll, NY: Orbis Books, 2005.

Warner, R. Stephen. "Religion, Boundaries, and Bridges." *Sociology of Religion* 58, no. 3 (1997): 217–238.

Warren, Elizabeth, and Amelia Warren Tyagi. "Why Middle-Class Mothers and Fathers Are Going Broke." In *Family in Transition*, 15th ed., edited by Arlene S. Skolnick and Jerome H. Skolnick, 399–418. Boston: Allyn and Bacon, 2009.

Watt, Ian. *The Rise of the Novel: Studies in Defoe, Richardson and Fielding*. Berkeley: University of California Press, 1957.

Weber, Max. "The Social Psychology of the World Religions." In *From Max Weber: Essays in Sociology*, translated and edited by Hans H. Gerth and C. Wright Mills, 267–301. New York: Oxford University Press, 1946.

Wolfe, Alan. *One Nation, After All: What Middle-Class Americans Really Think about God, Country, Family, Racism, Welfare, Immigration, Homosexuality, World, the Right, the Left and Each Other*. New York: Viking Penguin, 1988.

———. *Whose Keeper? Social Science and Moral Obligation*. Berkeley: University of California Press, 1989.

Wood, Richard L. *Faith in Action: Religion, Race, and Democratic Organizing in America*. Chicago: University of Chicago Press, 2002.

Wuthnow, Robert. *Acts of Compassion: Caring for Others and Helping Ourselves*. Princeton, NJ: Princeton University Press, 1991.

———. *Loose Connections: Joining Together in Americas Fragmented Communities*. Cambridge, MA: Harvard University Press, 2002.

———. *Sharing the Journey: Support Groups and America's New Quest for Community*. Princeton, NJ: Princeton University Press, 1994.

Yamane, David, and Sarah MacMillen, with Kelly Culver. *Real Stories of Christian Initiation: Lessons for and from the RCIA*. Collegeville, MN: Liturgical Press, 2006.

Young, Iris Marion. "Five Faces of Oppression." In *Justice and the Politics of Difference*, 39–65. Princeton, NJ: Princeton University Press, 2011.

Yukich, Grace. *One Family under God: Immigration Politics and Progressive Religion in America*. New York: Oxford University Press, 2013.

Zech, Charles E., Mary L. Gautier, Mark M. Gray, Jonathon L. Wiggins, and Thomas P. Gaunt. *Catholic Parishes of the 21st Century*. New York: Oxford University Press, 2017.

INDEX

Aberle, David F., 260n3
abolitionist, 1–2
abortion opposition, 79–80, 226; Bernardin on, 180, 278n32; complexity related to, 179–81; culture of life in, 180–81, 277n30; homelessness related to, 180–81; issue intersection and, 177–81, 277n28, 277n30; in JustFaith survey data, 85, 89, *89*; justice issue of, 178, 277n28; marginalization related to, 179; moral context for, 177–78; political parties and, 177; by Republicans, 167; social issue of, 178; structural issue of, 178; women's rights and, 178
accountability, 146
activism, 9, *94*, 94–95, 265n67; justice, 200; from small groups, 266n74; urgency in, 224
activists: volunteers compared to, 193, 279n49, 282n24. *See also specific topics*
Acts of Compassion (Wuthnow), 220, 238
affirmation, 146
agape, 2
age, 5, 255n7
alliance, 52–53, 58, 119
altruism, 156, 274n45
"Amazing Grace," 1–2
America: poor in, 182; "second language" in, 219–20
American Catholic identity, 136
American Catholics: Catholicism of, 225–26; in discipleship communities, 136; institutional strength of, 69; liberal/conservative divide in, 130–31

American Christianity, 191
American public policy, 172
Americans: Native, 204–5, 207; political involvement of, 199; republican style for, 28
Angelus, 114, 268n38
anointing, 68
anticommunism, 48
Augustine (saint), 128

back-pew Catholics, 253
Baggett, Jerome, 267n28
Bay Area congregations analysis, 96–99, *97*, 265n73
bearings letters, 213; on dilemma of efficacy, 188–89; as knowledge, 208–9
beliefs, 84–85; about faith and politics, 168–69, 173; about homelessness, 205–6, 238–39; knowledge related to, 203–5; practice of, 137–38; public opinions and, 165, 275n2
Bellah, Robert, 73, 219–20
Belonging (program), 252–53
Bender, Courtney, 261n16
Bender, Thomas, 282n30
Benedictine charism, 129
Benedict XVI (pope), 22, 276n10
Bergoglio, Jorge Mario (cardinal), 266n22
Bernardin, Joseph (cardinal), 180, 278n32
biblical and theological theme: Gospels in, 109–11, 267n28; theology in, 111–15, 268n31, 268n38
bishops' pastorals, 9, 56, 226
Black Protestants, 276n8

Hauerwas, Stanley, 10–11

heart engagement, 170

Hebrew scriptures, 67–68

heterodoxy, 49

high school students, 18, 248–49

Holy Spirit, 113–14

homelessness, 153, 163, 176, 222; abortion
opposition related to, 180–81; beliefs
about, 205–6, 238–39; individualist
and, 197–98; justice for, 230–31; JWalking and, 210; money related to, 281n23

hope, 67–68, 214, 238–39

house ownership, 190

Hughes, John (bishop), 29

human choices, 112

human conscience. *See* conscience

hunger, 2, 19

Hunter, James Davidson, 236–37

identity. *See* Catholic identity

image of God, 116; in theology, 112–13

immersion experiences, 159, 207–10, 248

immigrants, 26

immigrant style, 225; Catholic political activity and, 31; Catholic schools
in, 28–31; embattlement in, 28–32;
evangelical style compared to, 32;
modern expressions and evaluation of,
30–32; morality and, 30; poverty and,
28; relevance in, 32; republican style
compared to, 30; secularism and, 29;
strength of, 31, 39–40; subculture of, 31;
weakness of, 31–32, 39–40

immigration policy, 168, 276n15

inclusivity, 110–11

income: election voting related to, 231,
284n1; social class related to, 171, 182,
278n34

individualism, 232; asset of, 229; in compassion through personalism, 219–22,
231, 282n29, 283n41; drawbacks of,
229–30; homelessness related to, 222;
of transformation, 82–83

individualist, 218; dilemma of volunteerism and, 194–97, 200, 279n53;
homelessness and, 197–98

individuality, 73

individual moral authority, 35–37, 233

individuals, 154; in dilemma of resistance,
159–62; relationships of, 230–31; solidarity with, 157

information, 211, 280n8

institutional differentiation, 275n1

intensification transformation: "conversion careers" and, 79; worldview
widening in, 80, 82, 262n32

interconnectedness, 118–19

interfaith organizations, 62

interviews, 5–6, 255n6, 256n6, 256n10

intimacy, 143–45, 272n25; from stories,
212–13

Ireland, John (archbishop), 30

Jasper, James M., 283n42

Jesuits' murder, 14

Jesuit Volunteer Corps, 57–58, 235, 259n36

Jesuit Volunteers, 61–62, 260n48

Jesus, 62–63, 202; resurrection of, 128,
270n75. *See also* Christ-centeredness

Jezreel, Jack, 1, 255n1; award for, 18; at
Catholics Charities USA, 107–9; at
CTA, 45–46; education of, 10–11;
intentional community with, 12; as
itinerant preacher, 44–45; marriage of,
12; poverty and, 11; RCIA and, 11–13, 57,
68; on transformation, 68

JFM. *See* JustFaith Ministries

JFM core values: Christ-centered as,
62–64; community as, 59–60, 136;
compassion as, 58–59, 227; JustFaith as,
64–66; justice as, 60–62; transformation as, 56–58

JFM Prison Reform group, 41–43

John Chrysostom (saint), 115

John Paul II (pope), 107, 118, 121, 123,
276n10

rituals, 41–43, 144; Ephesians in, 133; items for, 133, 134, 135; in retreats, 133–36; in transformation, 67–68
Roe v. Wade, 177
Romans, 41–42

sacraments, 105–6, 108; confirmation, 249, 285n2
saints, 67–68, 75, 125–26, 128; stories about, 213
same-sex marriage, 177
Sant'Egidio, 39, 58–59, 60, 62
SASI. *See* Social Action Summer Institute
Schwarzenegger, Arnold, 164
science vocation, 152
scriptures, 34; in Christ-centeredness, 101–2; conversion experience and, 42; Ephesians, 133; Genesis, 41; Hebrew, 67–68; Romans, 41–42; social teaching in, 115. *See also* Gospels
Second Vatican Council, 103; church(es) in, 105–6, 129–30, 267n18, 267n22, 267n24; *Gaudium et Spes* from, 116–17, 123; from John XXIII, 104; laity in, 104–5; relevance of, 104
secularism, 125; financial giving and, 266n5; immigrant style and, 29; post-secular integration, 130
self-doubt, 237–38
self-selection, 90
sending. *See* discipleship communities sending; gathering and sending
servant model, 106–7, 267n24
sexuality, 177, 262n23
shalom (peace), 61, 174
sharing, 111, 134–35
shelter, 153; St. Vincent de Paul, 159; service in, 180–81. *See also* homelessness
shoes, 134
Shroud of Turin, 270n74
Sign of Peace, 42
simple living: in dilemma of efficacy, 188; poverty compared to, 185–87

sin, 41–42, 117, 123–25, 164
Skonovd, Norman, 261n15
small groups, 23, 85, 98–99; activism from, 266n74; commonality in, 217, 282n24; divergence in, 217, 282n23; in JustFaith, 13, 96; in *Prison Reform*, 43; stories in, 211
Smith, Christian, 103, 149, 235
Snow, David, 75
Social Action Summer Institute (SASI), 65–66, 112, 268n31
social class: Bread for the World and, 65–66; in evangelical style, 32; income related to, 171, 182, 278n34. *See also* middle class
social events decrease, 97, 98, 266n75
social justice, 12–13; in Catholic identity, 55–56; definition of, 32; "foot" of, 279n45. *See also specific topics*
social movement theorists, 137
social policy, 86–87, 87
social problems, 169–70
social sin, 123, 164; violence as, 124–25
social transformation, 84, 97, 97–99; gathering and sending in, 95–96, 265n61
socioeconomics, 35–36, 37, 257n44; recession of 2008 and, 21–22
solidarity, 144, 152–53, 250, 272n29; in Catholic social teaching, 118–20; crucifix related to, 126–27; dilemma of resistance and, 156–57, 161, 274n47; with individual, 157; paternalistic model of engagement and, 157, 274n50; relationship and, 283n42
songs, 101–2
soup kitchen, 197–98
spiritual goods, 171
Steinbeck, John, 231
stewardship, 185
stories: ambiguity in, 215–16; community related to, 212; about compassion, 201–3, 214, 227; in compassion through personalism, 221, 282n38; dialogue and

ABOUT THE AUTHOR

Maureen K. Day is Assistant Professor of Religion and Society at the Franciscan School of Theology and Research Fellow at the Center for Applied Research in the Apostolate. She is the editor of *Young Adult American Catholics: Explaining Vocation in Their Own Words.*